D0122886

ALL THAT MAKES A MAN

ALL THAT MAKES A MAN

Love and Ambition
in the Civil War South

STEPHEN W. BERRY II

OXFORD
UNIVERSITY PRESS

2003

OXFORD
UNIVERSITY PRESS

Oxford   New York
Auckland   Bangkok   Buenos Aires   Cape Town   Chennai
Dar es Salaam   Delhi   Hong Kong   Istanbul   Karachi   Kolkata
Kuala Lumpur   Madrid   Melbourne   Mexico City   Mumbai   Nairobi
São Paulo   Shanghai   Taipei   Tokyo   Toronto

Copyright © 2003 by Stephen W. Berry II

Published by Oxford University Press, Inc.
198 Madison Avenue, New York, New York 10016

www.oup.com

Oxford is a registered trademark of Oxford University Press

All rights reserved. No part of this publication may be reproduced,
stored in a retrieval system, or transmitted, in any form or by any means,
electronic, mechanical, photocopying, recording, or otherwise,
without the prior permission of Oxford University Press.

Library of Congress Cataloging-in-Publication Data
Berry, Stephen William.
All that makes a man : love and ambition
in the Civil War South / Stephen W. Berry II.
p. cm   Includes bibliographical references and index.
ISBN-0-19-514567-4
1. United States—History—Civil War, 1861–1865—Social aspects.
2. United States—History—Civil War, 1861–1865—Psychological aspects.
3. Confederate States of America—Social conditions.
4. Men—Confederate States of America—Social conditions.
5. Men—Confederate States of America—Psychology.
6. Sex role—Confederate States of America.
7. Man-woman relationships—Confederate States of America.
8. Ambition—History—19th century.
9. Soldiers—Confederate States of America—Social conditions.
10. Soldiers—Confederate States of America—Psychology.   I. Title.
E468.9.B37   2002
973.7'1—dc21   2002070048

1 3 5 7 9 8 6 4 2

Printed in the United States of America
on acid-free paper

I [know] of no more subtle master under heaven
Than is the maiden passion for a maid,
Not only to keep down the base in man,
But teach high thought, and amiable words
And courtliness, and the desire of fame,
And love of truth, and all that makes a man.

—Alfred Lord Tennyson, *Idylls of the King*

CONTENTS

List of Illustrations ix

Acknowledgments xi

Introduction 3

I Men and Ambition

1 All That Makes a Man 17

2 Two Separate Yet Most Intimate Things 45
  Laurence Massillon Keitt: Politics as Epic Poem 47
  Henry Craft: The Memory of Love 64

II Men and Women

3 Across a Great Divide 83

4 Purity and Desire 114
  David Outlaw: This Hollow Hearted Sodom 118
  Harry St. John Dixon: An Apple Before a Child 136

III Men and War

5 A Fountain of Waters 163

6 Looking Homeward 193
Nathaniel Dawson: The Unstudied Language
of the Heart 196
Theodorick Montfort: Something to Love and Pett 218

Epilogue 227

Notes 239

Bibliography 269

Index 283

ILLUSTRATIONS

1. Thomas Cole, *Voyage of life (Youth)*. Oil on canvas   27
2. "Young America," cartoon   33
3. Melee in the House of Representatives   49
4. Laurence Massillon Keitt   53
5. Caspar David Friedrich, *Wanderer Above the Sea of Fog*   58
6. Henry Craft's Marriage License   69
7. "A Terrible Moment," *Punch*, 1856   84
8. "A Winter in the South," *Harper's Weekly*, January 1858   112
9. David Outlaw   120
10. "A Kiss for a Vote," *Southern Literary Messenger*, July 1860   131
11. Passage From Diary of Harry St. John Dixon   147
12. Sketch From a Soldier's Pocket Diary   180
13. Confederate Soldier Returns Home   194
14. Gravemarker of Elodie Todd Dawson   231
15. Harry St. John Dixon in Confederate Uniform   233
16. Montfort's Fallen Casemate   235

ACKNOWLEDGMENTS

There is a land of the living and a
land of the dead and the bridge is love.*

R eaders with little stomach for gushing words of praise and thanks
should bypass this section altogether. First books are like first
children, and I mean to put a cigar in every mouth.

All That Makes a Man began as a dissertation at the University of
North Carolina, Chapel Hill. To my adviser, William Barney, I owe
an unrepayable debt. His archival leads and historical insights have
contributed significantly to this work, and I proudly call myself his
student. The other members of my committee—Peter Coclanis, Peter
Filene, John Kasson, and Joel Williamson—read the dissertation
closely and provided thoughtful comments that both saved me from
little embarrassments and sent me in new directions. In long conversations that ran the intellectual gamut, David Moltke-Hansen pushed
me to think broadly and deeply. Throughout the process, I have been
sustained by Peter Walker's contagious love of words and the ease
that came when he promised us that as writers and as people we
would all fail, for man would always fail and could only hope to do
it elegantly.

* Thornton Wilder.

xi

While I was at Chapel Hill, three institutions put up with me for long stretches. At the Center for the Study of the American South, Barb Call, Tony Young, and Joe Mosnier always made it easier to come to work. At the Institute for Research in Social Science, Jon Crabtree, Christine Cleveland, and Angell Beza gave both advice and encouragement. At the Southern Historical Collection, where I did the bulk of my research, I benefited from the unstinting generosity of John White, a man for whom, I am convinced, God has earmarked a particularly fluffy cloud. I also feel thankful for Chapel Hill itself—the little slice of heaven on which a voracious multitude daily feeds—for the red tape, fees and fines and hellish parking, bars, classrooms, and coffeehouses, where I finally figured out what I wanted to do with my life.

At the University of North Carolina at Pembroke I have found a new home, and my colleagues—Robert Brown, Micky Connelly, Bruce DeHart, Kathleen Hilton, Julie Smith, and Mark Thompson—have made it a happy one. *All That Makes a Man* has found its home at Oxford, where Susan Ferber has been a pillar of aid, understanding, and sharp criticism. I feel very fortunate to have her as my editor.

Friends have contributed no less directly to this work, offering encouragement, advice, and support. Gary Williams, my undergraduate adviser, instilled in me affections for history and the lilt of language. At UNC, Robert Tinkler had my back through too many years of graduate school, and Gavin Campbell's sharp criticism about my work and dry wit about this profession leavened many a grim moment. Over countless three-egg breakfasts, Terry Mehlman and Stacey Sewall listened as I presented my monthly (lack of) progress reports, and their company offered a welcome respite from the neuroses of writing. Stephen Rosbough has been everything one looks for in a friend. I have spent so many hours eating at his table, sleeping on his couch, and conversing from his deck chairs that I really ought to have paid rent. Michael McFalls, Sean Malloy, and I have walked from boyhood to manhood together, and I wouldn't know myself without them.

My family has been the mainstay of my life. Margaret and Clay Riley remind me every time I see them why *family* is the most magical word in the language. Patrick Berry has for time out of mind made our home a happy and productive one. Undoubtedly we're coming up on our millionth cup of coffee together, and I hope there'll be a million more. My parents did everything right—they raised a happy family—and this book is dedicated to them.

ALL THAT MAKES A MAN

INTRODUCTION

In 1857, North Carolinian Albert Luria fell in love with his cousin Eliza. He was fifteen; she may have been younger still. All questions of age were brushed aside, however. Albert's feelings were "too irrevocably fixed" on the girl "ever to centre on anyone else," and so he proposed. Unfortunately, Eliza's parents disapproved the match. The couple was too young, they said, and Albert's older brother had already married Eliza's older sister. Cousinate marriages were common in the Old South and generally free from stigma, but too much inbreeding could threaten a family's respectability. Dutifully, Eliza declined Albert's proposal of marriage and agreed not to correspond with him. Usually, such a decision would bring an end to the written record, and the couple would dissolve back into the unknowable past. Albert and Eliza both kept diaries, however. Denied the privilege of writing *to* each other they wrote frequently *of* each other, and thus their story can be sketched to its conclusion.[1]

In 1859–1860, Albert Luria attended military school in Hillsboro, North Carolina. The following year he joined the Twenty-Third North Carolina Infantry, hoping to "figure among [the] mounted men and dashing youths" swelling the chorus of the Confederacy. Despite

3

Eliza's final injunction that he should think of her "only as a sister," Albert held tenaciously to the idea that the Civil War presented an opportunity to win her love. "I have now set out in the world," he wrote ebulliently, "a pecuniary independence—a spotless moral character—and an unlimited regard for the views and feelings of Eliza are the prime objects ever present to my mind." In the festive first month of the war, Albert was thrown often into the society of other compelling and vivacious females, and it seems unlikely that Eliza was "ever present" in his mind. His vow of faithfulness, for instance, is difficult to square with a series of letters he exchanged with Loudie Lyons, culminating in their trading locks of each other's hair and daguerreotypes bearing the inscription, "Thine and thine only." "I do not restrict in the slightest degree my intercourse with [women]," Albert admitted. "I mingle freely, endeavor to render myself as agreeable as possible—make many pleasant and interesting acquaintances sometimes, and often very warm friends." Stationed in Virginia, Albert even made a warm friend of a Yankee girl living near his outpost who had the reputation for being "as lively as a cricket." Apparently the description didn't do her justice. "Well, it is actually so," Albert noted after calling on her, she is "a young lady, about 16 years old, beautiful . . . with an alacrity and gaiety about her every word and action that completely baffles description." So carried away was he by the Yankee girl's good qualities that he insisted on washing her dishes and milking her cow before he left. "I could not help feeling a little amused," he wrote, "wonder[ing] what the folks at home would say if they knew what I was doing."[2]

Certainly Eliza Moses would have been interested in what he was doing. Though she had conceded to her family's wishes—declining Albert's proposals of courtship and correspondence—she nurtured a secret from them all that finally burst upon the pages of her diary. Writing at night with one of her sisters as lookout, she confessed to her journal that whatever her outward appearance, however contradictory her behavior, she loved Albert Luria desperately. "I would give up the love of all others for him," she admitted. "The just God in Heaven knows this assertion to be true." The problem, though, went beyond familial objections to her own insecurities. She loved Albert—though she pretended she didn't. Did Albert love her? Or did he merely pretend that he did? "Would that I could see into the inmost depths of some persons' souls to find if they do love me," she wrote her diary helplessly. "I think there is one; but a doubt sometimes crosses my mind.... Why should one who has seen so much of the world fix his affections on me?... What merits have I above so many that he has seen?" Selflessly, Eliza called on God to help Albert forget her and move on. "If God should permit him to return," she wrote her diary, "I hope that his mind may be changed [and] his affections... fixed upon some one more worthy of them than I ever can be."[3]

As the war progressed, however, Albert became not less but more dedicated to Eliza. Though only eighteen when the war began, Albert Luria bore witness to events that would mature anyone quickly. "Visiting the Hospital [after Manassas]," he noted, "I saw piles of arms and legs laying about just as you have seen rags and papers laying about a floor where a little child has been playing." Sobering to the brutal realities of warfare, Albert began to turn his mind to the quiet simplicities of a life humbly lived. On stormy days, he wrote, the rain "acts as a sentinel at the door [and] the image of loved ones will arise—a beloved Mother & sister sitting around a genial fire sewing some clothes... or a Bro in my room, both of us smoking a 'Cuba Six' [and] discussing the merits of some trotting horse." These were scenes, he admitted, that he longed to enjoy again. But more than anything or anyone, Albert's dreams of life after the war centered on Eliza. "For how many of the happiest moments of my life am I indebted to this gentle young being. She little knows how much I prize them or how often in this stern life I recur to them."[4]

After the battle of Seven Pines, Albert's father traveled to Richmond to tend to a nephew who had been shot. While at the hospital he happened to pass some ladies standing over a cot, one of whom murmured, "what a handsome young man!" "I crossed over to the cot," Albert's father wrote, "and my shock was beyond my power of expression when I saw my son Albert lying unconscious with a bullet ... in his head." Albert Luria died at the age of nineteen from wounds sustained at Seven Pines. In his last months he had written of Eliza: "The heart I gave her more than three years ago is hers now and shall be hers until life has passed away and I shall be no more." After

Albert's death, Eliza received his diary and learned that he had loved her all along. "My life is all a blank to me now," she confessed. "It makes but little difference ... where I am or what I do."[5]

In 1850, fifteen-year-old Joshua Callaway was a mail carrier, making his rounds and kicking up dust on the familiar roads of Coffee County, Alabama. Ten years later, he was a husband and father of two, working as a teacher at Centenary Institute, north of Selma. By 1862, Callaway had responded to the governor's injunction to join the army or suffer the humiliation of a draft. "No man of true patriotism ... will stand still in such an hour of danger," the governor had intoned, "and suffer himself forced into the defense of his country." Once in the army, Callaway missed his family desperately. Surrounded by the din of men, he dreamed of "a little cottage home on some lonely island of the sea, with no human being near me but my beloved Dulcinea and little children." "It is a source of great comfort to me to look at the moon at night and think perhaps you are at that moment looking at the same object," Callaway wrote his wife. "Sometimes I become so spell bound that I see your Shadow, with children playing around you on the face of the moon. *Then how I do gaze!*" Compared with the purity of his family, Callaway found the army an immoral, sullied instrument. Eating out the fields and plundering the livestock of the land it was supposed to protect, the army seemed an amalgam of men's worst traits. "I have learned an important lesson by coming to the war," he concluded. "I learned more of human nature and deception than I ever cared to know." But for all the sins and iniquities of army life, Callaway believed he was in the right place, doing the right thing. The enemy was at the door, and he was willing to lay down his life in defense of his home. "I am as sick of the war as any man who ever deserted," he wrote. "But do not you think I have any notion of a similar course. No, never."[6]

In November 1863, the Twenty-Eighth Alabama was bivouacked near Missionary Ridge, and Callaway convinced some of his friends to climb to the top of Lookout Mountain. There they had a splendid view of the entire Chattanooga valley, and Callaway was struck by the fact that future poets and painters would stand exactly where he was standing "to have their geniuses inspired, and to immortalize the scene . . . in song and on canvas." Buoyed by such thoughts, Callaway felt a touch of the poet within himself: "While I was musing thus," he wrote his wife, "I could not help feeling a spark of ambition, a desire to make my name as immortal in future history and as classic as that of Lookout Mountain." But just at this moment, his eyes were arrested by a tiny figure emerging from a house on the valley floor—a general departing his headquarters. Callaway was flabbergasted. "I suppose he was a general," he told his wife, "but he looked so small, a mere speck, that I could not tell he was there at all if he had not moved. And when I compared him to the mountain and then to the universe, and thought of his pride and ambition, I could not help smiling at his impetuosity and sighing at his insignificance. He reminded me of an ant trying to shake the earth, and my ambition cooled off and I would be perfectly content to be at home with my wife and never be thought of after I die."[7]

Six days after his epiphany, Joshua Callaway was killed in a retreat from Missionary Ridge. Shot through the bowels, he was being carried from the field when he asked his bearers to put him down. His last moments (like the location of his body) are unknown. Presumably, he lay on the ground the Confederates had abandoned, staring at the sky and thinking of all who would go on without him. "[We are] hardly allowed to sigh at the fall of our friends and relatives," he had written helplessly before he died, "and if we do happen to shed a tear secretly, it is soon dried up to make room for one for some one else."[8]

On November 12, 1860, Thomas Reade Rootes Cobb delivered the most celebrated speech of his career. Standing before the Georgia legislature, he urged the assembled to put sentiment aside and dissolve the government of their fathers and grandfathers. "Long have I loved [this Union]," Cobb admitted. "Long have I worshipped it." But, he claimed, "the cruel hand of Northern aggression" had torn a thin veil from the idol of his youth, revealing a false prophet "whose deformity and ugliness . . . disgusted [and] pained" him. The speech was a resounding success. Deluged with invitations to speak across the state, Cobb accepted most of them. "He reminds me of the Methodist

Circuit riders I used to know in my childhood," noted his sister-in-law. He is "so thoroughly infused with the Spirit of the righteousness of the cause that no physical discomfort dampens his zeal."[9]

In many respects Thomas Cobb was an unlikely political zealot. His father had gone bankrupt in the Panic of 1837, and Cobb had turned to his older brother, Howell, and his father-in-law, Judge Lumpkin, for role models. Because Howell was a Democrat and Lumpkin a Whig, Cobb had for most of his life eschewed partisan politics and the speechifying that went with it. In the secession crisis, however, he found a political creed all his own, and he plainly delighted in his emergence from the shadows of men he loved too well. With Judge Lumpkin easing into his dotage and Howell committed to the Buchanan administration, Thomas Cobb was for the first time alone at the forefront of a political movement, leading not following, damning the consequences as he went ahead at full steam.

Given his idealism and inexperience, Cobb's disillusionment was perhaps inevitable. Secession could not chasten Southern governance or change the nature of man, but Cobb seems to have hoped for exactly such a revolution. While at Milledgeville to help draft Georgia's independence into law, Cobb could only complain of "the presidents in embryo" who jockeyed for Confederate office. "Believe me," he wrote home, "I am sick at heart with the daily manifestations of selfishness, intrigue, low cunning, and meanness among those who at this critical moment should have an eye single to the protection of their people and the preservation of their government." Nor did matters improve once Cobb secured a military position. One of the crabbiest colonels in the Confederate army—no mean feat—Cobb's letters are full of blistering critiques of his superiors: General Robert Toombs, he claimed, was a "desperate failure" who spent his days "drinking like a fish" and generally "making an ass of himself"; Robert E. Lee was "haughty, boorish, and supercilious" with "not the first feeling of a gentleman"; Secretary of the Treasury Judah Benjamin was nothing more than a "mean, low, sycophantic . . . Jew"; Vice President Alexander Stephens was "a poor selfish demagogue" bent on "opposition to everything"; and President Jefferson Davis was a "malicious dog," the very "embodiment and concentration of cowardly littleness [and] hypocrisy."[10]

The Civil War had not put an end to human greed or selfishness, had not remade the world. As his revolution died from within, Thomas Cobb, like Albert Luria and Josh Callaway, threw himself on the mercy of the only part of his life unsullied by war. "How I love you, Marion, you will never know in this world," Cobb wrote his wife from Virginia. "In another and a better we will know all things and my heart's deep devotion to you will be seen as it is now felt." Something about the conflict had convinced Cobb not only of the limits of man but of the limits of himself as a man. "I have never treated you right, Dearest," he confessed to Marion. "I have been cold and indifferent and sometimes churlish and many times thoughtless, but I loved you always . . . with all the strength of my nature. Remember this as long as you live." On December 13, 1862, Thomas R. R. Cobb was conversing with a group of officers behind a house when a random shell burst in their midst, severing the major artery of his thigh. He bled to death in a matter of minutes.[11]

Between April 1861 and April 1865, the life stories of 620,000 American men came to an abrupt end. Albert Luria's battle for his cousin's love—a battle he had already won—ended in a Richmond hospital where his father unexpectedly found him, another corpse in another bed. Joshua Callaway's defense of his family—a defense that took him hundreds of miles from their side—ended in a gasping, gut-shot breath on a field he had surrendered to the enemy. Thomas Cobb's bid to remake the world had rightly convinced him that it was himself who must be remade—and then a rogue shell unmade him altogether. For an astounding 35 percent of Confederate soldiers, their life stories ended prematurely, in murky ditches, crowded hospitals, unmarked graves.

Few subjects have received more historical attention than the war that killed these men. Unfortunately, the central fact that brought them to the field in the first place—the fact that they were men—has not been given due scrutiny. From the soldier's perspective the war was only partly a battle for this or that ideology. More immediately it was a test of manhood, a test an appalling number welcomed as an opportunity finally to measure up to their own standards for themselves. The conflict's staggering casualty rates—suffered in

repeated charges on well-defended positions—speak not to the soldiers' collective discipline but to their individual self-motivation. Ultimately, these men fought because, if in nothing else, they believed
in themselves. They believed they could face death, and so they did,
millions of them, some of whom survived to remember those who
weren't as lucky, for luck was all it was.[12]

Self-belief was not something the Confederate high command could
requisition and issue, like tents or trousers; it was something men
brought with them from home, with their Bibles and their hipflasks,
tobacco pouches and family photos. As such, this book begins its study
of male Civil War experience and motivation in the antebellum period, where the generation who fought the war learned what it meant
to be a man in the first place. The perennial question of why men
fought the Civil War cannot be answered without first answering
another question: Why did men of the period ever do anything?

Most of the books written on the Old South have taken men as
their subject. Largely, though, this has been unconscious. In the past,
scholars studied men because they presumed that men made history,
wielding as they did the lion's share of the power. Since the 1970s,
this presumption has been overturned. Today, women's historians can
claim, with right, that "in no way has the historical landscape changed
more radically . . . than in the emergence from the deep shadows of
the other half of the population." Not merely as wives and mothers
but as producers and thinkers, women contributed to the texture and
shape of their society in ways all out of proportion with the limited
power they were "supposed" to wield.[13]

Sadly, though, this revolution in women's studies has not been
matched by a comparable advance in our understanding of men *as
men*. Books on politicians or inventors who happened to be men cannot in any way address the changes over time in the pressures and
perquisites of masculinity, broadly conceived. To be sure, recent scholars have begun to examine Southern history from a gendered perspective—with impressive results. Cultural historians, for instance,

have discovered intriguing similarities between elections and other combative rituals, lending credence to the notion that ideals of public reputation were a constant in men's relations with one another. Then too, historians of the Civil War have highlighted the degree to which the aggressive masculinity of the South's political culture encouraged the region to see Lincoln's election as a personal insult that demanded an assertive and ultimately violent response.[14]

For all these advances, however, the story of Southern masculinity continues to be understood better in its postures and poses, more for what it claimed to be than for what it was. In their studies of duels and barbecues, hunting and stump speaking, scholars have examined with greater penetration the archetypically masculine aspects of Southern life than the dithering dreams and doubts that surely dominated men's inner experience of themselves. Of the consequences for the South of its hypermasculinized culture, much has been suggested. Of the consequences for the men living in and through this culture little is known. Of the general tenor of men's inner, emotional lives little has been said or written. As a result, men are denied a measure of their humanity, which, while in no way so egregious as that denied women for centuries, is nevertheless an impediment to understanding.[15]

None of this has been deliberate. Much of it results from the nature of the sources on which historians depend. Men of the nineteenth century were encouraged to cloak their hearts and stifle their doubts, to so carefully groom their public persona as to become it. The result is a staggering amount of evidence dedicated to the public, external, and projected aspects of men's lives and significantly less dedicated to the private, internal, and introspective. Self-reliance and self-doubt, self-love and self-loathing, are all and equally parts of any human enterprise. But because gentlemen of the Old South were encouraged to swallow half of these emotions and exaggerate the remainder, we get a skewed picture of their lives. "I know well what faculties I possess," Mississippian Henry Craft wrote in his journal. "[I know] how I can most please & how most successfully deceive those around me.... I seem happy & cheerful & hopeful. What a liar the *seeming* is." Without his diary, historians would have been inescapably among the deceived. The few records Henry left as land examiner, student, and lawyer could only be stitched together to give a history of the seeming and the lies.[16]

This book, then, is dedicated to the *inner* experience of masculinity, to the private landscapes men negotiated in their confrontation with what their society claimed a man should do and be. Although in no way intended as an exculpatory account of Southern manhood, it is intended very precisely to be an empathetic one. Here men are captured, alone and even lonely, pen in hand and pawing at their own minds, struggling to reconcile who they are with who they want to be, what they know of their circumstances with what they know of their hearts. When these men looked inside themselves, what did they see? What did they want to see?[17]

The remarkable thing about men is that however much they might want to obfuscate certain emotions, they want just as desperately to confess, to be understood. If one wonders what drives them, one has only to ask. "There are but two things worth living for," South Carolina planter James Henry Hammond explained, "love in life, immortality after death." By "love in life," Hammond meant a purely personal love, a "love to fill up one's yearning heart." This included friendship—the love of male for male—but primarily it meant the romantic love of man and woman. By "immortality after death" Hammond meant that a man should strive "to fill a niche in History to the end of time, not to die out with the death of [his] contemporaries." Hammond's "two things" were related, of course—love sustained the immortal drive, like kindling or coal. A bid for immortality could be cold going, and a woman warmed a man in his sacrifice and his suffering. This, then, was the male project in elemental form. There were only two features to the program, two quests, each beholden to the other. The woman, once acquired, would sustain and bear witness to the male becoming; the male would in turn reconceive his becoming as a tribute to her love. A great many men did not buy into this project, of course; a greater number *could not* buy into it. Among the poorest whites and slaves such ambitions would have seemed grandiose and absurd. Among educated white males, however, this thinking was pervasive. Few would succeed in these terms—many would make unhappy marriages and more would die unsung.

But all recognized these criteria—a love to fill the heart and a bid to live forever—as the standards by which success and failure would be measured. "No body *loves* me," Hammond complained, "no body will remember me who has not seen and known me." Loveless and unremembered, Hammond understood himself to have failed; death would claim him whole, as if he had never taken a breath of air. "My life," he lamented, "is a blank."[18]

But the braggadocio and the despair that vie for control in Hammond's diary are each part of a single romantic loop; dreams of immortality and love, lamentations over mortality and estrangement, wash over him in successive waves, bringing cathartic relief. Wallowing in lovelessness, Hammond discovers that someone does love him— it is Hammond. Writing out his mortality, he lives forever, in a diary that captures a man as fully as any other in the English language. Hammond's twin drives—for immortality, for love—which are so seemingly grandiose, turn out to be as much about human limits as human aspirations, as much about resignation as exertion. In each quest men search for a place not to impose but to subsume the self; they long for a project grand enough to make them worthy of the power they are supposed to hold. The fact that they so regularly failed and so regularly abused this power is certainly disappointing—but it is important to recognize that it often disappointed them too. All this suggests another and a more general problem—for all the biography that has been written on all the men of this time and place, manhood itself has been asked to conform to startlingly crabbed models, most of them unflattering and all of them incomplete. While it is undeniable that men of the period did some ghastly things, and did them with impunity, it may be worth considering that many were also trapped, and indeed occasionally crushed, by the patriarchy they ostensibly controlled.

PART I

MEN AND AMBITION

CHAPTER 1

ALL THAT MAKES A MAN

Idea! which bindest life around
With music of so strange a sound,
And beauty of so wild a birth,—
Farewell! for I have won the Earth.*

In June 1849, Georgia Congressman Thomas Butler King traveled to San Francisco to survey the political and economic prospects. California was poised on the brink of statehood, and King wanted to sample the region's ripeness for himself. The overland routes to San Francisco were so fraught with perils that most men of standing made the trip by steamer—itself a somewhat harrowing journey. The first leg took travelers from New York or Savannah to the Caribbean coast of Panama, where they picked up a flatboat on the Chagres River. The second leg took them downriver to the Camino de Cruces, where they mounted small ponies for the marshy overland route to Panama City on the Pacific coast. There they boarded another steamer, which carried them up the coast to California. In King's case, the men spent three days and three nights on the Chagres in water so low that they often had to switch from oars to poles to make any progress. They spent their evenings, King noted, in "Palm leaf huts" in real "*negro* villages," supping on "hard biscuits & coffee" and occasionally having to "drive out pigs & cattle to get a place to hang up" their hammocks.

---

* Edgar Allan Poe, *Tamerlane.*

Traveling the Camino de Cruces was, if possible, worse. King was given so puny a pony that the animal sank to its knees in the mud, and once threw him "head over heals...ten feet into a deep ditch," soiling his new white hat. The weather was typically tropical—hot and rainy—and when King finally arrived in Panama City he was "wet to the skin & completely fagged out." His wife, who was accustomed but not resigned to his long absences, marveled at his stamina. What could he be chasing that would carry him so far from home? What could be driving him that he would prefer a muddy ditch to her own loving company? But under all such deprivations and hardships, King remained positively buoyant. The country was beautiful, the air was clean, and the sense of adventure palpable. The ditch may not have suited him to the nines, but the life of a man of influence did, and a bedraggled hat was a small price to pay. Moreover, unlike his wife, King knew what he was chasing; he had a name for it: éclat.[1]

It is telling that King had to go outside his own language to describe how he felt. The comparable words in English—eminence, fame, glory, celebrity—sound pompous, self-serving, and vain. Éclat has an altogether different timbre—ephemeral yet manly, hinting at Old World breeding and New World energy. Wary of ambition, disdainful of vanity, and suspicious of accumulated power, Southerners liked their leading men not to make money but to be somehow affluent, not to work but to be somehow accomplished, not to give orders but to be somehow followed. Éclat had exactly this sort of conveniently vague flamboyance.

This chapter examines the éclat-based culture of men like Thomas Butler King. Here the focus is on ambition, one of James Henry Hammond's "two things," a constituent element of the antebellum male life. Like love or hate or hope, ambition has been a part of the human experience for time out of mind. This does not mean, though, that it remains unchanged through time or that it plays the same role in every age and culture. In the case of the Old South, I will argue, men's ambitions were grander, more appalling, and more personally destructive than is usually allowed.

Southern men generally—and Southern planters especially—tend to be seen as petty tyrants, animated by desires for authority, mastery, or, as one variation has it, "despotic sway." This is undeniably true in part, and men of the Old South could often be found perched on their self-conceived thrones like great birds atop a promising egg. As patriarchs, men were expected to provide a varied constituency—slaves, women, children, and (in some measure) poorer whites—with an array of goods and services: food, shelter, clothing, justice, moral leadership, and a sense of common identity and direction. To the degree that a man could convince himself that he was providing these things, he became (in his own mind) provider, lawgiver, governor, autocrat. To be sure, many of his dependents penetrated the fiction. Casting her eyes about the mulattos in her midst, Mary Chesnut was staggered by the degree to which she was forced to participate in a kind of male make-believe. Men not only fathered children by their slaves but then expected their wives not to notice. "And all the time they seem to think themselves patterns," Chesnut marveled, the very "models of husbands and fathers." Ludicrous and easily penetrated, the paternalist fiction was nevertheless meticulously groomed and thoroughly enforced. In its capacious folds, a man found ample space to explore his selfishness and his depravity, and enough delusional self-belief to feel affronted or hurt if anyone pointed them out.[2]

This does not mean, however, that the man himself could not have pointed them out; he could, and in all likelihood did, in bouts of self-recrimination and pleas to the Almighty for guidance and strength. The antebellum man may not have allowed others to question his authority, but he questioned it, deeply and often, cultivating the good within him and lamenting the bad. His was a sinning nature, and he knew it; he was compromised daily by compulsions made all the more irresistible by the fact that he could get away with them so easily. This sinning was something he pursued on the side, however, a lurid life he did not want others to notice because he did not want to notice it either. In the main, he wanted to do better, to be better, to link his name to something extraordinary. These men had power; they coveted and they abused it, but that does not mean that the lust of it constituted their reason for being. "They who liken us to the Giants of the school books," warned one planter acerbically in 1846, "and think of us as of a race of tyrants rejoicing in the clank of chains ... can scarcely have reflected on the life of a tyrant." Paternalism had its vanities but also its headaches, and for each instance in which manhood was wielded like a rod of iron there is another in which it was poured out like water. Power can be mediated variously—by carnality and greed, decency and love, frustration and failure—and Southern planters ran the gamut of that variety. To the extent that any generalizations can be made, it is safe to say that these men did not seek power for its own sake; their moral philosophy was too strong, their vision too grand, even when awfully so.[3]

Neither is it fair to say that Southern men were fixated on honor. They may have been touchier and more hot-headed than their Northern brethren. Their culture, after all, was more rural and therefore more primal, closer to the bone. Then too it was a culture situated atop the explosive possibility of slave insurrection, which made any slippage of authority seem potentially perilous. Quite probably, this made Southern men more sensitive to the respect accorded them by others, a sensitivity that could fairly be called an attention to matters of masculine honor. Although these attentions contributed to a Southern way of life, they did not constitute a reason for living. "Ask ninety-nine men in a hundred what honor is and they will give no intelligible answer," noted one Southern magazine in 1857. "There is nothing about which there is so much loose talk and confused thinking." Honor, its chivalric incarnation to the contrary, was not a code; it did not come with a handbook or guide. All Southerners had to determine what the word meant to them, and they did so with considerable variety and finesse. "There is a great difference between a desire for honor and a desire to deserve honor," noted one discriminating young Southerner in 1843. "There is no motive more elevated than that of desiring to merit the love of your fellow men, because honor can alone be merited by a truly moral and virtuous course of conduct, indefatigable application and perseverance." Here honor is not primal or rigid; it is not something to be taken by force or won by act of will but earned by dint of hard work. Writing to a young man entering the navy, South Carolina's leading lawyer, James Petigru, made the same point. He reminded the lad that not all could

expect brilliant opportunities in life and that few would sail into
Charleston harbor with a wreath of victory suspended from their
prow. "It will require all your fortitude to keep from repenting of
your choice, and to bear up under privation and weariness of spirit,"
Petigru reminded him, "but, honor is not honor for nothing."[4]

If the motive element of the male life was not power or honor,
what was it? This is exactly what Thomas King was wrestling with
when he hit upon éclat—a term comprising power and honor but
bigger than both of them. At first glance, King might seem a mercenary capitalist. He campaigned to improve the commercial attractiveness of the port of Darien, Georgia, where he happened to own
land. He lobbied the Texas legislature to finance the Southern Pacific
Railroad, in which he happened to have a promissory percentage. But
his schemes were not about making money per se (fortunate because
King did not make but rather lost a fortune); they were about exten-
sion, about breadth of imagination, about building an empire, personal
and national, about surrendering to something so much bigger and
better than the self that a man might be treasured up forever. Thomas
Butler King got out of the ditch, adjusted his hat, and blithely re-
mounted his scrubby little pony not because he was on a personal
power trip but because he could feel a nation's destiny surging
through him. The advance man of an entire civilization, King chan-
neled the energy of that multitude—and, like most great conductors,
it ran through him resistless and immense. One might argue, of
course, that these are exactly the sort of robust rationalizations in
which the best mercenary capitalists have always sought their succor.
But the country needed a better port at Darien, and it needed a
transcontinental railroad. How else could it fulfill its destiny? King's
self-interest and the country's bid for majesty were identical; King
had long since ceased to distinguish between the two, except perhaps
to notice that he had himself been made majestic by the pursuit.[5]

This spirit of éclat, while not peculiar to the South, ran deepest in
places where mastery over environment and slaves lent a certain
grandness to a man's vision. To be sure, slaveholding could degrade
the quality of a man's conscience. The presence of a subject class on
whom depravity could be practiced with impunity offered to all
and provided to many a tempting descent into a dark demimonde of

violence and sin. But the presence of a subject class also elevated a man's ambition, calling on him to conceive in terms of extent and exercise power in terms of majesty and domain.

When British naturalist Philip Henry Gosse traveled to Pleasant Hill, Alabama, in 1838, he found a crude community where even the planters lived in log homes of warped timbers and where every man was in such a hurry to plant that he did not bother to cut down the trees that hampered his fields—he simply girdled them and moved on. But Gosse could see that, despite their surroundings, these Alabamians were not rustics or rubes; their aspirations were grand, even preposterously so, and their simple communities, replicated hundreds of times over across the Southwest, were transforming the ecology of the region. "The Americans," he noted, "in commencing a hamlet or village, always look forward to its becoming a city; and hence the plan is laid out with an amplitude and grandeur that seems ridiculous." Less ridiculous, of course, was the effect of such amplitude on the land. American forests were expansive and unforgiving, to be sure, but so were the Americans intent on taming them. "This custom of girdling the trees instead of cutting them down," Gosse wrote, "gives the fields a most singular appearance. After the twigs and smaller boughs have dropped off, and the bark has dried and shrunk, and been stripped away, and the naked branches have become blanched by the summer's sun and winter's rain, these tall dead trunks, so thickly spread over the land, look like an army of skeletons, stretching their gaunt white arms ... across the fields." Here was Pleasant Hill in its truest colors—the pipe-smoking planter, kicked back to watch the sun set on an army of slaves or an army of dead trees, each in its own way a passable index of his own accomplishments. Such men, from Alabama backwater to Carolina estate, spoke King's language of éclat. "I am Columbus! Cortez!" exclaimed James Henry Hammond of his own efforts at Cowden plantation. "If I have been active & industrious, it has always been for higher purposes than to accumulate. ... I delight to accomplish, for accomplishment gives [me] all the emotions of a Discoverer & a Conquerer."[6]

In the nineteenth century, the Southern frontier was awash with such empire builders. Aaron Burr, a former vice president, set the tone for the century's imperial free-for-all when he rafted down the

Mississippi in 1807, perhaps scheming to cut off a large swath of the Louisiana Purchase to rule as his own kingdom. The plan failed, but Burr's unflappable audacity captured the country's heart; instead of being convicted of treason, he was coddled and plied with expensive wine for most of his trial. In the 1830s, John Murrell made land piracy a national cause célèbre in a series of intrigues along the Natchez Trace. Lacking Burr's aplomb, Murrell was strung up for his crimes, but his manly pluck lived on in the stories Americans liked best to tell about themselves. By the 1850s, swaggering imperialists bent on personal kingdoms rose and fell with stunning frequency. Filibustering forays against Mexico, Nicaragua, and Spanish holdings, especially in Cuba, kept the American government in a nearly constant state of international embarrassment. Every year, it seemed, a crew of scofflaws would set off in a rickety boat under the broad banner of manifest destiny and attempt to "liberate" a swath of foreign soil and rule it as their own. In 1850, for instance, William Walker led forty-five men into lower California. Capturing the Mexican governor at La Paz, Walker proclaimed himself president of the new republic of Sonora and began issuing edicts with all the pomposity of a Roman emperor. Walker and his men were eventually chased back across the border by Mexican troops, but in his subsequent trial, Walker was toasted and released to continue his scheming. Such episodes may seem ludicrous in retrospect, but this new class of roving adventurers acted as a sort of advance guard for America's more concerted imperial impulses. Exactly such skirmishes, after all, had proceeded and made possible the acquisition and domination of Texas, which, despite its titanic size, seemed to many just the beginning of the country's prospects to the South. "Gentlemen, what a vista does this open!" intoned James Hamilton before the Texas legislature. "[To the west and south of you lies a] country which by comparison dwarfs the imaginary nations for which Alexander may have sighed, and which stretches over a greater number of degrees of latitude, and through a greater variety of climate, soil and surface than the sword of Caesar ever measured in his boasted conquest of the world."[7]

"In due time," promised a tongue-in-cheek editorial in the *Southern Literary Messenger*, "our planet will be under the control of two Governments. The entire continent of America, with the West India

Islands, Polynesia, Australia, and Western Europe . . . will constitute its Republic. The rest of the world, leaving out Interior Africa, will be under the dominion of one man, and that man a Russian." The Russian regime, the article claimed, would be totalitarian in character, and would encompass those races—Turk, Persian, Tartar, Hindoo, Malay, Chinese, and Japanese—who, history proved, could only function within an autocratic system. Under a Russian tsar, such races could "continue to make toys and lacquer-ware; to raise tea, rice, and opium; to worship idols and commit suicide, with a felicity of uninterruption of which they have long since ceased even to dream." The planet's other government, while republican in character, would not only sanction slavery, but extend it benevolently to the rest of the world's unworthies. Southern gentlemen would of course constitute the master class in the New Republic, but they would be attended by Negro domestics, French cooks, Italian entertainers, Spanish butchers, German brewmeisters, and British butlers. Yankees, of course, would need to be subjugated as well. "Cowardly, thievish, superstitious, fanatical, destitute of a moral sense, or any fixed idea of civil polity," the article concluded, "[the Yankee] possesses all the worse and none of the better traits of the Negro, and stands more in need of a master." The problem, of course, was that the Yankee was not fit for much. Unable to distinguish right from wrong and generally atheistic, he could not be a preacher. "Too cruel and too morbidly energetic to be allowed authority over flesh and blood," he could not make a good overseer. Finally the author concluded that in "supervising machinery" the Yankee would probably "always find enough to do." Naturally, the name of the New Republic would be Virginia.[8]

The article is intended to be humorous. The accompanying editor's note describes it as a capital "piece of fun," and he hopes "that it will be read with enjoyment by our friends at the North not less than by the Virginians who are so exalted in its views of the future." Like most humor, however, the article is funny because, while distorted, it contains a germ of truth. By 1850, Southerners, like Americans generally, possessed an absolutely swaggering sense of expansionism. Unlike Americans generally, Southerners viewed slavery as an integral part of that expansion, a view that put them at odds with their Northern neighbors and provided a backdrop for the coming of the

Civil War. This should not distract, though, from the degree to which Southern expansionist rhetoric was consistent with American expansionist rhetoric generally. In its tendency to view the world as poised on the brink of revolutionary consolidation, and in its penchant for viewing race as the organizing principle of that revolution, the Republic of Virginia article offers a perspective as much American as Southern. The article's racism, too, owes more to race-based imperialism than to militant slavocracy. The author takes a relatively kindly view toward blacks: "The Negro, having been our earliest slave, and reared as it were under our own roof, will forever retain a more intimate relation to us than any other slave." And a much harsher view of southern Europeans: "With our Italians, we need anticipate no trouble. Popery being cast into the sea, they . . . will become at once manageable. It will be necessary to use fumigants and disinfectants freely, to rid them of vermin and the stench of garlic, but, after that, they will be very available as opera singers, fresco painters, and for the mechanical labour of sculpture." Slavery here has burst the confines of the plantation system to become a conceptually flexible, ideologically sophisticated aspect of manifest destiny in the Southern style. Placing the South's defense of slavery on the same foundation as the country's defense of imperialism, the article couches Southern peculiarities in an American idiom, making slavery seem the normative status for all of the world's lesser peoples.

Nor was this article particularly exceptional. An editorial in the December 1857 issue of Charleston's *Russell's Magazine* restated in all seriousness much of what the *Messenger's* Virginia superpower piece noted in jest. "The sum of the matter appears to be this," *Russell's* informed its readers. "The grand result toward which social events seem to be progressing, is the complete subjugation of the physical earth to the dominion of human intellect. The only portion of mankind capable of rising to this conception is that which composes the European-American civilization. Hence, in the grand progress, this portion must be the master-worker, and the law-giver, and every race not capable of attaining to this broad conception, must either assume a position, as under-worker, commensurate with its intellectual capacity, or as the only alternative, must yield the room it uselessly occupies to those who can be made to do so." For Southerners, then, "grand progress" began but did not end with the enslavement of Africans. Eventually all of the world's peoples would have to learn their place, serving according to their ability and receiving according to their unfortunate but innate disabilities. Historians, it appears, have sold Southerners rather short in suggesting that they were motivated primarily by a desire to defend their peculiar institution. True, the South's leadership sought to protect slave property, expand slave territory, and prevent class warfare by ensuring that land and slaves were available to nonslaveholders. But they believed they were— alongside their Northern brethren at first, better than their Northern brethren ultimately—building a Civilization.[9]

To the Victorians, "Civilization" was a word of vast, poetic power. Where an empire was measured in extent, a civilization was measured in majesty, and mid-century Victorians were nearly obsessed with the moral dimension of their sovereignty. "The term civilization," an author for the *Messenger* intoned, "has a philosophical signification—a signification fixed by history, developed by moral sciences, containing wide, boundless elements, and implying a compendium of man's best and noblest ideas." Admittedly, this definition is a trifle ungainly. The "signification," however fixed, and the "elements," however boundless, are left hanging in air; the compendium of ideas, despite the reassuring superlatives, is discomfitingly thin on specifics. As with éclat, however, Civilization gained much of its grandness from an unwillingness to ground itself in petty details. Comfortable in the clouds, Civilization had a gauzy celestiality, a quality that could not be defined by men precisely because it loomed so high above them.[10]

The *Messenger's* take on Civilization betrays more than a telling vagueness, however. This definition could only be the product of an antebellum education. Moral philosophy, progressive history, and noble ideas constituted something like the core curriculum of most colleges of the period, and this author mentions all three in one sentence. If he had added dead languages, he would have captured the full course load of the average antebellum freshman. While a complete examination of university curricula is impossible here, the basic contours are straightforward. Dead languages, especially Latin and Greek, opened the door to dead civilizations, which functioned as tutorials on the dos and don'ts of civilization building generally. The rise and fall

By 1850, American men, North and South, were caught up in the éclat of Civilization building. Inspired by women (embodied at right), men embarked on their quest to erect on the still primeval landscape a Civilization to stand for all time. As the painter shrewdly notes, however, they were mostly just building castles in the sky. Thomas Cole, *Voyage of Life (Youth)*, ca. 1839–40, oil on canvas 8⅜ in. x 10⅞ in. Munson-Williams-Proctor Arts Institute, Museum of Art, Utica, New York. 55.106

of each of the world's once-great powers was understood as a moral tale whose narrative arc resembled that of a grand epic. Each empire functioned as a heroic character, glorious and flawed, doomed from the beginning and destined to live forever in the memories of men who appreciated the poetry of making a play for it all. Thus the Athenian Greeks were an object lesson in the dangers of unrelieved esoterica, the Romans a paradigm for the pitfalls of rampant militancy. Although the message drawn from each hero's story was different, the moral was always the same—a perfect Civilization was possible, and a man was to search within himself to determine how he might best contribute to its attainment.[11]

By the 1850s, America had already made impressive progress as a would-be Civilization. The country's size doubled with the Louisiana Purchase and then doubled again with the Mexican cession. As important, the country's commercial development had been astonishingly rapid. To be sure, much of this development took place in the North, but the South's transformation was not without its own impressive features. The fact that two-thirds of the railway miles in the United States in 1860 were in the North, for instance, should not blind us to the remaining one-third stretched out across the South, amounting to some 10,000 miles. As in the North, these were miles that seemed to spring up over night. In 1850 Missouri sported a paltry four miles of track; by 1860 it had 817. Tennessee, similarly, went from 48 to 1,253 miles; Mississippi from 60 to 862; Alabama from 112 to 743; and Virginia from 341 to 1,743. More importantly, the rapid pace of development gave Southerners, as well as Northerners, a giddy sense of their own national prospects. "This railroad business is the *dispensation* of the present era," remarked South Carolinian William C. Preston, "and is to be the harbinger of mighty events, no less than a change—at least a very decided modification—of the plan of civilization. There have been two great dispensations of Civilization, the Greek & Christian, and now comes the railroad, or rather Locomotive." This was not the empty rhetoric of a stump speech; Preston had penned these words in a letter to a friend, and they were exactly the sort of terms in which Americans (Southerners included) had begun to think by the 1850s. Others might dicker with Preston's three pillars but probably not much: in the Greeks Americans had found their humanity, in Christianity their faith. Now they had the tool to implement them, the machine of all machines, the locomotive. More hung in the balance than getting cotton to market or fine fabrics from New York. A new world was being born, and Americans all were to be participants at the birth.[12]

The South's demographic maturation was as startling as its economic growth. In the 1830s, the South's population had been extremely unstable. The older states of the tidewater endured massive outmigration while the newer states of Tennessee, Kentucky, Alabama, and Mississippi were overrun with new residents. North Carolina's sagging numbers made it the "Ireland of America," and one resident described it simply as "one vast camping ground" on the way from one place to someplace else. For those who stayed behind, this "migratory fever" constituted something of a crisis. "Scarcely have [these migrants] squatted down," groused one South Carolina editor, "and built up their little 'improvements' than they hear of a new purchase, where corn grows without planting, and cotton comes up five bales to the acre, ready picked and packed—they pull up stakes and boom off for the new Canaan." "I cannot but think," he continued, that "every remove into the wilderness lessens the hold which refinement and society have hitherto held upon individual man." Such grumblings ought to have had a familiar ring. Decades earlier the Founding Fathers had been just as ambivalent about the wave of migration that sent Americans tumbling over the Appalachians and into the Ohio Valley. Washington hoped a good part of the settlers would be killed by Indians. Madison figured that the West would just have to become its own country. Monroe, seemingly forgetting himself, suggested that the east rule the west as a colony "similar to that which prevail'd in these States previous to the revolution." No such drastic measure was necessary, of course; the new states of the Northwest replicated and complemented the older states much more than they threatened them. The South had its own version of this crisis in the Southwest of the 1830s, and it witnessed a similar stabilization by the 1850s. Older states grew steadily and propitiously—in the towns no less than in the country—and newer states transformed their backwater settlements into prosperous communities. Just as the North had civilized the old Northwest, the South had transformed the Old Southwest from frontier outpost to a "future seat of empires." There was, to be sure, no Chicago in Alabama, but then neither was there a Natchez in Indiana. And the main point is a more general one: after a decade of transplantation Southerners set about the business of putting down roots, elaborating communities rather than transporting them.[13]

One did not have to be a city dweller to feel the effects of the South's rapid maturation. When John Shofner and his father came to Bedford County, Tennessee, in 1809, they confronted "a thick forrest of heavey timber and the powerfullest cain brake that was eaver saw." The round trip from Nashville to New Orleans took three months,

there were no grain mills, no place to market cattle or pigs (except
when the drovers drifted in), sugar was twenty-five cents a pound,
and women had to spin their own thread. When, in 1810, Governor
Lewis took a trip up the Mississippi on "the first steemboot that eaver
run the river," he caused a sensation. But by the time John Shofner
had reached middle age, there were so many steamboats on the Mississippi he could not count them; sugar was ten cents a pound; "wev-
ing factorey[s]" did most of the spinning; and it took twelve days to
make the round trip from Nashville to New Orleans (including the
time to load and unload 200 tons of cargo). There were grain mills
wherever there was water power, and where there wasn't water power
there was steam. Railroads were springing up everywhere, and Shofner was confident the day was not far off when he could put his "hole
crop in the cares [railcars] and in three days go to markit, sell out,
lay in, and come home." "Histrey cold not relate aneything to excell
the progress," Shofner goggled proudly, and "we are still going
ahead."[14]

John Shofner was (with the exception of his spelling) absolutely
right. His country had made a startling debut and seemed determined
to take its show all the way to the top. The South was fully a part
of that project. However cavalier their attitudes toward the Union
during the secession crisis (a subject to be taken up in due time),
Southerners right up to the Civil War believed that America either
was or would soon become the greatest civilization ever to grace the
earth. Ancient Greece had its intellectual attainments, Rome its empire; but America might have it all, and its progress had been stunning
to behold. Traveling to New York in September 1858, South Carolina
planter William Elliott was present for a two-day celebration of the
laying of the first Atlantic cable (between Ireland and Newfoundland).
Looking down from the upper window of his hotel on "the thronging
multitudes that—filling the streets—were distributed on the very
house tops," he began to sob. "[I] remembered this City as I had
known it in 1806," he wrote his wife, and "whether it was patriotism
or what other feeling—I know not—but the tears streamed down
from my eyes. Possibly it was a commendable pride at witnessing the
extraordinary progress of the Country." And Southerners had every
right to be proud. They had participated fully in the besting of the

redcoats, the founding of the Republic, the rise of American military and commercial power, and the steady conquest of a western empire. Americans, Southern and Northern alike, had for years told brazen tales about their special destiny as a people; by 1850 it was beginning to seem as if the tales might be true. No longer a passive exemplar—a City upon a Hill—America began to dream itself an empire for the ages.[15]

To the observers living through it, however, the country's rapid growth seemed often more frenetic and disorienting than directed and progressive. The attainments were lofty, the rhetoric loftier, but still there was something in the speed of the advancement which seemed reckless in itself. Americans were a simple, republican people at heart. Their progress, while fortuitous, had overtaken their ability to assimilate and make sense of it. To North Carolinian Robert Morrison, American advancement seemed less like an unfolding destiny than a "Go *a-head* mania." "The reckless, growing & insatiable thirst to drive every thing at *Steam Speed*," he griped in 1853, "produces disregard for law, order, safety, and human life.... Cautious men, moderate measures, wise counsel, prudent forethought, and common sense are commodities too old for consideration & too contracted for this expanding age." To a writer for the *Messenger*, the alterations were so profound they threatened the very nature of man. "To one that can look back for the last thirty years," he noted in 1854, "the changes ... are beyond the wildest imaginings. The new and extended powers ... together with the wonderful inventions of man, have added to his nature [and] made him almost another being." Underlining this angst, of course, the deepening sectional crisis tainted each national success, giving the American project an awful, self-defeating aspect. With each new conquest, a manifest destiny that might have been expected to bring national unity brought deeper division. With each new development in transportation, manufacturing, and communications, North and South became more deeply engaged, more deeply implicated, in each other's appalling peculiarities. Poised to achieve greatness, America was instead threatened with self-destruction.[16]

The constrictions of the 1850s were a particular problem for coming-of-age males. More educated than their fathers, they were also under more pressure to live up to the version of civilized patriarchy

that had become so integral to the South's sense of self and to its
defense against the North. In the face of such constrictions, young
men did what they always do when times are tight and opportunities
few and beneath them—they hung around the house, living lavishly
on their parents' ample account. Needless to say, this did not go over
well with the parents themselves. "The babe of to day," griped one
Southern editorialist, "whilst it gazes admiringly at little sister Sue in
trains and a hoop; opens its eyes approvingly at the youthful Fanny's
declaration, that the great purpose of her life is to be a 'fast woman,'
and pats brother Georgy encouragingly on the back, as he swaggers
into the nursery, redolent of cigar smoke." While such indictments
suggest in part that Southern children were growing up too fast, the
real anxiety was that Southern children were not growing up at all,
creating a generation of perpetual infants, incapable of controlling
their urges and unwilling to accept responsibility for actions which
were typically childish and destructive.[17]

This concern was especially common in the planting class, where
wealth allowed young men to display their impertinence in all its
foppish finery. Hammond, for instance, called his sons "dead weights"
who "growl, grumble, sulk and *do nothing*. . . . They don't pull off their
coats and go at it. They shoot birds, buy fish, and gerrymander the
County . . . they are mere dillitanti—theatrical planters . . . [and] negroes, overseers, and neighbors see that as plainly as I do." Of course,
such subjective disgruntlement proves very little; it's quite possible
that Hammond's father said the same things of him. But in the late
antebellum South such complaints were rife, and men more farsighted
than Hammond correctly discerned that the problem was not the
young per se, but the steady constriction of the prospects they faced.
"The time I fear is past," noted William Elliott in 1849, "when a
Gentleman can succeed as a planter. The pains taking of an operative
manufacturer must be added to the duties of the agriculturist—or he
will reap nothing but disappointment and vexation." The master of
fourteen plantations spanning several states, Elliott practiced diversi-
fied farming, experimented with different systems of crop rotation
and irrigation, and not only kept up with the agricultural journals
but contributed to them. And still he could claim in 1854 that he felt
like a man on a treadmill: "Though I have not squandered, but on

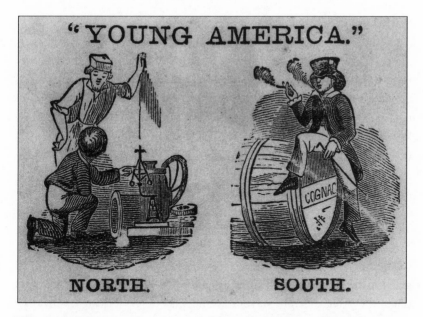

This antebellum cartoon captures the emerging distinction between Northern and Southern adolescents. The Northern boy is penitently posed, worshiping at the altar of capitalism, devoted to learning a trade, and respectful of his elders. The Southern boy is a fop and a rake, all lacy cuffs and careful coiffeur, content to ride a barrel of brandy to his destiny. Note the suggestive position of his hand and riding crop. Clearly, smoking and drinking are but two of his many destructive appetites. "Envelopes of the Great Rebellion," Southern Historical Collection, UNC.

the contrary have trebled my paternal inheritance—such is the unproductive state of our agriculture that our incomes are reduced to almost nothing. . . . A new order of things prevails and young men of the first families must work or starve." The crisis then (to the extent that it could be called one) was not so much generational as systemic. Slave prices had ballooned, the international cotton competition had stiffened, and land seemed ever scarcer, dryer, poorer. None of this is to say that the planting life was somehow doomed; the Southern economy, with or without slavery, would likely have adapted and continued to expand. But it does not take a market breakdown to set the mind of a master class to turning; in an era of ever-rising expectations and ever-collapsing opportunities, relatively small constrictions tend to take their psychic toll. "Oh for a snug little farm," Hammond lamented in 1853, "where I could indulge my fondness for the country ... without the anxiety created by the idea that the 'main chance' depends on having every screw tight & and the whole machinery moving on clock-work principles." And so here at last we have Hammond's real complaint—it was not that his sons worked so little but that he worked so much. He resented their ease because he was himself ill at ease in a world where the gap between planter and clock maker had closed.[18]

——————◆——————

Why couldn't Southern men content themselves as clock makers? Unfortunately, while economic modernization in their region had proceeded far enough to make Southerners anxious, it had not proceeded so far as to make them adjusted. As a result, North and South diverged not merely on the role slavery would play in American Civilization but on the role men should play in Civilization's attainment. In the North, boys were encouraged to pattern themselves after what might be called *civilized* manhood. Men were supposed to exemplify and embody the *effects* of civilization, underscoring their self-possession and self-restraint by holding up to the world a paragon of gentlemanly conduct, abstemious habits, and Christian rectitude. In the South, boys were supposed to follow a subtly different pattern, one of *civilizing* manhood. Southern men were obliged not merely to affect Civilization but to cause it, the emphasis falling on not merely the composition but the imposition of the self.

In 1858 Josiah Gorgas, later Confederate chief of ordnance, reread a biography of Benjamin Franklin he had first plumbed as a boy of thirteen. Then the book had been part of his father's library, one of a host of biographies that acted as national models for manhood. Gorgas had devoured the book then, reading it more than a dozen times, each time coming to a greater admiration for the subject. But when he read the biography in 1858, he found that he did not like Franklin's character as he once had. "There is throughout his life too much of the sense of worldly success," Gorgas noted. "Nearly all his maxims relate to success in life, & many of his precepts, in fact most of them, are too deeply tinctured with policy. It is not a brave, open and generous nature that lies open before us in these pages and stirs us with sympathy for its struggles, & with admiration for its success." Franklin's was a Yankee sort of manhood. Caught up in the pennies and the precepts, he had known nothing of éclat, nothing of the good a man could do when he had the mettle to run wide open. Franklin's maxims for success, while functional, were too stingy, too tight in the shoes, the pockets, the pants. Successful in his lifetime, Franklin was nonetheless a poor model for boys because he had been unwilling to give fully and openly of himself in a great gamble to build, love, live.[19]

The problem with this Southern model was that it bore little relationship to the changing reality of men's occupational lives. By the 1850s, planting families were sending increasing numbers of their sons to college, where they blithely glutted themselves on the poetics of Civilization building. At the same time, these same sons were with increasing frequency entering professions other than planting, where they came up against mundanities of a workaday world that little comported with the models for manhood they had been taught in school. How could Southern men live up to increasingly romantic ideals of civilizing manhood when the expansive work of winning the empire was giving way to the more mundane work of administrating it? How could they be contented clerks and mechanics—as their Yankee brethren seemed to be—when their expectations for themselves ran always toward energy and éclat? "To be great, there must be a great work to be done," Mississippian Joseph Baldwin complained. "Talents alone are not [enough]....Great abilities...need a great stimulus." These stimuli had certainly been present in the founding period, and they had been present right through the 1830s and the South's great land boom. "In a new country the political edifice, like all the rest, must be built from the ground up," Baldwin observed. "While nothing is at hand, every thing must be made. There is work for all and a necessity for all to work." By the 1850s, however, the Old Southwest had been tamed; society had stabilized and grown respectable; rules governed behavior and competition for positions and resources had become stiff. Greatness was no longer to be seized but earned and then, Baldwin noted, after a "long and tedious novitiate."[20]

Across the South in the late antebellum period, young men faced such novitiates with a sort of dejected resolve. Contemplating his 1853 graduation from West Point, for instance, J.E.B. Stuart had little notion how the grand ideals he had learned were to be applied in the world as it was. "After next June I have not the remotest idea what will become of me," he wrote his cousin. "If you are good at divining I wish you would try the art to determine my fate." Ticking off the possibilities, however, Stuart realized there was only one avenue open to him. The life of a farmer had a certain nobility but "presupposes the possession of a *farm* which ... is not always practicable [for] the young man for whom capital has not already been accumulated." This left what Stuart called derisively the "*hireling* professions ... Law, Medicine, Engineering, and Arms." "The lawyer has his cases but *seldom* receives his fees. The physician has his patients & his sleepless nights but his patients are very patient in *waiting to pay him.*" And the Engineer was in an altogether impossible situation: "[He] must first have a reputation before he can get desirable employment" and, of course, he couldn't establish a reputation without first being employed. For Stuart, this left only arms. "The officer has his toils but he [also] has his rewards." Stuart concluded, "There is something in 'the pride and pomp and circumstance of glorious war,' which makes 'Othello's occupation' the most desirable of all."[21]

Stuart was relatively lucky in finding a profession that comported with his notion of what a man should be. Most of the South's college graduates were not so fortunate. They went out into the world armed only with unachievable ideals and dreams of greatness so lofty they had little practical application. The brashest men compensated for such circumstances with sheer pluck, but men of melancholy or sensitive disposition sometimes gave way to despair. In "Leaves from a Dreamer's Diary," a writer for *Russell's* admitted that his education had almost ruined him for real life. "Of all the places on earth in which to settle an indolent youth," he noted, "an American College is the worst." There, he claimed, boys were indulged and coddled; they basked in the shade of magnificent oaks and, when they did make it to class, were plied with fanciful stories until their imaginations became almost "morbidly acute." Nothing in their boyhood or education prepared these young men for the sharp constriction of circumstance and insipid grind of their mundane professional lives.

"I had pictured to myself, with fancy's vague pencil, some great obstacles, which determination and energy would overcome," noted the
writer of his college years, and "I was unprepared then for the slow,
consuming cares which gathered around me. . . . the little cares of life
. . . which [would] waste away [my] heart."[22]

Tennessean John Lincoln suffered a similar shock as he left college.
For three years, he said, his days were spent in alternating bouts of
reverie and depression. He would imagine himself a teacher and the
toast of a college, delivering a powerful oration before the whole
student body. Then he would fancy himself a great lawyer, standing
"two feet and a half taller than [renowned jurist William] Wirt." But
from this dizzying height, he would always come crashing down in a
spell of the blues that left him indifferent, torpid, and "distant to the
whole human race." "You've no idea, Sue, how much I suffered by
the nasty blue (black they were to me) devils," John wrote his cousin.
"They were caused by the bodily weakness attendant upon a student's
life. . . . My mind dwelt in the ideal world so much that it chafed at
the sober realities of life. I was full of happiness and full of misery,
sometimes the one, sometimes the other. . . . I dwelt . . . in golden castles of the delusive future, . . . my mind . . . more enlarged by great and
noble views of life, yet, . . . strange as it may seem, the vividness of
my conception of the responsibilities of life made me wish to shun
them . . . and the brightness of my ideal made me despair of reaching
it." College had raised Lincoln's expectations and his ambition to an
almost dizzying altitude, leaving him little grounding in the practical
everydayness of manhood as it really was. Stuffed to the gills with
Napoleon, Washington, and Hale, Lincoln had barely a first notion of
how to set about being contented as a clerk.[23]

Taking up the practicalities of manhood had a similar effect on
Mississippian Everard Baker. "Here of late, a change has come over
me," he noted in his diary, a change "which is in its nature anything
but agreeable." Baker's youth had been "interspersed with . . . many
scenes glowing with the merriment & hillarity of a gay & sportive
disposition." But when he compared "that view with the life that now
feebly glimmers in these long expected years of manhood—which
allured in the distance with such flattering anticipations—" he conceived, he said, "almost a hatred for myself." "Now I am a dull,

insipid being," he confessed in his diary. "My days pass in a state of torpid[ity] & sluggish[ness]. Unable to entertain company with dignity or pleasure & a drag upon those whose company I seek, [mine is] a listless, lethargic state of mind, unable to pursue a profitable train of thought or to follow the suggestions of another. [This] unaccountable debility . . . disables me from anything like mental employment & very often sheds a brooding melancholy hue over my whole self." Unable to adduce one good cause for his disagreeable thoughts, Baker felt himself "to be aught but a happy man."[24]

Any college student, of course, experiences some despondency when he turns finally to the problems of building a career and raising a family. These problems were exacerbated, however, by an antebellum system that almost monomaniacally stressed the glorious histories of the world's great men—even as the opportunity for glory began to fade. As it did, children raised to emulate great men began instead to envy them. "[Napoleon] grew up in a time of turmoil, and had a chance to fight his way to the Consulate and Empire," Richard Elliott griped. "I grew up in a quiet time, when there was no chance to pick up a crown at the point of one's sword." For depressives like Stuart, Lincoln, Baker, and Elliott manhood seemed almost a quiet curse; raised to project their aggressions outward an untold number began to redirect them inward upon themselves.[25]

To be sure, women suffered from fits of despondency too. But when a woman's world was not as she wanted, she still had hope to comfort her. Unhappy women, of whom there were undoubtedly many, lived much of their lives in a counterfactual future where the passage of time had reordered their circumstances and happiness had returned, as if of its own accord. Wearily accustomed (though never resigned) to surrendering themselves to the will of men and the whims of fate, women had one great advantage over men—they could surrender themselves to the march of events without losing their self-esteem. For the powerless, hope becomes a touchstone, the future a magical alternate world, which, if it never comes to pass, is still an endless source of comfort. "What would we be without hope," noted Anna King in a letter to her daughter. "Hope which concerns this world—& hope which concerns the world to which we are all hastening!" Men, however, tended to find hope an unsatisfactory solution to the problem of present unhappiness. Hope was too passive, requiring a kind of patience and submission to fate that ill-comported with the male ideal. Men did not wait for things to change; they changed them. They understood themselves, and were understood by others, to be in command of their own destinies; the fault for adversity lay, as often as not, at their own door. To be sure, men prayed for good luck and railed at bad, but they could never fully abandon the idea that it fell to them to deal with the difficulties and dissatisfactions that beset them. Hope, then, was a weak man's refuge, and indulging it was as likely to bring self-recrimination as satisfaction. "What is hope itself but a happy sort of discontent," grumbled William Gilmore Simms, "tell[ing] us of unattained objects and conditions." "You call it hope— that fire of fire!" noted Edgar Allan Poe in *Tamerlane*. "It is but agony of desire."[26]

But if men could not turn to hope, neither could they turn easily to other men. Given the Southern male's prickly sense of self, relationships between them had a peculiar dynamic. On the one hand, the emphasis on the difference between male and female concerns meant that men, and especially young ones, were often in each other's company, engaged in male pastimes and pursuits. They played together, hunted together, went to college together, and often managed farms and businesses together. On the other hand, men were constantly on their guard, watching each other for signs of respect and disrespect, competing with each other for mates, honors, and distinctions. Even in friendship, there was a standoffishness, an unwillingness to appear weak, vulnerable, or emotionally needy. "I have always been afraid of committing myself in talking even to my friends," noted Wallace Cumming, "not that I would have said more than I meant but that from some (imaginary) cause or other I might receive a rebuff." To be sure, there was a rough camaraderie between males, especially between college chums. But most understood that when they left the university for their respective destinies, they were unlikely to continue such friendships on anything like an intimate level. As William Elliot explained somewhat sadly: "There is something of mutual self-deception, and exaggeration in *early friendships*, which the experience of after life dispels. And while the conflicts of interest or ambition estrange us from some—and the grave separates us from others—we seek not to replace those broken links with others that may prove as brittle."[27]

Unable to hope without appearing idle and fatuous, unable to seek counsel from other men without appearing vulnerable and weak, men often heaped blame on themselves for their perceived failure to live up to standards for manhood they all recognized as surely as their own face. Turning against the standards was not an option; all knew from the beginning that a bid for greatness would be cold going, all agreed that its legitimacy as a life goal was beyond reproach.

The case of Giles Patterson illustrates the degree to which ante-bellum men of a certain caste actually preferred being failures to giving up the dream of immortality whose standards had made them failures in the first place. As a student at South Carolina College, Patterson would lie in his dorm room for days, drifting dreamily, indulging equally in vainglory and self-reproach. He wanted to be an orator or a poet, and he believed he had abilities in these arts. His parents and professors believed so too, and Patterson admitted that he had received his share of "plaudits and praises." But he knew also that the chance of ever exercising his abilities in a bold and open arena was remote. He had little confidence that the world would give him such an opportunity, less confidence that he had the brass to seize such an opportunity if it was offered. Thus the encouragements heaped on him by others seemed wasted—instead of "nerv[ing] up" his "young heart to desperate struggles and new efforts to gain distinction in the world" they had rather the opposite effect, teaching Patterson that "my futile attempts at honor or immortality are vain, and that I must give up the pursuit." But he did not give it up; he merely shifted the arena of that pursuit to a land of fanciful dreams. Having steeled himself to the fact that he hadn't the moment or the mettle ever to become great, Patterson allowed the realization to slip quietly from his hand, like the book of a child grown drowsy, and fell instead "into a reverie of some happy chance that will be offered which if it did really come to pass would be as miraculous as a fairy tale."[28]

Patterson's preference for oratory and poetics is revealing in itself. The orator was the South's ultimate public man, capable of "rais[ing] armies" or "subvert[ing] governments" through "the potent agency of [his] tongue." The greatest orators, of course, did not deploy such power wantonly; rather they crusaded for truth, tearing from their own breast the passion and the commitment they hoped to instill in others. "The man of purest motive, of sincerest conviction," reported the *Messenger*, "will be [the] greatest orator. The earnestness of a mind fully convinced, spreads to and through an audience with the rapidity of [an] electric spark," holding listeners "spell-bound, as if entranced by a heavenly vision." The poet had similar abilities— heavenly visions and electrifying acts of imagination were his stock in trade. This is probably why orator and poet made such tempting choices for young men like Patterson. Both immortalized their passions in a high tongue; both pursued an intellectual agenda with a purity impracticable among the "hirelings." There were, however, some critical differences between the poetic and oratorical arts. The poet was a solitary figure, an orator in spirit, but turned inward upon himself. He would never draw the world into his lungs and bellow it forth in an exuberant rush of air. What he drew into himself tended to stay there, haunting and caged; his words blasted through his vitals only to emerge in silence to take up their careful positions on a page. Then too the orator's primary concern was Truth, a slippery, contested thing in any age, but never more so than when a country is drifting toward civil war. The poet's muse, on the other hand, was Beauty— a softer mistress who invited a man to behold for himself, without backchat or bother. Patterson's inward turn to the land of dreams and his poetic proclivity were part of the same impulse that drove the depression of Everard Baker and John Lincoln. Unsure that he would have the chance to be an orator, unsure that he would be equal to it if it came, Patterson redirected his orator to the indulgent audience that awaited within, ever receptive and respectful. Patterson had not lost his desire to create something intellectually pure, had not lost his impulse for empire building, but in a world as sullied and as complicated as his had become, he was relieved to think that he might build that empire on the relatively uncontested terrain of his own self-loathing imagination.[29]

The éclat-based culture of Thomas King, then, had a dark and destructive flipside. For all the promise of immortality and indulgence it held out to men, it also instilled in them an unconscious and

irresolvable resentment of standards for manhood that could not reasonably be met. As men struggled vainly against the omnipresent
possibility of failure, they occasionally fashioned imaginary empires
out of their own self-hate. No Southerner better represents this tendency than Edgar Allan Poe. To everything he was ever accused of,
Poe bleakly responded, I did it—not merely because he did do it but
because, having pointed the finger at himself so long and so ably, he
was ever ready to confess to anything. When the *Boston Daily Star*
charged Poe with appearing at the Lyceum in a "*gentlemanly* condition of liquor obfuscation," Poe was furious. "In the first place," he
told his readers, "why cannot these miserable hypocrites say 'drunk'
at once and be done with it? In the second place we are perfectly
willing to admit that we *were* drunk—in the face of at least eleven
or twelve hundred Frogpondians [Poe's nickname for Bostonians] who
will be willing to take the oath that we were *not*. We are willing to
admit either that we were drunk, or that we set fire to the Frogpond,
or that once upon a time we cut the throat of our grandmother. The
fact is, we are perfectly ready to admit anything at all." Poe's point,
exaggerated for effect, is accurate—a man can't very well be accused
of something he has already admitted to, and Poe's tales, poems, and
essays read like one long, terrible confession.[30]

But the perversity that plays out so prominently in Poe's life and
fiction masks a feature far more chilling: an authorial control as tight
and total as a death grip. His themes were hot passions—murder,
obsession, torment, and madness—but he always rendered them
coolly, with precision, discipline, and a discomfiting sanity. His subjects were often fantastic—balloon rides and voyages off the edge of
the world—but he always described them in meticulous detail, with
objectivity, authority, and compelling reasonableness. "You often re-
volt at his subjects," remarked an 1854 review in the *Messenger*, "but
no sooner does he enter on them, than your attention is riveted....
[Held in] his glittering eye...you forget everything—your home,
your friends, your creed, your very personal identity, and become
swallowed up like a straw in the maelstrom.... And during all the
wild and whirling narrative, the same chilly glitter has continued to
shine in his eye, his blood has never warmed and he has never exalted
his voice above a thrilling whisper." Poe had not given up the project

of being a man, had not given up his imperial impulse, his rigid control, or his expansive vision. Rather, like Patterson and countless other Southern men, Poe had turned these drives inward upon himself, seeking to erect a personal empire of sorrow, a kingdom of pain over which he had sole mastery. The self-destructiveness so often associated with him was simply the creative drive working in reverse; out of destruction and death he fashioned an anti-empire with all the appointments and glories he had been cheated out of by life. Thus his House of Usher collapses into the tarn, his City Upon the Sea slips quietly beneath the dark water, never to reemerge. In the decline of Civilization lay a Civilization all Poe's own; here he was an aristocrat, not declining but expanding, a dark prince presiding over a collapse of the universe as magnificent as its birth. His rage, he admitted, was a "sacred fury," a sort of alternate religion in which he indulged his dream of a release more permanent than death. Poe, a contemporary critic marveled, had somehow slipped "below the suicide point [where] death open[ed] up no hope for him [because] his quarrel [was] not with *life* on earth [but] with *being* anywhere." But even in his vast condemnation of being, Poe did not turn against the ideals for manhood that had been taught him in his Virginia boyhood. "I only beg you to remember," Poe wrote his stepfather at nineteen, "that you yourself cherished the cause of my leaving your family—Ambition. If it has not taken the channel you wished it, it is not the less certain of its object. Richmond & the U. States were too narrow a sphere & the world shall be my theatre. . . . My father do not throw me aside as *degraded*. I will be an honor to your name." In building an empire of his "sacred fury," Poe created the mightiest Civilization of all, a Civilization of decay at war with God himself.[31]

From Alabama backwater to Carolina estate, Southern men also spoke *Poe's* language of éclat. "I came into this world without my knowledge or consent," noted planter James Henry Hammond in his diary. "If . . . a Superior and Designing Being created me and placed me here; if this is *all* or the best, *I do not thank him.* I wish I had been let alone. I should not object—hating the pain and lurking fear of death, to be remanded at once to my original nothingness, for this is a world of ineffable misery and from my experience I abominate it and most that it contains. If there is a Hereafter, then the God who placed me here owes me large compensation for the sufferings I have *involuntarily* undergone on Earth." Hammond, like Poe, has slipped below the suicide point, indulging an appetite for self-destruction as voracious as his appetite for self-aggrandizement. Throughout his life, Hammond built up his personal and political empire, only to then preside over its dismantling. As governor of South Carolina, he was poised to spring into national politics, but preferred instead sticky fumblings with his nubile nieces, resulting in disgrace. From his disgrace, he threatened to rise again, only to alienate his wife and society in sexual forays in the slave quarter that none could be expected to ignore. Hammond's cycle of self-destruction and resurrection was in perfect sync with the imaginative cycle of the antebellum male more generally. The bid for immortality took them from a bloated to a despairing sense of self and back again; unable to live up to their own standard for manhood, they often indulged a depressive melancholy as romantic, as fanciful, as self-involved, as the notion of immortality itself.[32]

CHAPTER 2

TWO SEPARATE YET
MOST INTIMATE THINGS

How was it that Ambition crept,
Unseen, amid the revels there,
Till growing bold, he laughed and leapt
In the tangles of Love's very hair?*

In his first published poem, *Tamerlane*, Edgar Allan Poe adopted the persona of a defeated and world-weary warrior lamenting life from his deathbed. A shepherd in his youth, Tamerlane lived high above the world on a mighty mountaintop, sleeping soundly under a vast and open sky. There he wanted for nothing. He lived a life of simple pleasures and cares with a woman of unsurpassed beauty and goodness providing him all the companionship he could ever need. In her he glimpsed the heavens; in himself he found a better man for her company; together they shared the delights and pains of which human life is wrought. But one morning Tamerlane awoke with a fire in his heart. The clouds above him seemed like banners, unfurling to reveal his name; the distant thunder seemed a blasting bugle call, sent to wake his slumbering ambition. The world was his, the sky seemed to say; he had only to rise and take it. It was not for himself alone that he would conquer the world, however. Speaking to his beloved of his aspirations, he began to see that in her too was a light too bright to shine and fade in a desolate wood. She must have a

* Edgar Allan Poe, *Tamerlane*.

throne—and he must win it for her. Thus did Tamerlane's love and ambition become tied up together: "And, so, confusedly became / Thine image, and—a name—a name! / Two separate—yet most intimate things."[1]

The bugle blast that woke Tamerlane from his mountain reverie was heard by countless young Southern men. In 1848, Mississippian Henry Hughes heard the call: "I will rise above doubt, dread, sense, sin," he promised his diary. "I [shall] stand upon the pinnacle of Fame and look down on Washington & Napoleon. . . . I will be the greatest mortal man that ever was." Not surprisingly, Hughes's ambitions, like Tamerlane's, centered on Civilization building. "The Condition of Europe arouses and encourages me," he noted of the 1848 Revolutions. "I will be the President of America and Europe. The Republics of earth shall all be joined in one Government. I will be their ruler. I feel that for some such destiny as this, God has marked me out." Equally unsurprising, Hughes, like Patterson and Poe, Hammond and Tamerlane, fell from such dizzying heights, fetching up only when he had slipped below the suicide point. "Nothing seems to me so grateful as annihilation," he confessed. "I am homesick for the grave."[2]

As the last chapter noted, this cycle was an endemic aspect of masculinity in the late antebellum South. Having ascended with the romantic tenor of the times, men's dreams of pride and power became ever loftier as their opportunities became ever more constricted; their frustrations had almost inevitably to be projected outward or in, with results that were usually destructive. What went unexamined in the last chapter, however, is the insight that lies at the core of *Tamerlane*. Men did not travel this cycle of elation and despair alone; they brought their women with them—real women if they were available, fantasies if they were not—folding them up in great, covetous visions of masculine becoming. Through the eyes of their women, men could appear grand and unconquerable, even in a clerkship; in making their bid for greatness in a woman's name, men could feel that their quest was less about self-aggrandizement than self-sacrifice; and in their inevitable failures, men could rebuild on the bedrock of a woman's love and faith. "Have I ever had a pleasure in which woman was not an element," Henry Hughes asked, returning to the top of his cycle. "Ambition and Love, these are my life."[5]

The confusing mess men made of ambition and love was, of course, distinctly personal and should not be overgeneralized. While the pressure to live up to the South's masculine standard was common to the region, personality played a crucial role in shaping how individuals responded to that pressure. The following extended treatments of Laurence Massillon Keitt and Henry Craft give but a flavor of that remarkable variety, providing a glimpse into the complex ways in which men experienced what they regarded as the central fact of their lives—the fact that they were men.

Laurence Massillon Keitt: Politics as Epic Poem

In February 1857, a general melee broke out on the floor of the House of Representatives. For three days the legislators had engaged in a heated debate over the admission of Kansas as a slave state. The Buchanan administration had rammed the bill through the Senate with relative ease, but House forces were evenly matched and perennially ill-humored. One representative captured the general mood when he suggested that each man check his sidearm at the door—he was only half kidding. On the third day of the debate, opposition forces gained an unexpected advantage—an unusual number of dinners and dances had seriously depleted the Democratic ranks. Frantic, Alexander Stephens sent messengers to the likely salons to round up the wayward congressmen. Most probably, Laurence Keitt was among these reinforcements. His passion for politics was equaled only by his passion for fashionable life, and he was one of the city's most notorious gallants. Regardless, by two in the morning the "leader of the Palmetto State's young chivalry" had dragged himself into the House where he lay sprawled across two tables, half drunk and half asleep, one of his shoes having fallen to the floor. The Republican floor leader, Galusha Grow of Pennsylvania, was conferring with opposition-minded Democrats on that party's side of the House when John Quitman of Mississippi offered another in a long line of silly motions designed to forestall a vote. Tired, frustrated, and not a little belligerent himself, Grow objected "with considerable tartness" to such parliamentary pettiness. Apparently the objection came as an unwelcome intrusion to the napping Keitt—with eyes still closed, he inclined his head just long enough to growl, "if you are going to object, go back to your own side of the house." "This is a free hall," Grow answered the prostrate congressman, "and I have the right to object from any part of it when I choose." At this Keitt was up in a flash, fumbling for his footwear. "Wait until I put my shoe on, you Black Republican puppy," he snarled at Grow, "and we will see about that." Slightly amused, Grow held his ground, claiming he would be damned before some "nigger driver" fresh off the plantation would crack a whip about his ears and tell him where or where not to stand in the House of Representatives. Keitt, normally adept at such verbal sparrings, was at an unusual loss for words and instead launched himself at the defiant Republican, meaning to choke him. Accounts vary dramatically as to what happened next. Republican papers and Grow partisans claim the well-proportioned congressman caught Keitt with a hard right, knocking him to the floor. Keitt backers claim Grow's fist went wide of the mark and that Keitt had "merely tripped." Regardless, their tussle set off a general melee in front of the speaker's podium in which dozens of congressmen fell upon each other, one wielding a heavy spittoon. The older representatives were just beginning to get wheezy when Cadwallader Washburn of Wisconsin grabbed William Barksdale of Mississippi by the hair, preparing to deliver him a heavy blow to the face. Unfortunately Barksdale's wig came loose in Washburn's hand and the startled Wisconsin representative swung at nothing but air. Convulsed by laughter, the rioters attempted to regain their composure as the embarrassed Barksdale reacquired and repositioned his crumpled hair. The next day, Keitt apologized for the incident, admitted he was the aggressor, and claimed that any blame belonged to him alone. But even Keitt's friends shook their heads at his conduct, confirmed in what they had always known about the impetuous congressman. "I like Keitt for many things," William Trescott told his friend Miles. "He is frank in his nature, honest in his politics, and I believe true to his work." But "he has sadly depreciated the old Carolina standard ... and I see no hope of [his] improving." Indeed, Trescott noted, men like Keitt

By the late 1850s, brawls on the congressional floor were relatively commonplace. In this editorial cartoon entitled "Opened with Prayer," the
representatives are skirmishing before the chaplain can even complete the
opening benediction. "[Such] Preliminary Piety," noted the accompanying
article, "[is useless] when the voice of the Divine is likely to be drowned
at any moment by fierce eructations of Illinois wrath, or the sharp snaps
of South Carolina Derringers. It [is only too] clear . . . that the Christian
precepts of the morning have no effect in repressing Mr. Kellogg's tendency to muscular overthrow of his foes in the afternoon, or Mr. Keitt's
anxiety to bring forth his compact little death-dealer from his coat pocket
in the evening." The benediction, the article concluded, was as ill suited to
open a session of Congress as a "Biblical inscription at the entrance of a
Brothel." From *Vanity Fair*, December 31, 1859.

make "[me] apprehensive of some new mortification whenever I hear
that a South Carolinian has been distinguishing himself."[4]

It is for incidents like this one that Laurence Keitt earned the
sobriquet "Harry Hotspur of the South." There is much in his career
to justify the title. Born near St. Matthews, South Carolina, in 1824,
Keitt seems to have had a rollicking and happy youth. Of his earliest
boyhood we know only that he was "famous for foot races, the gift

of gab, and for never wincing when . . . flogged." Still they are important details. Keitt was a child of privilege, at ease with his mind
and body, self-assured enough to take punishment stoically, even
proudly, self-aware enough to realize that if he wanted to be on the
administrative end he would have to be on the receiving end of some
of life's hard knocks. (These would be important lessons for a man
whose lifelong philosophy was "if the world buffets you, buffet it
back.") Like many of his rank and region, his natural brass would be
given a little polish at South Carolina College where he threw himself
into the proceedings and excesses of the Euphradian debating society.[5]

By his own admission Keitt entered politics a "mere boy," elected
at twenty-four to the Orangeburg district statehouse seat by a constituency that almost to a man disagreed with his political viewpoint.
Keitt, however, believed that it was precisely this audacity that "drew
the people" to him and gave him a hold on them greater than any
of his predecessors. From his very first canvass, then, Keitt learned
never to "stoop to a mamby-pamby dalliance" with public opinion
before making up his mind. "I assume," he claimed, "that my position
is as much to teach . . . as to be taught. . . . [and] I have never stopped
to inquire, when a vital principle was at stake, whether the multitude
would think as I did or not." Keitt would give speeches in his district—"even the gods of old sometimes showed themselves," he
noted—but he would not cavil or grovel with the "melodramatic
flirtation" of the cringing office seeker. "No dreamy dalliance, no
sated worship, pampered by the spicy condiments of whim or fancy
will do in this life," Keitt noted. "Life, in the very texture of the
word, means struggle, motion, purpose, object." From his first day in
politics, Keitt's object was the secession of the South from the United
States.[6]

Once in Washington, however, Keitt threw himself as much into
socializing as politicking. The city had an infectious energy that
matched Keitt's own. Parties were "as thick as leaves in Autumn"
and the ballrooms were always "full of Belles." The young congressman was a "favourite . . . among the ladies" and a constant companion
of Buchanan's niece, Harriet Lane, who oversaw all White House
social functions. "In reality," Keitt marveled of Washington, "this is
a great place; I never saw any one who got tired of it." While some

men of his age were on their way west, preparing to cut their own swath out of the American dream, Keitt thought the frontier held out only the scrubby alternatives of hardscrabble living or ignominious dying. For his part, Keitt would stay in Washington, where "whoever likes gaiety can have enough of it" and the "rich geniality" of the social scene could not help but fascinate a man who could "make a figure" of himself.[7]

To be sure, Laurence Keitt cut quite a figure in Washington. As an orator, he was nearly unmatched, with a "rapid and fervent manner" that was "riveting," "irresistible." His voice was deep and powerful, and when he took up the subject of abolitionism (which he did gratuitously) he paced around his desk, scattering papers before him "like people in a panic" and pounding "the innocent mahogany" until pens, pencils, documents, and even "John Adam's extracts shuddered under the blows." Accounts of his forensic displays tend to be indulgent in their detail—not so much from partiality as from the smug satisfaction of the writer who has bumped into a walking archetype. "[His is a] pyrotechnic style," remarked a writer for *Harper's Weekly*. "His speeches are melo-dramatically effective, made up of the entrances and exits of ideas that sparkle vividly while they are on the stage and go off in a tumult of applause, leaving an intoxicating sense of beauty and of daring, yet nothing distinct but a metaphor or a bold antithesis." Is the reporter describing Keitt's speeches or Keitt himself? Hasn't he conflated the two? Isn't he implying that Keitt was himself melodramatically effective, strutting his hour upon the stage, beautiful and daring, sparkling and vivid, but ultimately just a bold antithesis? This sort of thing happened regularly to Keitt. He was the fiery Southern orator perfectly essentialized in the qualities of a single man, and one suspects that if had he not existed he would have been invented by a society that had given him the uncommon license to stand as his own caricature.[8]

The truth, though, is that Laurence Keitt *was* invented, first by a young man playing at politics, then by a constituency living vicariously through his frothy indignation, finally by historians who have always been content to regard him as his contemporaries regarded him—the fire eater essentialized. Undoubtedly he deserves his reputation as a swashbuckling secessionist. It would be difficult to find a man of the period more dedicated to the separation of North and South and impossible to find one whose rhetorical flourishes relied so regularly on the imagery of the embattled knight. However, our stereotypes of the Southern cavalier—the honorable warrior of a doomed civilization or the laughable dandy jousting with windmills—all tend to sell rather short the intellectual depth and motive power of the South's unique blend of chivalric traditions. Keitt's case is an excellent one. As a student at South Carolina College, Keitt developed a lasting respect for only one professor—the barely closeted Unionist, Francis Lieber. In Lieber's class, Keitt sat among the busts of intellectual giants and watched transfixed as the armies of darkness and light moved across Lieber's vast collection of maps. In the Euphradian debating society, where political questions dominated the discussion, Keitt held forth only on literary and historical subjects. Would Socrates have been justified in leaving prison when solicited by Crito? Was Coriolanus justified in fighting against his country? In truth, Keitt found the college's conservatism, its disunionism, one of its least compelling features, at least when compared with the study of Roman imperialism, Grecian intellect, and Shakespearean poesy. Keitt was a romantic humanist searching not for *a* motion, purpose, or object but *any* motion, purpose, or object, so long as it corresponded with his (admittedly overblown) conception of what it meant to be a man. In Keitt's mind the qualifications for this last, august office were quite strict. Most of the politicians he met were milk-and-water types, confirmed imbeciles who moved like amiable mutes through the world, "decaying through inaction, rusting out through sloth." "Such a thing," Keitt noted, "whom Nature wrangled about in fixing his positive gender and compromised upon the neuter, has no attractions to me." True manhood did not dally or dicker, Keitt believed, but acted, and then decisively. In South Carolina this made him a secessionist, and certainly Keitt set about the role with his typical exuberance. But beyond the bravado and bluster one detects a literary and historical sensibility fueling his vision.[9]

Keitt was somewhat obsessed, for instance, with the notion that

Laurence Massillon Keitt. From a lithograph appearing in *Harper's Weekly*, December 22, 1860.

"white men [had] occupied South Carolina" in the tenth century and that the documents to prove his contention were rotting away in a records room in Copenhagen. He suggested to the legislature that many such "memorials of our history" were languishing in European archives and requested that "some proper person be appointed to collect [them] all." When Keitt's proposal was rejected, he had the nerve to deride the legislature for being too caught up with sectional questions to dedicate proper energy to documenting the past. Even Keitt's proslavery arguments tended not so much to rest on historical justifications as to be overwhelmed by them. In a speech to the Virginia Military Institute, he set out to prove that the South would be a perfect commingling of ancient Greek and Hebrew traditions. Any enduring civilization, he claimed, rested on moral, mental, and material pillars. While the Greeks were accomplished in mental and material pursuits, they could not construct a perfect society because they had no true knowledge of God. The Hebrews, by adhering to God's word, had constructed an incredibly strong moral society, but

mental and material foundations were weak. The South was in a
unique position to bring the great traditions together; from the Greeks
it would borrow the "instinct for Beauty" and from the Hebrews the
fear of God. Forcing blacks to perform the more onerous duties necessary to any society would give the intellectual elite the freedom to
go about the business of civilization building, and a standing mudsill
caste would spare the South the class conflict that plagued other
nations. As a proslavery argument, the speech was no different from
a thousand others and, indeed, by the 1850s positive good defenses of
the institution had become so reified that an orator contributed only
his passion and a little window dressing. But Keitt's historical super-
structure was no mere rhetoric or rationalization; it was to him as
important as the defense itself, perhaps more so. To understand why
requires an in-depth understanding of a subject far removed from
politics or slavery—Keitt's abiding love of poetry.[10]

On six occasions between 1851 and 1854, William Gilmore Simms
delivered a series of lectures he titled *Poetry and the Practical*. It was,
he admitted to audiences across the South, an odd title, a seeming
oxymoron. Of what practical use was poetry? Poesy, after all, was a
mere "pomp of words...wandering through eternity...a vain and
empty discourse...which appeals not to the common reason." And
America, Simms acknowledged, had become a very practical place.
For three generations it had dedicated itself to the quest for empire.
Once just a motley collection of "little spots along the Atlantic shores,"
the country had spread "with the flight of an eagle...to the far
waters of the Great Pacific." "We have conquered the savage nature
[of] the wild forests," Simms claimed, and "have gone fearlessly forth
upon the high seas, declaring them our common." "We have achieved
wondrously" and have won by dint of "iron will" and "unbending
earnestness" an empire for the ages. But the country had lost something along the way, Simms told his audience, and something very
like its soul. Indulging its imperial appetite, America had become
monstrous and engorged, with a passion only for conquest and a taste
only for blood. "The nation living thus dies out and must die out,"
Simms claimed, when in a gluttonous paroxysm it turns on itself for
a final meal. Having won an empire, the country needed now to
deserve it, to earn a dominion measured not by its extent but by its

beauty. And the poet could teach them how, could give them the practical advice they needed to save the country from self-destruction. The poet's arts, Simms noted, are "superior to those by which our possessions have been won." The poet can teach us to "secure what we possess . . . to strengthen our bulwark with Beauty and to sharpen our spears with Love." Simms understood that his audience wanted to hear nothing of such trifles, but they were going to hear it, he claimed, because they had forgotten what it meant to be Beautiful and because poetry had become the most practical subject in the world.[11]

Laurence Keitt may or may not have attended these lectures, but he undoubtedly read them. Keitt and Simms corresponded occasionally, met regularly, and shared a passion for poetry generally and Simms's work specifically. With most of South Carolina, Simms found Keitt a somewhat volatile character. "He is a good fellow," Simms noted, "but likely to flounder his Batteau in smooth waters." Keitt, on the other hand, viewed Simms with wonder, almost as a student does a stern but brilliant schoolmaster. "He is a remarkable man," Keitt wrote typically. "He has the most varied talents [and] the fullest information of any man in the state . . . with a generosity of spirit and a guilelessness of heart which hook him to those who know him most staunchly." Keitt, moreover, believed, with everything he had, that he not only understood *Poetry and the Practical* but lived it.[12]

Like Simms, Keitt believed that poetry was the divine in man struggling to sing. Much of the time, of course, it did not sing very well. Most poets were mere "sonnatteers of the hour," Simms noted, "possessing but a moderate command of language . . . manufactur[ing] verses upon the ordinary emotions and the received commonplaces of society." Keitt concurred. "Modern poets," he claimed, "seem to me to be like David, not like Solomon. They gather and accumulate and heap up, but they cannot construct and proportion." Their problem was not a lack of talent per se, but a chronic self-involvement, a mental pettiness. "Continual introspection," Keitt noted, "is dangerous; it is what Bacon calls the merest cannibalism—the heart eating itself up." By writing from the self alone, these modern poets consumed their own humanity and their poetry became the "nightmares" and "hysterics" of the soulless. What they did not understand was that "one may learn from everything, from the mountain and the valley, from the flower and the shrub, from the bird and the insect, from any living and creeping thing in physical nature." The Greeks had understood this. By peopling the woods with divinities and the waters with nymphs, the inherent Beauty of nature had been given a form and face and substance men could touch and be touched by. Certainly this made the Greek gods more human, but it also made humans more godly, made them dream more broadly, imagine more grandly. For Keitt, the *Iliad* and *Odyssey* were the "Genesis and Deuteronomy of the ... indestructible Bible of Art," and provided a model for a poetry of divine and titanic majesty. The true poet, for Keitt, was not some scribbler "twist[ing] and twin[ing] arabesques of metaphysical subtlety" and was not some exorcist chasing the ghosts and goblins that haunt men's minds. The true poet was vatic, bardic, practical, himself a living poem, a man grasping at the essence of Beauty primeval and thrusting it before his fellows.[13]

Keitt did not muse on the subject of poetry, he did not dabble. Though he never wrote a line, Laurence Keitt is best understood as a practicing poet. His politicking was never about the campaign or the canvass, this bill or that legislation—it was not even particularly about democracy or even secession. Rather it was about giving birth to Beauty, conceived in the solitude of the poet's mind, brought to "life and vigor and passion amid the shock and hum of men." For Keitt, America was no republican experiment, a Britain with a better constitution. America was a promise God had made to man, an epic that began in 1776 and ended when the country took its rightful place not merely among nations but among civilizations. In other eras the poet had helped build such civilizations through literature or history; in Keitt's era the practical poet exercised his muse in the arena of politics. "Public life ... in a country like ours," he said, "is a grand and glorious field. Two hundred years ago Milton said he who would write an heroic poem must make his whole life heroic. This is equally true of our own time, and true of politics too, for politics now is our epic poem."[14]

History, Keitt believed, was punctuated by events, by Promethean moments when the world was returned to the potter's wheel to be remolded, remade, and fired again. By 1855 the entire Atlantic community was on the brink of just such momentous change, "rocking with the throes of ... august developments" that could "no more be stifled than the spirit of the earthquake." In the coming storm, lesser men would be overwhelmed. They would miss the opportunity to shape the world and, as suddenly as it had come, the drama would be over, "its agencies, like waves, rocking and rolling themselves heavily to sleep." This was the poet's moment, Keitt's moment, to marry his name "to mighty events, to mighty measures, and to an immortal future." "He who cannot stand with steady eye and ... steel nerve upon the glacier of power," Keitt noted, and "lift the banner of truth and humanity above the mist and vapors and clouds of prejudice and popular passion ... is not and cannot be a statesman."[15]

To prepare himself for this glacial moment, Keitt spent the summer of 1855 at a secluded mountain resort near Greenville, South Carolina. For six weeks he received no mail or newspapers and gave no thought to politics. Instead he read six thousand pages of literature, history, metaphysics, and philosophy, comprehending them not as the student but as the "master." Keitt believed the "intellectual gladiator" needed these moments of study to exercise the bulging muscles of his mind. But Keitt was no sword for hire. He was, he claimed, not so much ambitious as questing; his energy was not self-serving merely but "of kin to divinity and to a higher purpose." Time was quickening, becoming elastic, the "tone of the world was changing" and Keitt would be damned if he would sit around slackjawed and let the "milk-and-water" men control the nation's destiny. "The materials of heroic life," he claimed, "were scattered all over the field of public life." Some men saw only "grass and stubble and straw, or in office only gewgaws." But the "soaring intellect" felt a "quickened pulse [and] throb of quenchless energy" at the thought that "his country [might] treasure him up as a portion of her precious heritage and remember him proudly when with jeweled brow ... conquering tread and imperial stature she join[ed] the great Panthenaic procession of the nations." Near the end of his stay in Greenville, Keitt rose early to catch the sunrise. The view, he said, was magnificent. He stood "on a cliff 1100 feet perpendicular," a mountain chain surrounding him on three sides. A sea of clouds had settled in the valley and, agitated by winds, they lapped up against his precipice like waves. It was a

Keitt's description of his stirring moment on a Greenville precipice is eer-
ily similar to that evoked by Caspar David Friedrich's *Wanderer Above the
Sea of Fog* (1818). Hamburger Kunsthalle, Hamburg, Germany.

sight Nature presented to Keitt alone, an ocean in the sky, stretching
out like the unmapped waters of a great Civilization.[16]

Laurence Keitt was, by his own admission, a "visionary and a the-
orist." Secession was to him but a blip in the grander becoming of
the world; his ambition was epic, his aspirations colossal and grandiose. But every urge to dismiss his vision as the messianic exuberance
of youth should be quelled; this man was elected to office, then re-

elected, then elected again. He insulted the people, brawled on the floor of Congress, and postured himself a god—and he usually left his audience hungry for more. Far from being held accountable for his audacity, he was elected for it. In the wake of the Sumner caning, Keitt hoped the northern men would rise en masse. If they did, he promised "the city would...float with blood." Sick of "stagnation," the prospect of a general bloodletting in the capital offered a tantalizing release. The tidy, modest revolution that had birthed the republic would not do this time; Keitt was looking for something more cathartic, wrenching. In the summer of 1856, he found it.[17]

———◆———

Susanna Sparks was, by every account, a stunning woman. One breathless newspaper editor, utterly overwhelmed by their first encounter, pronounced her "magnificent...[with] fair brow and lovely arms, a sweet glow mantles upon her cheek...a bewildering beauty flashes from her eye and encircles her" like a dream. Even the curmudgeonly editor of the *Charleston Patriot* seemed susceptible to her "necromancy," gazetting her every ball movement and indulging himself in paeans to her face and form. Uncommonly attractive on the outside, Sue was nevertheless an emotional wreck. She had been engaged to the son of a wealthy and prominent South Carolina family when without warning or explanation the young man had married someone else. The humiliating episode left Sparks darkly depressed and deeply distrusting of men, and she resolved thereafter to be "strong, hard, and cold." Whether Keitt was first attracted to her uncommon beauty, biting intellect, or studied coolness, we do not know; their earliest courtship remains something of a mystery. But by December 1854, Keitt was thinking he might be in love. He had been fond of many women, but for Sue he felt an odd sort of "electric sympathy," a spark of something divine. He resolved, however, not to confess his feelings until he could test them in "the most terrible of all trials—the flatteries of the brilliant and the éclat of triumph." That winter he threw himself into the Washington social whirl, searching his heart thoroughly, determined to see if Sue's image faded amid the honeyed compliments of beautiful belles and the high praise of men known round the world. But whatever Washington had to offer, it did not throw even a shadow over his feelings. On March 9, 1855, "doubtingly ... tremblingly," Keitt proposed.[18]

Sparks did not accept his proposal—nor did she reject it. Instead, she began a period of dissembling and recrimination that would last for two months. Keitt, she claimed, was a man of roving fancy, indiscreet in politics, notorious in the drawing room. If he loved her at all, it was for her beauty, and his fascination would fade as soon as he found some shiny new bauble to pursue. She had been betrayed before, by friends and by a lover who gave her all manner of assurances. She had recovered from that heartbreak, had even grown stronger by it, but would never again surrender to mere "sentiment whipped into froth." Having studied music and painting for a year at Barhamville Academy in Columbia, Sparks was determined to give up the flighty life of the belle and continue her studies in Europe.[19]

Keitt was crushed but defensive and set about his courtship with the same zeal (and many of the same tactics) he employed in politics. He sent Sparks long letters countering her every objection, drawing deeper from philosophy and literature than his own feelings. Sue was like a "mannikin boy" with "hair erect, eyeballs staring, and tickled nerves" whistling bravely by the graveyard at midnight. As soon as she conquered her fears and threw off her torpor, she would learn, as Keitt had, to shine, not "in an untutored and rough society but in the circle of the Muses and Apollo where power and fashion are constellated." He understood that she was crushed, weary, spent, and hurting, but whose fault was that? She was selling herself short to blame others for her heartache. The struggles of life were life itself; those who did not learn from them were not living but dying, slow as a tree. Keitt recognized that he was being forward to offer these observations, but believed it was exactly what she needed to hear. "Verily, Miss Sue," he told her, "I have read your nature—may I say so?—better than you have yourself." As for her rendering of his nature, Sue had been taunting and unfair. He did not "look upon all life as a dancing school" and was not "one of those whose life begins at 10 at night and closes in the morning at 4." Whatever he may have done or been in the past, he had given Sue "no reason for such treatment" and could not understand why she would trifle with his emotions. "I have thought, I have thought again. Again I have thought," Keitt told her—his love was no "galvanized sentiment." He was prepared to share with her "everything that constitutes my manhood and my nature."[20]

After two months of such importunings, the beleaguered girl reluctantly accepted Keitt's proposal, but she promised him only her presentiments of disaster and feelings of hopelessness. This was enough for Keitt. "Your letter," he claimed, "has poured upon me a brightness as gladsome to my little worth as that which streamed upon the universe when the morning stars first sang together." He understood she was still soulsick and that the "spectre" of her earlier experience would occasionally rise before them, but he promised to treat her with "patience, gentleness, forebearance, and unselfish and unmixed devotion." "That [morbid thoughts] should rise up now and then, I cannot complain of," he noted, "for the waves of the ocean still roll for a time after the storm has passed away and calmness has breathed upon its surface." "And now, dear Sue, as the flower under rude influences closes in upon its heart, enfolding there its fragrance, so would I, content with you alone, enclose you in my inner heart."[21]

For the next year, Susanna Sparks chafed within her new confines. She postponed the wedding date twice, forgot to answer Keitt's letters, and spurned his friends and family whenever the occasion presented itself. Confronted by this barrage of insults, in the face of all her cruelties, Keitt appears to have done what he had never quite managed to do before—he fell in love with her. His affections, he claimed, were not based on her physical beauty but on her superiority as a human being. When her eye had lost its brightness, when her hand had lost its roundness, and fortune had done its worst, then he would take her all over again, as joyously and as tenderly as he had when young, as the culmination of all his life's earthly blessings. He admitted he had been presumptuous in their early courtship. He had so ably learned to read men's hearts in the political world he had thought he would be able to read hers and direct it to his will. But what he had not realized was that she was better than he was, purer and more holy. Her love was not something to win, but to be worthy of, and he dropped the speechifying and sophistry, and threw himself on her mercy. His allegiance, he said, was bound to her unalterably, as to a superior being, and though she might stab him through the heart he could never reproach her—his love for her had become his religion, it had made him a better man.

On his way to the capitol one morning, Keitt stopped at the burned out wreck of a fellow House member's home. The owner, Colonel Benton, was shuffling through some of the things, and Keitt expressed his condolences. "I care not for brick and mortar," the Colonel replied, "for earthly things; my manuscripts, which have almost become my children, I could lose too. Yes I could have lost all these if the dresses of my wife had been saved. They hung by each side of my bed, and they were the last thing I saw at night and the first at morning." It was a simple gesture, but Keitt was moved almost to tears, claiming the incident would never pass from his memory. "In him the curse and crime of selfish ambition has been mitigated and brightened" by the love of a noble woman. "Dear Sue," he wrote her after the incident, "you much mistake me if you think, even for a moment, that I am not submissive to your lightest request. . . . I would give my proudest hopes and my starriest ambition to win back freshness to your heart."[22]

Taking him at his word, Sue exacted one final, staggering price—if he were serious he would give up politics forever and move with her to Europe for as long a period as she desired. Keitt reeled, but only for a moment. Politics, he said, had always held a strong attraction for him. The trappings of office might be contemptible, but the exercise of "power, raised by the scaffolding of thought and will and suspended like [a] mighty dome in . . . Heaven" was the work of his very soul. "I once thought nothing on earth could tempt me from" such a life, he wrote his beloved, but "for you I will give it up wholly, completely, and forever. [For you] I will snap now, as soon as you wish it—tomorrow—the wand of office, carry you to Europe, and linger with you around Tumuli—its mounds, its columns, and its ruins. . . . for you I will make any sacrifice, and deem it no sacrifice" whatever. Keitt was not bluffing. He told friends and colleagues he would not be returning to Washington the next term and even met with the president to determine whether there might be a diplomatic post vacant in Italy. Forced to "choose between private and public life," Keitt flung the latter aside—"the former will be perpetual, and to me it is a safety." Soon, he promised Sue, he would transport her to Europe, plant her in any soil and in any clime she might choose, and preside over the recuperation of her heart. If, once there, "any rude blast visits you roughly, it shall be only because I cannot shield you from it. If the hand of sorrow presses heavily upon you, I shall feel its weight as painfully" because our lives will be joined together.[23]

Everything had come easily for Laurence Keitt—his material comfort, his charismatic good looks, his intellect and education, his career and uncompromising politics—everything was his for the taking—except Susanna Sparks. In her he had met a will as titanic and as immovable as his own, and what options did he have but to love her for it? He could not debate her, he could not challenge her to a duel, he could not cane her or race her for the privilege of her hand—he could only submit. It is critical to note, however, that this submission, when it finally came, was not begrudging or bitter; rather, Keitt seems to have been relieved, thankful, finally to surrender to something or someone without it costing him his manhood. "You are so much better, so much purer, so entirely holy to me," Keitt noted, "that I can scarcely bind to my soul the sacred belief that you have mingled hopes and aims with one so much inferior.... Oh Sue, how much more do I owe you than I can ever pay." But did he really owe her? The bombast and bullying of his early courting certainly warranted an apology, but did it amount to a debt? Did he owe her for ignoring his letters, for snubbing his friends, for requiring that he quit politics? No, he owed her for the opportunity she gave him to be whole, for the chance to stretch his love, exercise his weakness, and indulge his very human sympathy for surrender. "Hard struggles since I have been a boy," Keitt admitted, "in a field where rough blows are dealt, have indurated me all over save in this one point ... my inner affections have become [as] preternaturally keen as my nature otherwise has become cold and self-collected." This is a remarkable insight for a man who considered self-reflection a kind of cannibalism. His love for Sue, his pursuit of her, was, by his own admission, directly related to politics. Every brutal beating he took in the political arena, every enemy he made or criticism he withstood, fed his need for the woman

that might minister to that inner core, who might make him feel, by
some whisper or touch, that he withstood the blows for reasons beyond
his own ambition.[24]

But does this adequately explain Keitt's willingness to give up politics forever? Not if Keitt is understood first as a fire eater or a politician—not if one reads only his encomia to slavery and state's rights.
But if he is understood as a man, and a man of poetic sensibility at
that, the decision becomes explicable. Susan's demand did not rankle
or chafe; she had given Keitt something politics had not, an opportunity to make a grand and sweeping gesture—a moment in which
time stood still and waited on his answer. Keitt was not surrendering
his epic poem to Susanna, he was folding her up within it, transferring
his poetic purpose from politics to romance, a distance perhaps not so
very great. Granted he would never save mankind, but he might save
this woman, and he had the sense he would save himself in the
bargain. "You have given me an object," Keitt admitted to Sue. "My
struggles were becoming aimless. I had won a crown here and a
chaplet there. I had broken a sword in this fight and beaten down a
castle wall in another contest, and I was becoming somewhat indifferent both to feast and fray. You have been a promethean spark and
I have relumed a spirit which was slightly waning and given a
brighter blaze to fires which were somewhat fitfully burning."[25]

On July 7, 1856, the relumed Keitt received a letter from his fiancée—she wanted to discontinue their courtship, this time indefi-
nitely. Keitt drafted two replies, both drained of emotion. "Justice
requires me to say that I trust we have met for the last time," he
noted in both, "and should we ever meet again, it must be as strangers." Laurence Keitt returned to politics the following term, rededi-
cated to the separation of North and South.[26]

Henry Craft: The Memory of Love

Seen from the outside, Henry Craft lived an incredibly average life.
His father, Hugh Craft, was born near Vienna, Maryland, in 1799,
and removed at an early age to Milledgeville, Georgia, where he
became a prosperous merchant and planter. Hugh's first wife bore
him a son, Henry, in 1823, but she died shortly thereafter. Hugh

subsequently remarried and was just beginning a new family when the bottom fell out of his finances. Surrendering most of his worldly possessions to his creditors, Hugh collected his family and headed off to Holly Springs, Mississippi, the heart of newly acquired Indian country. Though somewhat awkwardly the only child of his father's first marriage, Henry seems to have had a happy childhood, and he greatly enjoyed growing up on the South's frontier. Holly Springs was quite possibly the most booming of all the boom lands of the Old Southwest. In January 1836 it was estimated that only twenty white men lived in the area; six months later the number was up to thirty-one hundred. The census of 1840 revealed that Mississippi's population had nearly tripled in a decade, making it the fastest growing state in the country. Henry, then seventeen, literally helped his father carve a plantation out of the bush, and he would in later years remember these times as "the free roving of my woodsman days." His father set up a sort of real estate business and taught Henry to be a land examiner.[27]

By 1847 Henry was twenty-four, had made a tidy sum in the land business, and was part of a social circle that met at neighboring plantations throughout the spring and summer for parties and dances. They were, he claimed, "the gayest of the gay," and it seemed as if "the laugh[ing] and danc[ing]" would "reign unbroken." He was particularly interested in one member of his gay party, Lucy Hull, who lived nearby at Tuckahoe plantation. At first Lucy had seemed all "outside show," "a brilliant, careless, gay & rather heartless girl." Gradually, though, he discerned a "certain under current beneath the surface ice." Henry had been in love before. He had from his earliest recollection possessed an "ideal of a woman" he could love, and occasionally he would in the throes of a new crush fancy that the object of his desire measured up to that ideal. Time spent in her company, however, usually revealed that it was his own ideal he loved, that he had tricked himself by dressing his crush in the trappings of his perfect woman. At first he believed this was what he was feeling for Lucy. Like all the others, she would soon reveal her true self, and he would be filled with the same old "painful doubts & vacillations" that had accompanied his other crushes. But as the spring dragged on, Lucy appeared "more & more in her higher & better & hidden character" until she had actually eclipsed his ideal. Lucy taught Henry that "women might be what before I had never imagined." "I [am] not deceived," Henry confessed jubilantly. I will "elevate my love to reach the elevation of its object."[28]

Desperate to confess his affections, Henry was devastated when Lucy spent one evening deep in conversation with a gentleman from Memphis he had never seen before. It became suddenly so apparent that Lucy loved this man, had loved him, and "was perhaps engaged to him." Henry was "miserable, utterly miserable as I had never been before." Lying awake that night, he vowed to speak to her the next evening and discover whether he had really "loved so utterly in vain." Reaching the gate at Tuckahoe, he glanced up at the moon and it "seemed to smile so sweetly" that he felt it was an "omen, an encouragement." He had since early childhood worshiped the moon, and he interpreted its smiling countenance as an acknowledgement of his devotion, "a promise of success." The interview with Lucy must have gone well. After sitting with her on her couch for hours, Henry mounted his horse with a lighter heart. He had not told Lucy of his love for her but had learned that his "fears of another were groundless."[29]

The next morning Henry arose with the intention of confessing his love. Lucy was leaving with her family for a vacation at a local spa and he could not wait for her return. He saw her at church that morning, but she was surrounded by her parents and he could not find an opportunity to talk to her alone. Instead, he slipped her a note, explaining that he wished when she returned to speak with her about a subject close to his heart. If she did not accept this proposal she was to leave his note on her front porch; if she accepted it she was to leave a flower. Anxiously, Henry rode to Tuckahoe that afternoon to see what her answer would be. Evidently, Lucy was a levelheaded girl. She had not left a flower, but a sprig of arborvitae, the tree of life. "What a thrill of joy it sent to my heart," Henry confessed. "It was the beginning of a happiness which none but those who have loved and been loved can appreciate." Riding home, Henry found "all nature was bright & happy." He was, he confessed, in love with all the world.[30]

As soon as Lucy returned, Henry requested an opportunity to talk with her alone at Tuckahoe. He longed for the chance to see her and his "heart beat rapturously when" he "thought of hearing from her own lips the sweet confession which her sprig of arbor vitae" had given him. Again the interview must have gone well. They were, he said, "hours vouchsafed but once to the mortal pilgrim," and when he left Tuckahoe he had her ring on his finger, "a pledge of her love." A week later Lucy and Henry were engaged to be married.[31]

The afternoon before the wedding, Henry procured the marriage license and readied their luggage for the honeymoon. He waited at the stage office for Lucy's bags, but they never arrived. As evening wore on he went home and found a Tuckahoe servant waiting for him with a note. Lucy's father and brothers had strenuously objected to the marriage and had talked Lucy into calling it off. Stunned, Henry sped to Tuckahoe and confronted Lucy's father in the grove, "pacing to and fro over the wet grass" and demanding to see his fiancée. He received only a note from her—it read simply "oh, misery."[32]

Crushed, Henry left for Memphis to cool off. While there he received a letter from Lucy—she had made up her mind. Her love, she said, was "unchanged & unchangeable," and she had resolved to throw herself upon Henry for happiness "come what might." Henry sped home with the "deep rapture" of knowing "that she would willingly endure the frowns & reproaches and even desertion of those whom she fondly loved" to be with him. What "fearful agony" she must have suffered, he thought, "when she knew that she must choose between them & me." Henry could not get over the "devotion, the true woman's heart, which characterized her conduct under those trying circumstances." Lucy's parents talked the couple out of being married immediately, but a date was set for early fall, and Henry was overjoyed.[33]

Two weeks before the wedding, Lucy collapsed. Henry blamed her brothers and parents for Lucy's illness; they blamed him and forbade his seeing her, claiming that it "was imprudent to excite her." Henry felt the "peculiar relative of hostility" that they entertained for him, however, and he grew bitter, hanging around outside Tuckahoe, hunting birds for the time Lucy might be up to eating them. Despite her family's admonitions, Lucy was true to Henry, sending letters to him, claiming that he was in her dreams and that if possible she loved him more than ever. She planned a day when Henry could fetch the buggy, carry her from her sickbed, and drive her slowly through the grove. When that day arrived, she was not better. Henry was allowed to come and see her, but by then she was "insensible, the film of death . . . gathering in her eyes." Henry could not bear to see her in that condition and left the room, but everywhere in the house echoed "that heart rending sound as she gasped away her life." At 2 A.M., Lucy was laid out on the living room sofa in her bridal attire. "Her countenance," Henry wrote, "had resumed its natural appearance & was smiling & beautiful in death." He thought she seemed in a pleasant sleep. His grief had exhausted itself, his "rebellion . . . against Providence" had not commenced, and he spent an hour with her body, "calm and quiet." "It was," he said, "the holiest hour of my life."[34]

Lucy's death marked a turning point for Henry, a revolution in his humble history "as important and momentous to me as [those of] 1688 to England, 1789 . . . to France, 1776 to the U.S." Unable to enjoy Holly Springs without Lucy, Henry "sought refuge" at Princeton. He hoped to "find in the emulation and competition of a class" relief from his thoughts, a respite from mourning. However painful the last year had been, he vowed to "go on with an upward brow & a callous heart, ready to meet whatever" might confront him. His utmost hope was that the next year at Princeton would launch him upon a career. "I have suffered affliction & bereavement such as few perhaps are called to undergo," he wrote, but there are "tender ties still binding my heart." "The future," after all, "is the future."[35]

Though only twenty-five, Henry was older than most college freshmen. While he enjoyed the company of his fellow students and found in competition the incentive to study and discipline of mind he had always lacked, he felt alienated. "I am an old man as it were coming back to the employments of his youth," he noted, a man "whose life is far advanced among those just *preparing* to live." The perspective was one he could not shake, a feeling of always being outside looking in. He had come to Princeton to embark on a career, and he envied fellow students who seized upon professions and threw their shoulders to the wheel. But there was also something absurd about their zeal. "With what strange alacrity & thoughtlessness men run such a race,"

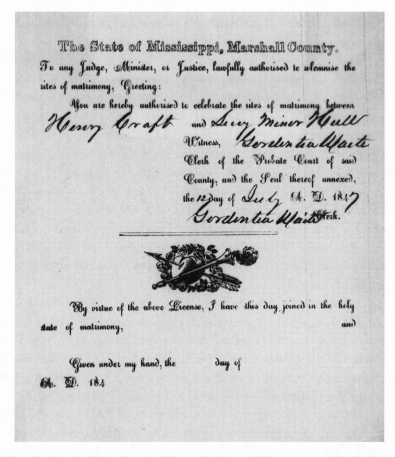

After the death of his fiancée, Henry Craft carefully preserved his half-completed marriage license. He never recovered from the loss of his first love. Craft, Fort, and Thorne Family Papers, Southern Historical Collection, UNC.

he noted. Doubting his own worthiness to embark on such a project, he doubted equally the worthiness of the project itself. The result was a kind of paralytic self-loathing. He would spend hours in his room, "trifling away" his thoughts "upon nothing." Daydreaming and "castle building" were his "besetting temptations," and he indulged them liberally. Part of his difficulty, of course, was that he was still in mourning. Seven months had passed since Lucy's death, but Henry treated himself to long descriptions of her in his journal. Henry, though, was not merely maudlin. He had remarkable powers of self-perception and could be incredibly frank in analyzing himself. One spring night after writing of Lucy he admitted that not having her to love, he had fallen in love with his own sorrow and was loath to give it up. "The memory of her love," he noted, "is my greatest treasure."[36]

Henry might have turned to religion in his mourning, and he tried reading the Bible at night to find some solace. But he could not shake the suspicion that prayer was a human vanity, a ludicrous "farce of uttering solemn words upon the air." Listening to the "confessions & petitions made" in church he could not help but wonder, "what is all this?" We address the Creator of the Universe "as though he were absolutely present & listening," but do we believe it? At least heathen worshiping on a stone, he noted, have a God "sensibly present with them."[37]

After five months at Princeton, Henry received a letter from home, proposing that he return to Holly Springs to form a law partnership with a local attorney. Henry decided to accept and went to New York to make the arrangements. His journey home was a long one, but it felt good to be back in a place he understood. "It may be weak & childish, the feeling of homesickness," he noted, "but nevertheless I acknowledge that I have ever been subject to it." After being in the North he almost enjoyed how "old & drearyed & scattered & uncomfortable" his hometown was. Some associations, however, ran too strong. The stores and the streets, the people and their homes, all were "connected with thoughts of *her*." "Her image is ever rising up," he noted, "and ever rushing down upon that bed of death.... Thus has it been every day & every hour."[38]

But what gradually dawned on Henry was not that Lucy's death had affected him too much but rather too little. Like the people he saw in church all "prone & grovelling in the dust," he was going through the motions of feeling but had never grappled with the truth. Lucy's death, however much he dwelled on it, had not made him see the value of time or life, had not elevated his character or brought him closer to God. Rather he had dwelled on death because he was trying desperately to conjure some kind of emotion from a heart that had turned to stone. The truth, he believed, was that he was a mere harlequin of a man, apt to "chatter and laugh an idiot glee & stumble & roll & chatter & laugh again & hate myself & know that I am a fool." In these moments he felt like leaping "joyfully into the embrace of Death," but he did not have the heart. "*My heart!*" he exclaimed, "if I have one, it is a hard rock of selfishness encrusted by a thin mould of sentimental sensibility in which mushroom feelings spring up & perish in a day." "My worst enemy," he confessed to his diary, "could not have a meaner opinion of me" than I do.[39]

Henry spent his first months back in Holly Springs living with his parents. His stepmother had prepared his old room, "improv[ing] it wonderfully & [making] it much more comfortable." But his relationship with his father became strained. Henry was prone to getting up late, not so much out of laziness, as his father seemed to think, but because, nursing an ailing heart, he preferred the solace and dark quietude of evening time. Henry would sometimes vow to change, to rise early and throw himself into the day as his father did, but every time he did so it seemed as if his father was "so ready to exact another & still another sacrifice" of his habits that he sank back into his old routine. "He has no sympathy whatever with me," Henry noted, "no indulgence for my foibles, no pity for my weaknesses." Henry loved his father and recognized the sacrifices he made for his family, but confessed "I do not know how to appreciate his firmness & principles, how to yield to the exaction of his character." Frustrated, Henry was too much the indulgent romantic to assume the "callous philosophical commonplace every day-ishness" that his father associated with the ideas of a man. Unable to come to an understanding, Henry moved into a boardinghouse.[40]

Henry was no more satisfied with the time he spent at work. He was supposed to be reading to pass the bar, but each time he picked up a book he lapsed into a listless apathy, his eye wandering over the page, his "mind rov[ing] hither and thither in childish" vacancy. He had no energy or ambition, he claimed, and felt no enthusiasm or hope in his new profession. Again, laziness was not the problem. When there was mindless work to be done, he could "work as industriously as any other machine." But Henry was quick to see the absurd in human enterprise; he was the kind of pessimist who could be consistently disappointed by the bad he discovered in things, even as he expected to find it there. Henry had revered the law as a boy; it had seemed like "a noble and venerable edifice ... gradually built up by the successive labors of many generations of great intellects." His imagination had pondered the "forgotten laborers whose work survives them" and the "generations of inhabitants who have called [this] shelter their home." But upon entering this great edifice, he found the rooms dedicated not to ennobling the intellect but to degrading it. As he strolled on "from door to door he encountered the tokens of humbug & trickery and meanness and intrigue at every step." His ideal temple of justice was in fact "a mart where learning is sold and impunity for villainy purchased, an exhibition room of human depravity & degradation and a prostitution house where for fees, principles are distorted, precedents seduced, and ingenuity and trickery and humbugery made the pimps of the wealth which passes for success."[41]

It seemed to Henry as he moved between the "monotonous routine of office duties during the day & lonely, sad evenings" that he did not "live in [the] actual world." Having for so long made his home in a land of melancholy reverie, he felt out of step with the people striding down the sunny streets. Henry was dissolving from their world, becoming invisible; he lived now "among the shadows" where "every thing" was "unreal & unworthy [of] interest or thought." "Events have overtaken" me, he confided to his journal, and flit through "my memory in the semblance of the changing scenes of a dream." The past held out only narcissistic pain; the future seemed but "a massive impenetrable wall, built right up in my very face." Utterly without prospects, Henry began to have presentiments— which were wishes—that he would not live long; residing in a world of shadows, he found that mortality was the only thing he could see with any clarity. The "dark tide of Death," he wrote in his journal, "sweeps every where beneath the sham & parade, the national greatness, the political existence & the intellectual march which constitute the world as it is spread out around us." "No doubt all of the untold millions who have gone before me have ... gazed into [the] gloomy stream [of time]," he noted, as "bewildered, stricken, stymied & stupified as I [am] now. What a sad record then must be the book which

is kept on high by He who knows all the thoughts of men [and] all
the emotions of their hearts."[42]

But of course it was not God but Henry himself who was the keeper
of sad records. His diary, after all, was a transcript of his depression,
a witness to his mourning, a series of bleak love letters he sent to
himself through the way station of the dead. But the intensity of
Henry's melancholy could not be sustained, however much he enjoyed
it. By the first anniversary of Lucy's death, he found that "the eclipse
of sorrow is passing or past." "This day brings with it no new sadness
as I had supposed it would," he confessed. "My first waking thought
was . . . 'One year ago she died.' But there is no new pain which memory can inflict, no new echo which can answer those words 'she died'
in my heart." Henry gave his diary partial credit for the change. It
was, after all, his and Lucy's story, however sadly short, a narrative
of their "love & . . . disappointment . . . right up to the closing scene."
"I here dedicate" this journal, he wrote, "to the memory of the past
year, here inscribe it as the tombstone which I raise over the grave
of my former life. . . . [And so] let me take my farewell of Tuckahoe,
bury the past & turn toward whatever may be my future." There was,
he admitted, a "sweet, sacred joy in communing with the dead," and
he would miss it sorely. "In the busy hours of the day & the quiet
midnight, in solitude & in crowds" Lucy had been always in his
thoughts. But now he had to bury with her "the memory of what has
been," and "summon up the energy & hope & strength for the new
existence" which lay before him. "Farewell Tuckahoe," he wrote, "the
past, the bright, the dark, the joyful sorrowful past—farewell."[43]

For two years, Henry had kept a diary of his innermost thoughts,
his gift for writing and for self-perception providing insights into the
mind of a young gentleman of the Old South as he grappled with
love, death, religion, the nature of man, family, and the professions.
Without this diary, nothing would be known of him. Certainly none
of his contemporaries could have guessed at the tortured entries in
his journal. "I seem" to the outside world "happy & cheerful & hopeful," Henry confessed to his diary, but "what a liar the *seeming* is."
"I know well what faculties I possess," he wrote, "[I know] how I
can most please & how most successfully deceive those around me. I

know too then those in whose partial judgments I am capable of
much, but I feel that I act the hypocrite when I encourage such
opinions. I believe I can talk tolerably good *nonsense,* write a passably
flimsy letter & beyond that am fit for nothing but a machine." In
passages such as these, Henry's journal became part of his self-therapy,
a place to confess the unconfessable in a world that was unsympath-
izing and absurd, a place to purge his despondency over his own
worthless nature. Clearly he intended the diary for his eyes only. The
cover page contains just two words, "my journal"; no name, no date,
just a self-referential declaration of possession. "I have endeavored,"
he explained, "to make these pages a true transcript of my feelings."
His days full of so much *seeming,* he filled his nights and his diary
with the truth that existed beneath "the sham & parade." But in
1849, after keeping a two-year record of these brutal truths, Henry
disappeared from the historical record.[44]

Henry Craft resurfaced in 1859. Of the decade-long disappearance,
he says nothing. An attorney in Memphis with a new wife and new
baby boy, Henry began a new diary, this time to maintain a record
for his son. The ten years, though, had not made Henry any less
gloomy. In the first pages of his new journal he recorded his thoughts
as he watched his new home being constructed. A new husband and
father, Henry could have seen the house with all the hopefulness of
a man starting over with his new family, building a new life from
the ground up. Instead, "a shade of sadness" stole over his thoughts.
"Of what events in our history may it not be the scene. What joy and
what sorrow garnered for us in the coming time may reach us there.
Shall the years glide over us within those walls bringing calm content.
. . . Shall sickness lay its hand upon us there, and death come to claim
its victims one after another from our circle." "These are questions,"
Henry confessed, "that sometimes seem to be uttered for my ear by
the bricks as they are piled upon each other, and the wood as it takes
it's shape & place under the workman's hand." Typically, Henry was
both sadly cynical and sadly correct. Construction of the house ran
$5,000 over budget, and he was nearly ruined.[45]

Tight finances were not the only reason the house triggered such
despondency—Henry Craft seems to have made a very unhappy marriage. His new wife, Ella, was an indulgently ill woman, a bundle of

mysterious symptoms providing rationale for behavior that would otherwise appear selfish. Despite a "legion" of attempted remedies, nothing "seemed to help her at all," and it was hard, Henry noted, "to see her just gradually fading away without apparent disease." To cope with her affliction, Ella turned to the Bible with the sort of monomaniacal vigor of the new convert on her deathbed. Henry had hoped that Ella would be God-fearing, that she would possess the sort of "genial, cheerful, loving home religion that brightens the family circle & so much beautifies woman's character." But Ella became a fanatic on the subject, adopting the "religion of gloom & austerity and asceticism—of fasts & vigils & penance—of constant seclusion and perpetual engagement in devotions." "If she could only learn & feel that while she is *in* the world she *must* be to some extent *of* the world," Henry wrote, if she could just understand "that she has other duties besides those of devotion there would be no trouble." Instead she was but a step removed "from the spirit of the hair shirt and self-flagellation," preferring the role of Christian to that of wife and mother.[46]

Occasionally, the Crafts would attempt to make amends, and Henry would record a meek hope that they were at a new beginning for their marriage. "No doubt I have been greatly in fault," he admitted to his diary. "I must try to be satisfied ... that her thoughts and affections are enjoyed by much higher & worthier objects" than myself. But always shortly after the reconciliation, the coldness returned. "I feel the estrangement between us grows day by day greater and more hopeless," he noted. "I am satisfied that it is useless to think of our being happy together again." By 1860 Ella had determined to remain almost exclusively in her own upstairs room, not coming down even to eat. Compounding such problems was the fact that Henry's mother-in-law, Mona Douglass, both disapproved of him and lived on his property, always contributing where she could to the sense that Henry was unwelcome in his own home.[47]

Long business trips seem to have provided Henry with some relief from his failing marriage, but it was a home he had always wanted. "My nature," he admitted, "is peculiarly dependent for its happiness on affection and sympathy, and I find myself wholly cut off from them." He would in his intercourse with other men hear them talk of their homes and their families with a pang at his heart. "Others seem to be hurrying home as the benumbed man seeks the fire," he noted, "but . . . I would sooner be almost anywhere else than at home. Home! What a mockery to talk of my having a home!" Occasionally, Henry contemplated going into town at night and finding "the pleasures . . . which some men seem to enjoy," but he understood that he was "too domestic" in his habits and tastes to do such a thing. He contemplated leaving Ella, but that seemed too irresponsible. He contemplated suicide but seemed to think himself unworthy of such a grand gesture. Instead, he spent his nights at home, as alone in his room as he had been at Princeton and at Holly Springs in 1847 and 1848, and confessed his soul to his journal.[48]

Henry Craft also seems to have found some solace in opium. The hours spent over a writing desk, he claimed, had so soured his stomach that relief could only be found in laudanum. But as with Ella, the exact locus of Henry's pain is difficult to pin down. He describes it variously as "torpidity of the liver," "Protean . . . Dyspepsia," "spinal disease," "nervous derangement," and finally, almost admitting the insurmountable problems of diagnosis, simply "my pain." Regardless, opium was always the preferred remedy, with the explanation that he had been forced to resort to it. "I sometimes feel that my whole internal economy is deranged and diseased," he admitted, "and that I must soon experience a general breaking up. I am obliged to keep my liver going by constant dosing."[49]

By the fourth year of his marriage to Ella, Henry had to admit that his life was a wreck, "physically, intellectually, morally, socially, and emotionally." He was not in control of anything, but rather "drifting along upon the stream of chance and accident." "My life is a failure in every point of view," he confessed. "I have not achieved even the poor success of making money. In Memphis I am cut off from all the associations and friendships, and professional ties that rendered life in Holly Springs pleasant if not successful. I have no friends here. In my profession, I am not known. I utterly abhor and loathe and detest the place, and yet I am tied down here beyond all hope of getting away." Like the bricks of his new house, the days had piled on days, the months on months, the years on years, a great temple built to unworthiness, unhappiness. We are caught in a "web of difficulty," he said, "from which extrication is improbable if not impossible."[50]

Only one thing seems to have given Henry Craft even a modicum of joy—his son Douglass. "Today," Henry wrote typically, "I have nursed and amused Douglass a good deal." He is "my only resource. He seems to love me very much and that is very gratifying to me—all the more so perhaps because of my feeling of isolation." While at home Henry stayed close to his own room, living a life as isolated as when he was a bachelor. But occasionally Douglass would come to his room and "his 'pa pa' " would remind Henry that he was not alone. Henry had hoped that Ella would help him keep up his journal, and there are a few early entries in her hand, but she determined that diarizing smacked "too much of the sentimental" and gave it up. So Henry took up the journal, intending it not only as a place to purge his thoughts, but as a record for his son. As with all the endeavors of life that Henry found worthy, however, the journal quickly became to him absurd and self-defeating, a testament to his ongoing humiliation. "Should you ever see this Douglass," he wrote, "and feel no responsive emotion—feel no appreciation of it, thank God that you are fitter for life than your father was." And so Henry wrote a volume to his son, the sole source of his happiness, pouring out his true feelings on pages he hoped the child would never care to read. Indeed, a consistent theme of the diary is the hope that Douglass would somehow be spared his father's overtender heart. "Let him be practical," Henry urged, "common place, real, if he can & so all the more suited for the practical, common place & real which he will encounter." The language Henry uses here corresponds perfectly with that used in his first journal when describing the "common place every dayishness" of his father's male ideal. Henry's father had been a man; Henry hoped Douglass would grow to become a man. Henry was himself something tragically less. "I always thought," he wrote his sister in one of his few surviving letters, "I would have made a much better woman than a man." It is the kind of startling remark easily made the more so by quoting out of context. But Henry's failure to measure up to his own conception of manhood was a theme to which he constantly returned. "It is [on] the tender side of my own nature," he wrote, that "I have been most often wounded." He wanted desperately to change, to be tougher, to dwell not on the burdens and sorrows of his past, man's past, but upon a future that was his to seize and build, as his fellow students at Princeton had seized and built. "But I am too weak and irresolute for all this," he admitted. "I have dreamed and drifted too long now to be a man. . . . Indeed, I feel and have always felt that I am not a man; and have no business with a man's affairs or responsibilities." "My dear boy," he wrote to Douglass, "how willingly would I see you dead rather than know that you have inherited my character; and yet how much I prize you & cling to your love no one can know."[51]

On December 31, 1860, Henry Craft sat in his room, the house quiet, everyone else having gone to bed. Douglass began coughing and Henry took him some medicine, then returned to his journal. He had just come back from a five-day business trip, but there was no word of greeting from his wife. "I go away and come back now without a word of affection," he wrote, "as a stranger indeed, and feeling that when I go all are glad, and when I return all are sorry." This has been "the most unhappy year of my life." Though he sat at the threshold of a new year, a new beginning, the gloom of the past twelve months extended "its pall into the future." His thoughts, he said, dwelled now upon his mortality because "the things of this world [are] so unsatisfying and empty." He knew that he was ungrateful and rebellious, sinful and selfish, and that many would see in his home and family something to envy. But Henry could not summon the strength to be thankful. "I feel broken down in health—broken down in spirit—sick at heart," he confessed. But in that peculiar spirit of defiance that runs through his character, Henry somehow summoned the strength to go on, throwing down the gauntlet and challenging the new year to do its worst. Sitting alone in his room, ignored, unloved, unknown, his marriage and finances a wreck and an addiction to opium reaching an alarming level, at the close of the "most momentous year in our Country's history," and with dark clouds gathering on the political horizon, Henry Craft decided to "let the old year go with its chapter of the world's history to the great archives where that history is kept—the world's history made up of what individual men have done & been & thought & felt." "Come on new year," he demanded, "with whatever of weal and woe for me and mine thou mayst be charged; come on." Henry Craft ended his second journal with this entry, and again disappeared from the historical record.[52]

Conclusion

Laurence Keitt and Henry Craft were distinctly different personalities. Keitt was what one might expect of the Old South—cavalier and brash, a living caricature of the swashbuckling secessionist at midcentury. Craft, by contrast, conforms to none of the stereotypes of the Old South. He was no dandy or patriarch, parvenu or hotspur, but a forgettable nobody, soulsick and broken down in his struggle with the indignities of life. In the full flower of his youth, reared on lands just wrested from the Indians, Henry Craft dwelt with loving excess on the subject of rot and decay. Like the coffins of the period, outfitted with bells that might sound an alarm if the occupant returned to life, or Poe's detailed horror stories of a narrator entombed, so Henry was hyperconscious of his own living death, of the rot of his sick body and the zombifying monotony of his profession. In him, the pressures of being husband and father, professional and breadwinner—in short the pressures of being a man—were finally so great that he was crushed by an obligation to virility he could never discharge. It would be hard to imagine a greater contrast to the flamboyant, unsinkable Keitt.

But in important ways the two men are also curiously complementary. Each was an incurable romantic—Keitt of the British school, Craft of the Sturm und Drang. Each sought a romantic reunion of the self with forces of nature that were brutal and beautiful and capable of swallowing a man whole. Keitt, for instance, once claimed that he would be happy for his body to be atomized and scattered to the four winds. Craft once confessed that he would be content to slip below the earth to be consumed by the worms. But if Keitt's psychic direction was always upward and out, and Craft's was always inward and down, the two were equally fixated on stagnation—Keitt warring with it, Craft succumbing to it. In coping with and compensating for that stagnation, moreover, both chose to pour their emotions onto the written page, creating romantically elaborate narratives from the mundanities of daily existence. In their letters and journals, if not in their lives, these men had direction—Craft ever sinking, Keitt ever rising—toward something undefined and immense, something like immortality or death, which, after all, borrow deeply from one another.

Equally important, both Keitt and Craft could never keep their dream of a woman's love separate from their dream of manly (in)distinction. Craft, of course, was pining for a woman who was dead, or later, a woman who was not his wife, in either case a fantasy woman who might finally make him the lord of not merely a house but a home. If he had not been cheated of this masculine essential, Craft seemed to think, he might have risen on steppingstones of his dead self to the status of a real man. Keitt's trajectory, as might be expected, was just the opposite. Having established his masculine credentials on his own, he realized that his achievements were meaningless and hollow without a woman to bear them witness. Both men's lives, however, illustrate a larger point: men's oft vaunted independence was in fact an elaborate ruse. They, as much as women, depended on members of the opposite sex to validate and make meaningful their struggles and successes, to aid, comfort, and believe in them, even and especially when self-belief began to fade or fail.

PART II

MEN AND WOMEN

CHAPTER 3

ACROSS A GREAT DIVIDE

Love seeketh only self to please
To bind another to its delight
Joys in another's loss of ease,
And builds a Hell to Heaven's despite.*

To readers familiar with negotiating personal spaces through public places, the *Punch* cartoon on page 84 must have provided a
quick laugh. On careful examination, however, the image holds a
fascinating key to understanding gender relations among the elite of
the Victorian era. The man's umbrella, his top hat, his beard, his girth,
the dark and muted colors of his frock coat and peg-top trousers all
suggest the stolid and mature man of means who by the 1850s had
become the fashionable world's male ideal. Early in the century the
ideal had been quite different—plates depicted lithe, clean-shaven,
boyish men sporting tighter trousers and brighter colors. By midcentury, however, a gentleman was seen less as a gentrified pleasure
seeker against a rural backdrop than an urbane professional against
an urban backdrop. Here he needed to be solid, immovable. His was
a mature society—prosperous, conservative, and market-oriented—
and his fashion reflected it.

Women's fashions matured over the period as well. In 1800 the
fashionable female had a slim, girlish body made all the more so by

* William Blake, "The Clod and the Pebble."

"A Terrible Moment," *Punch*, 1856.

a tubelike dress of airy material. She was generally portrayed in a well-groomed garden, looking sprightly and sylvan, as innocent and virginal as a fawn. With the maturation of her society, however, came an elaboration of her costume. Her husband had gone out into the harrowing world of stocks and banks, railroads and financial markets, and he needed a lieutenant who could oversee the details of the household he left behind. Bonnets, which before had been worn like a horse's blinkers, now slipped back on the head, suggesting the expansion of vision commensurate with the wearer's increased responsibility. And like her male counterpart, the midcentury Victorian lady was allowed to take up some real estate. The vast hoops of her crinoline could be thirty feet in circumference, making her wider than she was tall and accommodating a matronly figure as easily as a girlish one. In the streets and shops the skirt provided a buffer between her and a world she was in but not of; she sat atop a kind of cloud, moving without motion in her portable, domesticated space.

The situation depicted by the image is certainly ludicrous—the simplest of gestures is made awkward and self-defeating. But there is something sad about it too, as the title of the illustration—"A Terrible Moment"—makes clear. Surely the man has as much to do with the lady's wearing the skirt as she does herself. His businesses bought the cloth, cut it, and shipped it. He more than she, it seems safe to say, believes at some subconscious level that she needs to be isolated from the temptations and trials of the manly world she moves through. In this image, it is as if the two sexes meet across a great divide, the man making an elaborate display of closing the gap of his own creation, the woman barely reaching out from the sanctity of the ruffled spaces that keep her safe and secure but also unapproachable and alone. Somehow the simple act of touching the opposite sex had been made "terrible."

To be sure, men and women of the antebellum South were separated by a wide divergence of interest and attachment. Raised in and to their separate spheres, there was a chasm between them, the contemplation of which could leave either party with a sense of vertigo. This said, it is important to remember that men and women have a habit of finding their way to each other, whatever the distance or difficulty. It has been suggested, for instance, that men of the nineteenth century wanted their women to be pure, pious, domestic, and submissive. What historians sometimes miss, however, is what men of the period understood perfectly: a woman who was truly pure, pious, domestic, and submissive was also uncommonly boring. Men paid homage to this feminine ideal, but they lived it less in the observance than in the breech. Women were to embody such virtues always, to practice them where convenient, and to above all rise above proscriptions and proprieties to be, privately among their menfolk, at least, open-tempered, compelling, and reasonable, engaging and unguarded, human and whole, mischievous and lively, interesting to talk to and diverting to spend time with.

But more important than all this was the gulf introduced in the last chapter. However flexible on some subjects, men believed that women were supposed to bear witness to male becoming, to cheer men to greatness, and to comfort them along the way. Every free white man had a personal empire to build, whether it was a private plot on a scrubby canebrake or a personal dominion on a vast tract of good earth. And each man had another empire to build in a woman, through whose eyes he could see himself succeed. That the two imperial projects should become tangled up together, as in *Tamerlane*, was not so much surprising as inevitable. Having projected their own aspirations onto their women, men could not help but see them as part and parcel of the larger project of immortality.

This confusion comes out very clearly in the way men talked among themselves about courtship. A woman was not merely to be courted, as the saying went, but wooed and *won*. As with everything else a man might win, calculation and stratagem were an expected part of the process. After falling in love with his future wife, South Carolina rice planter J. Motte Alston began plotting how best to ensnare her, worried lest he be "out-generaled" by her other suitors. Louisianan Roberdeau Wheat viewed his courtship of various women as a "matrimonial campaign." He did not love any of them, but that did not matter. "I want some woman who will love me so much that she will in time teach me to love her," he confessed. When finally he found a good candidate, it was not her own rare qualities that attracted him but her credulity about men. "She is not beautiful," he noted, "but she is good, not brilliant but amiable, not witty but looks as if she would think her husband so even when others said he was dull and stupid. . . . I have not courted her yet but feel that I shall win her." Military metaphors, as in the cases of Alston and Wheat, were undoubtedly the favorite in referring to courtship. A woman was a sort of fort besieged, and men understood that it would take no common set of tactics to secure her surrender. "An earnest lover has all the senses of a North American Indian," reported a writer for the *Messenger*, "with tenfold more sagacity, acuteness and cunning, and will march steadily on to his purpose, and leave no trace of his goings which can attract the notice of hostile eyes. Day or darkness, alone or in a crowd, in the parlour or along the way,—anywhere, everywhere, opportunities present themselves, where a man is ready for the work."[1]

And indeed, men fully expected courtship to be work. They did not begrudge the effort, however, because without effort there could be no sense of achievement, no sense of pride when the battle was won and the spoils taken. South Carolina jurist James Petigru thought he saw exactly this dynamic at work in the story of a thirty-two-year-old woman who had become the most sought-after sweetheart in Virginia. To all pleas and entreaties the woman remained steadfastly single, though she "consign[ed], every year, new lovers to despair." Her unusual power over men, Petigru surmised, had nothing to do with attractiveness, wit, or wealth. "She is not beautiful," he admitted, "she never was and nobody, not even among the great rejected, would probably say he thought she was." Neither did she possess a great fortune—her father was a simple judge who had "nothing but his salary . . . and can't resign because he would starve." Nor was the woman a vivacious conversationalist. Indeed, Petigru noted, "she is remarkable in no way; makes no effort to shine and does not shine, but dresses, talks and sits like a staid, sedate, imperturbable person." This, in fact, was the wellspring of her appeal. There is "no doubt in my mind," Petigru remarked, "that [her] secret . . . is to be found in that principle that leads men to take pleasure in a difficulty overcome. . . . It is because she is so hard to please, that all the world are smitten with the desire of pleasing her."[2]

The winning of a woman, then, was a quest not unlike any other male quest for distinction and éclat. She was a great, glittering prize, like Keitt's bright chalets and diadems, and men set about success in the romantic arena just as they had set about it in their professions. Lord King, for instance, saw courtship as a clash of wills, stylistically similar to lobbying for a railroad contract or an important bill. Traveling with his father as a representative of the Southern Pacific Railroad, he made the comparison quite explicit. "The uncertainty of Legislation," he wrote his brother, "is so great that that of women is a fool to it. With a woman you may understand 'yes' for 'no' and return to the charge, but with Legislation, if you let it floor you, you have to stay down." For a writer at the *Messenger*, hunting provided a better metaphor. The courting male, he noted, needed to be ever vigilant about women, "lest as . . . wild steed[s] of the prairies, they dash away beyond your power to subdue them." But if a man was careful and "pressed his suit with vigor," he might gain a favorable answer "before she could reach the shelter of her home." For another gentleman, the world of banks and bonds provided the best model for courtship. "If I could go to the old gentleman's counting-room in business hours, state my wishes, and leave the whole matter in his hands, I shouldn't mind marrying," he noted, "but if I must ask his

daughter, then I'll be hanged before I'll be married. Not that I would
object to asking her, if I could do it as readily as I enquire the price
of stocks, or the latest European news; but I cannot do that, and
indeed, to be honest, the only time I ever tried, I found myself getting
. . . red in the face."[3]

This mixing of professional and romantic metaphor makes perfect
sense from one perspective. Men were expected to be the pursuers in
courtship; their quarry, like fame or fortune, was something to be
achieved, won, prized, treasured, taken. "Women, by the inalienable
delicacy of their natures, do not act the part of wooers," the *Messenger*
reported. "But as to men, if they deserve the name, they can in a
great measure control their own destiny. . . . Among other things
which they can do, they can marry." And marry they should, suggested most antebellum Southern magazines. In a piece entitled "On
Old Bachelors," F. W. Shelton noted that for all the criticism they
endured, old maids were not the problem. "*Let them alone*, since God
has so willed it," he advised. They are a "chirping and vivacious class
of women who, from mere accident and the force of circumstances
over which they have no control, bloom solitary in the desert." Shelton
was not as sympathetic when it came to old bachelors, whom he called
an "unfortunate class who will be esteemed by many as scarcely worth
the labor of an essay. And they are not, except as a solemn warning,
a painful yet salutary lesson to others. They are, for the most part,
mere fragments of humanity, scattered links of the golden chain
which connects the family of man." There was no good excuse, then,
for a man not to marry. He had only to roll up his sleeves and go
at it. To be sure, the world of courtship could be a brutal and competitive one, but no more so than the world of banks and politics, and
antebellum magazines were full of advice for the timid courtier.
"Women, like dreams, go by contraries," intoned one magazine sa-
gaciously. "If the man be humble in his petitions, the woman will be
haughty in reply; if he be bold in questioning, she is modest in answering. . . . Humility in a man subjects him to the suspicion of cowardice, and women hate and condemn cowards more than men do.
Bravery and manliness . . . they adore, but an effeminate milksop they
detest and despise." Successful courtship, then, depended on the same
qualities of character that men were expected to bring to their pro-

fessions. If a man was bold and pressed his suit with vigor and determination, he might succeed in any arena, even romance.[4]

As in the case of Laurence Keitt, however, most men found that a courtship based on bullying and bluster was not only ineffective but altogether unsatisfying. Despite the advice given them by magazines, heedless of the need always to appear manly, men longed for a rest from their own competitive drives and masculine pursuits. Romance gave them this opportunity, and men usually seized on it when they stopped playing at love and gave themselves over to it whole. Victorian proprieties could be rigid; the public culture of romance could stress a tight reign on the passions and a battery of tricks and tactics. But, as in any age, love will out and write its own rules. As high as they could be built, as fast as they could be written, antebellum men and women scaled the walls of Victorian propriety and damned the advice of the magazines, and struggled, sometimes with success, to find each other whole.

For many middle-class couples, this struggle and this search took place on paper. For a variety of reasons, correspondence was, in the antebellum period, an integral aspect of courtship. Most obviously, couples were often separated by unnegotiable distances in an era of slower, more restricted travel. Then too Victorian proprieties and the prying eyes of small town life made the letter one of the most private, and therefore most sacred, romantic spaces. But these were not the only reasons romantic parties often preferred writing to meeting. Raised to their separate spheres, men and women had a vast psychic distance to close, a distance that could seem overwhelming when they met face-to-face. Letters allowed couples to come at this distance more obliquely, more tentatively. In letters, personal attention could be paid without the discomfiting awkwardness that attended public presentation; in correspondence, men and women hid behind an authorial voice, an anonymity of sorts, that helped compensate for the natural shyness they felt in the first flush of romance. "I believe that I can write to you more freely than I can talk," Harriet Alexander noted in a letter to her beloved Wallace. "Everything reads smoothly, no matter how often the pen falters in the writing, & the written page cannot reflect the color that mounts to the cheek of the writer. . . . I believe that I am a *little* frightened of you yet, & I wonder how I

ever have written & do write you the vain & idle things with which
I often fill my letters. . . . I believe [I] play that I am writing in my
journal & that what is written will not be for inspection." A woman
identifiable only as "Toosie" employed a similar method of make-
believe in her letters to Lord King. Writing late at night, after everyone had gone to bed, the stillness hypnotized her, allowing her to drift
to her lover and back in the comforting abstractness of her mind. "It
still rains on, and the clouds are thick and dark," she wrote him, "I
am beside an open window, sister is sleeping, and I hear *nothing*
except the quiet & measured falling of the rain . . . until I ha[ve] almost forgotten *you* in the Lord of my imagination. . . . I am scarcely
aware *who* I'm writing to. You are again becoming ideal, and I *wish*
I could write you a volume." Letters, then, were a sort of incubator
of romantic interest and attachment; there shyness and reserve could
be peeled back, layer by careful layer, until a person's inmost self was
revealed.[5]

Such revelations could become quite intense, especially for men.
Obliged to be so often stoical and self-possessed, courtship offered
them one of the few arenas in which they could explore and disclose
the softer side of their psyches. Laurence Keitt, remember, thought
introspection actually dangerous, a sort of cannibalism in which the
heart turned on itself to feed. Henry Craft was living proof of Keitt's
theory; self-examination brought him only loneliness and grief. But
in courtship letters, men could take an inward turn that did not suggest retreat. Here weakness could be confessed and indulged; here
introspection was not merely safe but essential. As North Carolinian
Wes Halliburton noted, the letters he exchanged with his dear Cousie
brought him his greatest peace because they gave him an excuse "to
retire into [him]self."[6]

In romance, then, the constrictions on a man's heart and expression
were lifted. To a woman he could surrender, with all the force of his
being, and be no less a man for the fall. New to such a feeling, men
clung to it desperately, damning the advice books and relishing the
most submissive, even the most servile, aspects of courtship. "Do you
feel as if I *belonged* to you?" one Mississippi youth asked his beloved,
"and that you have a property in me? If you do, you should give
me full directions how to behave myself." After a man's surrender,

no task was too menial, no sacrifice too great, where it was performed in her service. She was his superior, especially morally, and he knew it, said it, and admitted it to himself and her, over and over again. "I am perfectly willing, nay it is *imperative*, that you be *above* me," wrote a Tennessee boy to his sweetheart, "for man, *civilized* man, always looks *up* for something to adore, and *I* have found that something in [you]."[7]

It is important to recognize that in no way was a man surrendering his masculine drives. He had merely shifted the arena of their pursuit, as Keitt did so effortlessly, to the personal empire he fashioned out of woman. In her he hoped to create something all his own—a Civilization as magical as any he might found on earth, a great kingdom of love where he could surrender and still reign supreme. A student at the University of North Carolina, Wes Halliburton had as prickly a sense of honor as any of his classmates. "I have learned by being taught in adversity's school to depend upon myself," he claimed. "I never have and never will ask a favor of any man if asking that favor is a mark of inferiority." But with Cousie, Haliburton could ask anything, give anything, do anything, be anything. Cousie had given him something the rest of the world hadn't, and his opinion of the world suffered as a consequence. "I love to think that every body hates me," Halliburton confessed to his beloved, "I love to be alone. I love to be called 'Ishmael.' I love to look out on the land and in all eyes see *hatred*, on all brows a frown, on all lips anathemas. I love to believe that I am of no use to any body save you. I don't care, yes I care, but I would not turn on my heel to gain the love of a living man. Cousie, sweet darling, I love you. Every breath, every fibre, every chord, every throb, is yours and only yours. . . . When you write all is joy and love, when you write I feel independent of all the world." In marrying, Halliburton underscored his manhood, took possession of his first, most important dependent, and achieved the most basic, the most primal, of empires. Far from compromising him, his surrender to Cousie actually established his independence.[8]

There was, of course, another model of legitimate surrender available to men—surrender to God. It isn't too surprising, then, that antebellum men often borrowed from the language and power of Christianity to help them sacrilize their romantic projects. Their love, they knew, was not merely physical but spiritual and required therefore a spiritual vocabulary. "Keep your sweet heart buoyed up," wrote one husband, "with the reflection that I *love* you *fondly* & will *cherish* and *reverence* you as the good christian does his maker." "To love you dearly and consider you as the 'idol of my affections,' " wrote another, "requires no effort: it is natural as it is for me to breathe. Every breath I draw is perfumed with the holy incense of this sacred affection, and every wish invokes the protection of a thoughtful Providence upon your head." For some men the similarities between religion and romance ran so deep that spiritual vocabulary was not enough. Their love of woman had progressed past the merely spiritual to the devotional, requiring more liberal nicking from the established faiths. Romance had become, for them, itself a personal religion, complete with intercessor (the beloved), church (the home), conversion experience (falling in love), and sacraments (engagement, marriage, physical intimacy, writing letters, and mourning).[9]

For most men, romance did not replace organized religion but bled into it until the two were indistinguishable. Their wives became their conduits to God, and that was often as close to Him as they really wanted to be. William Pender's determination to become a Christian, for instance, was less a religious quest than a romantic one. Possessed by a love for his wife that surpassed his ability to explain it, his search for answers ended, as it often does, at the doorstep of the Almighty. Perhaps God could explain to Pender what he felt and why. But because it was his heart and not his soul that led the quest, Pender could not find his way to God to ask Him anything. Fanny's gravity was too strong; Pender's orbit around her too stable. Each time he set out to find religion, he found only Fanny; all roads led to Romance. "Honey, whenever I try to reflect upon the future and to resolve to do better," Pender wrote his beloved, "I think of you first and your image rises up and intrudes in upon my thoughts of Christ and the future so that I have almost come to feel that you are a part of my religion." Pender was being modest. Fanny was not so much a part of his religion as the whole of it. He wanted to love God, but the truth was, God had His drawbacks. God was remote, stern, inscrutable, and publicly available, traits He shared with Pender and most other males. Could Pender really be expected to love another male, to surrender to Him? The whole notion violated something fundamental to Pender's basic being. Fanny, on the other hand, was real, warm, manipulable, and, most important, her divinity existed for Pender alone. "I have not had that love for Christ in me that I ought to," Pender admitted to his wife. "I know I am grateful for all the mercies He has shown us, I love his name, but it has not a part of my existence like my love for you. My feeling for my Savior partakes more of that arising from a sense of duty, but for you it exist[s] and how it commenced and upon what principle high up I hardly know or think about. I know you are my wife, that I love you and am anxious about you and desirous of pleasing you because I love you." Here, then, was a suitable foundation for a religion. No stuffy churches. No hypocritical preachers. No parishioners meddling in each other's affairs. Just Fanny, Pender's personal intercessor with the Almighty.[10]

When a man attempts to make an intercessor of his wife, he may run into problems. His beloved may not be particularly religious, for instance. William Nugent experienced this difficulty with his fiancée, Nellie. Younger than he and more frivolous, Nellie not only attended a dance in his absence but also took her turn on the floor. William was beside himself. What was the fiancée of a "poor, sober-sided Methodist" doing "whirling thru the mazes of the dance" and pressing the flesh "with the devotees of fashion"? His reaction, though, was not that of the jealous lover but of the disappointed acolyte who stumbles on the rector tippling in the vestry. "You occupy a sacred position in my affection; Almost that of an idol," William reminded his intercessor. "If it is broken and destroyed, who will be the iconoclast?" George Peddy had the opposite problem—his wife, Zerlina, was caught up in her own faith, whose doctrines conflicted with his own devotional enthusiasm for Romance. "The fact that nothing can elicit such soft expressions & such pleasant ones from you as [talking about God]," Peddy wrote his wife, "teaches me that your affections are concentrated upon divine things. Hence I am forced to the conclusion [that I] share only a finite portion of your pure affection. If this be so, alas for me: better far that I never had been born." And even if a man's wife had just the right amount of religion, she was still his wife as well as his intercessor, creating grave problems in the confessional. Pender himself ran into this problem while seeking spiritual guidance for his sexual gluttony: "Honey, the same that causes you so much trouble [Fanny was pregnant] is my stumbling block in this world.... I do feel humbled and mortified to think that the most dangerous of all our passions and the most sinful when indulged, should be the one that I cannot conquer." Fortunately, he claimed, whenever he had impure thoughts he had only to conjure up Fanny's face and the mood passed. For her part, Fanny seems to have overlooked these references, telling her husband to go forth and sin no more. But when Pender admitted to having had "a very nice time dancing and flirting with a very nice girl" at a party, she demanded penitence: "Now, I ask you candidly, in your sober senses, why you wrote me such a thing as that? Was it to gratify your vanity by making me jealous, or to make me appreciate your love still more? You are very much mistaken.... Nothing you have ever said—nothing you have ever done, nothing you have ever written in this whole of our married life—ever pained me so acutely or grieved me so deeply." Pender was staggered; in his religious ecstasy he had severely misjudged the temper of his confessor. His next letter was an impassioned act of contrition—"Fanny ... you have torn my heart ... you have brought tears, bitter tears [to] the eyes of one who has loved you and tried to honor you"—and he subsequently confined himself to confessing sins of omission rather than commission. "It is certainly lonely enough [here] to satisfy a monk," he grumbled after things had blown over.[11]

But even as he sat groveling at the hem of his confessor, the surrendering male had his eye on his ambitions. These women were not saints. They may have been more morally upright than their menfolk, but they had done nothing worthy of worship and were, few of them, comfortable with the notion. Rather it was the men themselves who had made gods of their women and placed them so carefully in the heavens. Their professions might be mundane; their quests for greatness might rise or fall. But their women were always their own, and in romancing them men found a spiritual quest, a poetic purpose, with all the éclat and energy of empire building. And when finally they became great, as each man believed he one day would, his woman would be close at hand to witness and reward his suffering and his sacrifice.

—⇒·◇·⇐—

The imperial drives and poetic ambitions of antebellum men had tremendous consequences for antebellum women. To be sure, a woman had her own sphere, a domestic one, over which she exercised considerable power. "Home—that is [a woman's] empire," remarked Robert Mallard in a letter to his fiancée, "there she governs with ... all but despotic sway." And in ways that are just beginning to be appreciated, antebellum Southern women used their dominion over domestic concerns to justify the formation of benevolent societies that exercised a significant influence in the period. In these pursuits women were generally encouraged, and, as in the antebellum North, female education was expanded to include more than the social graces. Indeed, by the 1850s, a woman's curriculum looked a lot like her brother's. Southern women were encouraged to keep abreast of the political developments of the day, their counsel was often sought and followed, and, in the very differences of their outlook, their behind-the-scenes influence was seen as a natural corrective to the brutalities of a man's world. "In families, as well as empires, there is oft a power behind the throne greater than the throne itself," intoned George Fitzhugh in *DeBow's*, "and that power is usually clad in petticoats." Men's judgments, Fitzhugh argued, were often of little worth because men believed too much in their powers of analysis to derive answers from complex systems. "These old fogy lawyers," he complained, "get cramped and stiffened equally in body and mind. . . . They have a self-important, turkey-cock strut, 'walk wide between the legs as if they had the gaffs on,' and bear their heads as carefully as a milk-woman does her pail, for fear of spilling their redundant brains, of which commodity each member, it is obvious, believes that he possesses a close monopoly." Women, on the other hand, reacted instinctually, trusting in their innate goodness—of which they did possess a close monopoly—to lead them to sound conclusions.[12]

Then too, the rigid proprieties that so stifled and contained women could also be used as a weapon. Annoyed by a pestering beau, Laura Cole told her would-be swain that there was nothing she should like so well as for him to recover her missing pencil. The boy spent hours blithely looking for an implement that didn't exist, happy to be of such minute service to the fair sex. "He ... searched very diligently," Laura confessed to a cousin, "for what had not been lost. He peeped under chairs, tables, sofas, annoyed the old ladies by removing their foot-stools, got a reprimand from his grandmother, a gentle reproof from his gentle mother, and a sour look from his aunt." To be sure, Laura could not come at her disaffection for the young man directly. But in sending him on a fool's errand, she drew on a wellspring of feminine power which, so long as it was exercised obliquely, could thwart and dull the wills of ostensibly more powerful men.[13]

In the main, though, a Southern woman's province was a precariously small one. All of the spaces from which she exercised her power also circumscribed and contained her. Everything about her was supposed to be smaller—her influence, her appetites, her interests, and, especially, her size. Calling his dear Nellie "my own little wife," William Nugent explained that he did not mean "little in the sense of a precious consort, & agreeable companion." In this Nellie filled "every sacred corner of" his heart. Nor was she little "in those qualities of mind" that made him contented in "the contemplation of a long life of prospective happiness." Rather she was "little only in that best & to me dearest of all senses, *Size*." Such endearments and belittlings were not all bad, of course. Some women relished the adoration of the opposite sex and were never so contented as when swinging in the arms of their larger, stronger husbands. "It seems to me if I were with you I could not suffer you to do anything in the world," wrote George Peddy to his beloved Kate, "not even walk. I should want to carry you tenderly with my own hands." For her part Kate rather liked the idea. Twisting her ankle on the fireplace, Kate became dizzy with pain, and her daughter was "distressed to death for fear" she would cry. But all at once the little girl "looked up with a brightened face and said, 'Mama, hush, Pappie will tote you.' " "She is like her mother," Kate wrote her husband, "[she] believes you [can] make all things right." But there were occasions, too, when a woman's physical powerlessness seemed not a consolation but a curse. In an altercation with her siblings, Harriet Alexander discovered just how frustrating her small stature could be. Standing next to her younger brother Porter one evening, she remarked that if he grew any taller she would no longer be able to kiss him on the forehead. The statement attracted the attention of her older brother, Felix, who responded, "Never mind, poor little thing, I'll put you up on my shoulder[s] & then you'll be as tall as any body." "I saw what was coming & tried to drop on my knees," Harriet noted, "but before I could utter one cry for mercy, there I was, mounted on [his] shoulder[s] & in such an agony of fruitless & impotent wrath as ought to have crushed him with its weight. He carried me round & round & would'nt put me down & I felt so insulted that I would'nt deign to scold a bit.... If my ability had been as good as my will, they would have had a sound drubbing apiece." But of course her ability could not match her will, however titanic it might be. Her brother was stronger and bigger, and if he chose to exercise these advantages, she could do little to stop him.[14]

As with size, so it was with other aspects of female powerlessness. When mediated with respect and restraint, a woman could enjoy being adored, even possessed. But when mediated otherwise, she was left only with Harriet's "agony of fruitless & impotent wrath," which, finding no outward expression, had to be simply swallowed. Unlike a man's world, where action and projection were staple themes, a woman's world was marked by restraint. Her frustrations could not be sublimated in a boxing match; her drive for excellence could not carry her to the White House. For this reason, women's imaginative lives were crucial. On flights of fancy, they could travel to far-off places and sample novel experiences. But the imaginative life, while vivid and vibrant, seemed so frail and weak, founded as it was on airy nothings, that it could occasionally come crashing in on itself.

The life of Anna King suggests the degree to which this internalization could weigh on a woman. Anna Matilda Page had been a happy, confident child. She lived her whole life at Retreat, a plantation on St. Simons Island, Georgia. She was educated at home, a live-in tutor and a neighbor's knowledge of French equipping her with the learning and polish befitting a belle. In 1823, she was sent to Savannah to display these accomplishments, to throw herself into the oh-so-brief quickening of time and loosening of restraints that attended a woman's coming out. "I dance a great deal," Anna exulted to her mother, "and [am] much pleased of course as is always the case when I can dance as often as I feel inclined." But after her marriage, Anna began to slip into a despondent sort of trance. Her husband, Thomas, was inclined to be away much of the time, leaving the planting in the hands of his wife and their overseer. "The birds are very troublesome to the corn which is now filling," she noted in one of her reports to Thomas. "Sanders broke your double barrel gun all to pieces so that I have no means of destroying them. John Demere shot the best ox I have yesterday. This fact he acknowledged himself to Dunham [the overseer]. The animal is not yet dead. Now put all these things together & you must think I have enough to try even old Miss Job."[15]

But it was not the petty trials of plantation management that overwhelmed Anna—it was the fact that she had no one with whom she could share these things. Anna's concept of her social circle was family oriented and intensely nuclear. She did not seek or find sisterhood in the wider society of women; she did not fraternize with extended kin or with the other members of her community or class. Despite the concerns that weighed her down, she derived comfort only from her family, lamenting the presence in her home of anyone who was not a member.

This made it more difficult when family members left her, as Thomas did on business, or as all her children did for their education. But Anna's concern for her "absentees" went beyond her own unmet need for social support or companionship; she was nearly paralyzed with worry that one of them would be struck down by disease. In her letters she discusses health and sickness, her children's, the neighbors', the slaves', with what might seem an obsessive frequency. These were times when illnesses were omnipresent and deadly, and Anna acted as the family doctor, nurse, and pharmacist. She often spent a great part of her day ministering to the sick of her extended household, occasionally passing entire nights at the bedside of the "stricken." Anna's preoccupation with the subject, however, ran deeper. Her first-born had been taken at an early age, sending her into dark depression. Suddenly all her children seemed to her like "shades," suspended somewhere between life and death, under her care but ultimately beyond her control. If one could be taken from her then so could another, and another. She got over her grief but was left with a "soul harrowing fear that harm might befall" another member of the family, a fear aggravated by their frequent travels. To her husband, she admitted the concern "drives me almost crazy. I can settle down to no employment," and she berated her children sharply if they did not send constant updates on the state of their health. By the 1850s, Anna would often ask one of her children to skim incoming mail before she read it to make sure it did not contain dread news. As soon as the letters had been given a once-over, she devoured them with a great relief that her loved ones were yet safe. "God has been most merciful," she told a daughter with characteristic pessimism. "Our numbers are still the same. May this blessing be continued to us yet a while longer. We cannot expect it to last forever. No, my child, *a change must come*. We know not at what hour or who will be the first to go." For Anna, life was a precarious enterprise and she saw her loved ones as being in a nearly constant state of deadly peril.[16]

Certainly loneliness aggravated these anxieties. After evening tea, if Thomas was gone and all the children were in bed, Anna would lie awake, unable to read or write or sew for fear her eyesight might worsen with the strain. This, she said, is "my most lonely time." "You have so much to divert your mind," she wrote her husband, "but poor me I have no change—the same dull roteen [sic] of ordering break-fast, dinner and supper, looking after the servants and then darning socks *and thinking*." Indeed, it was the thinking that most plagued her. "My mind seems in a constant confusion," she noted in a common refrain, "if I could just be relieved of this fullness in my head." Anna's anxiety was not an occasional or affected phenomenon. Helplessly, in letters to her husband, daughters, and sons, she formulated and re-formulated her "nervous derangement" until the words lost all meaning: "I have much to take up my attention & find it harder to collect my thoughts every time I have to put them down on paper"; my mind "is so clouded from various causes, I can scarce find ideas to form a sentence"; "if I could only keep from thinking I would do better"; "I cannot control my thoughts"; "I can't think or look for anything but further trouble"; "I do believe my head cannot be right. I feel no dependence on my own judgment"; "I feel like a vessel tost on the waves to be driven as the wind or circumstances may"; "if I was good enough to die what a world of troubles I would escape"; "I have interest in nothing and no one has interest in me"; "I feel such anxiety for the living"; "I must say I am tired of my tread mill life";

"I am the *greatest slave* on the plantation"; "I wonder . . . if I shall ever know what peace is"; "My life seems entirely wrapped up in the lives of you beloved ones. I live in constant dread of what may happen to you"; and on and on. For all the years of her married life Anna fretted and stewed over matters beyond her control, trapped between her understanding of the passivity of woman's proper role and the realities of her active life. However ably she ran the plantation and ordered her house, her gardens, her table, she returned at night by channels well-worn to worrying about the plantation and house, gardens and table, the sick, the dying, and the absent. Her own health was uncommonly good—in thirty-six years of letter writing she never noted suffering even a sniffle. And she could even deal with gruesome death, so long as it did not stalk her own family. When the steamship *Magnolia* exploded, Anna helped turn a cotton barn into a makeshift hospital. Such accidents could be incredibly gory affairs and the *Magnolia* was no exception; great billowy mounds of cotton were soaked in blood, and days after the explosion limbs were still washing up on Retreat's beaches. An entire torso was retrieved from the inlet—Anna examined it minutely to determine if the decomposing corpse had any characteristics that might help identify the deceased.[17]

But for all her strength, Anna wanted most to be weak, to be dependent, to feel that a man was taking care of things, even if less ably than she could take care of them herself. "We want a head among us," she noted of her family. "I have no mind of my own. Neither have I *experience or judgment*. . . . Alas poor me I have no head for anything." A woman, Anna had taught her daughters, was supposed to set a passive example, to exercise her influence by moral suasion and demur suggestion. Forced by circumstances to adopt a stronger role in her own family, Anna regarded her own authority as something usurped and improper, and she exercised it apologetically, tentatively. "I do indeed feel that mine is a most responsible situation," she wrote Thomas. "Responsible to my God! To my husband! To my children!!! The spirit truly is willing but the flesh is weak. I cannot do all that is required of me. I find myself constantly looking *for aid* from you my beloved! What a misfortune to all of us your being so little at home! When Oh! when will you again remain at home!" The answer, of course, unspoken but understood, was never.

But Anna would not, could not, admit it. And this, finally, was the underlying cause of her "soul harrowing" fear that one of her absent family members might be struck down. So long as they lived there was a possibility that her stewardship over her husband's family might one day come to an end, that they might return to make her a wife again, a mother again, a woman who again made sense to herself.[18]

In the meantime, Anna struggled to cobble a family together out of paper, almost literally writing out her eyes in long letters to her "absentees." "It gives me very little trouble to write," she told her daughter, "& it is so much pleasure to hold communion with you beloved ones . . . that I could spend my time in doing little else." Anna could be petty about letters—she sometimes numbered hers to show how often she wrote and scolded family members if their letters were deficient in quantity or quality. If letters became the measure by which their love was judged, however, it is understandable. "Your dear Father & beloved selves," she wrote her daughter, "are all I have on earth. . . . As much as you think you love me *your love is as nothing* compared to the *ardent love I feel.*" Devoted entirely to her family, Anna demanded reminders that they were devoted too, that they in some small way echoed her feelings. Otherwise, "stuck down on this lost end of the world," she could convince herself that she had only imagined them all in her scribblings. As she put it, if her family did not write, she "didn't exist."[19]

As much as her letter writing testifies to Anna's commitment to her family, it also suggests her detachment from the wider world. Unable to bring her absentees to her side, she absented herself; her mind flew to them and back, leaving little behind but a life spiraling always into itself. She would go to church, but members would inquire after Thomas. "Our neighbors congratulated me on having heard from you," she wrote wryly, "for I believe the most envious must *pity* me." She could not explain Thomas's absences, could not quite condemn them openly, but she understood that they reflected on her, shamed her, and she stopped going to church. She complained that the island had "just enough people on it to make it disagreeable," but found she could not easily leave as "the passage in a boat has for me so many terrors I can't think of it." Hers was a world within a world, a place that year by year grew smaller and smaller, more and more isolated. Certainly this was true spatially—"If I had all my family with me," she admitted to a daughter, "I could live for years without going outside the front door." But it was also true temporally. "I must not look back," she noted after a series of reminiscences, "and I fear to look forward." Anna's entire world was collapsing in upon a single point—wait and hope, wait and hope, nothing could be fully resolved until Thomas would finally return and make them a family again. In the meantime, Anna could not have been surprised that her sons and daughters pitied and babied her—Anna did no less. Constantly thrown back on herself as she searched in vain for advice, companionship, or support, she could only threaten and scold, gestures that by their very emptiness became the kind of quaint character trait her family could indulge but not take seriously. Even when the family (excluding Thomas) went on vacation, Anna could not escape the role she had made for herself. "No one thinks of asking me to go [anywhere]," she confessed to a daughter. "I suppose they all look on me as [just] as much of a fixture here as I am when at home."[20]

On January 20, 1859, Anna's waiting ended. Her oldest son, Butler, stood brushing his hair before a mirror when he felt an odd twitching in his left eyelid. He turned to his brother to "point out this strange symptom" but found he could not speak distinctly. He was quickly placed in a tub of hot water—a galvanic battery was hooked up and he was given a mustard emetic. His hands were paralyzed so one of his brothers put a finger down his throat. "A little blood came the first throw—then it came up in volumes." "Great God! What a sight," Anna noted. She felt sure her son had retched up his heart. Laid out on a bed, Butler seemed to be resting peacefully when he was seized by "awful convulsions" that persisted until "his mind left him" and "his noble soul left his body." Suddenly Anna could stop worrying over where or when the ax would fall. Butler's death gave her something real to lament and with it came an odd sort of relief. In her anguish, she felt "none of the torturing anxiousness which ofttimes" made her miserable. "How many years of happiness," she wrote with uncharacteristic clarity, "have I wasted in gloomy anticipation of misfortunes . . . that spirit of continual fretting and moping over fancied ill, that temptation to exaggerate the real or supposed dangers which surrounded my beloved absentees, the disadvantages of our condition, magnifying the trifling inconveniences of our everyday life into enormous evils."[21]

Months after Butler's death, Anna's letters continued thick with religion and despair. She wrote Thomas that she was "looking to Jesus! for help in this our deep sorrow, looking to Him to guide us in the strait and narrow path which will lead us to His mercy's seat. Sometimes I feel comforted, then again all is dark, dark." Anna held regular prayer meetings in her dead son's room, believing his glorious spirit descended from the heavens to be near his family. She called her grief "a deep sorrow which time does not lighten" and chastised her daughters for wearing anything but black. When, a few months after the funeral, Thomas returned to politics, she did not bother to ask when he would return. Anna had once written her daughter, "Oh! that I could once more see you all around my table, I think I would then be content to die." Butler's death had ensured that such a reunion would never happen; despite the writing and worrying, the waiting and hoping, her family would never be all together again. Now only heaven afforded such a possibility and Anna clung to the idea tenaciously. "Tho my heart's idol has left me to return no more," she wrote her daughter Georgia, "each day takes us nearer to the new home Christ has given him.... I long for that better world." On August 22, 1859, seven months after the death of her son, Anna King passed away. Given her impeccable health, it is difficult not to concur with her daughter that she had died of grief. Her life had finally collapsed upon itself bearing her away to her long-sought reunion with her "departed treasures."[22]

Anna King's case is undoubtedly extreme. Her husband was unusually inattentive; her disposition was unusually morbid. To be sure, there were also cases, like the Perrys of Greenville, where wives demanded that their husbands absent themselves and not come home until they had achieved something miraculous. But Anna King's psychic trajectory was all too common in the antebellum South. "I do not know if I have any positive disease," noted Sarah Gayle typically, "but I have my own proper share of nervousness, weakness, swimming in the head and a dull, sleepy sensation.... My family claims untiring attention." The life of a planter's wife consisted of routine—and more routine—and she rarely had the opportunities her husband did for altering patterns worn with overuse. A planter's business took him often to town. His profession took him often farther still. The plantation became for him a place to put his feet up and recuperate from the trials of his various absences. But for women, the plantation could be a place of excruciating dullness, a world within a world where the petty cares of children and slaves seemed all but inescapable. Returning from a trip to the city, Mary Chesnut quailed at being once again bottled up on her plantation. "Already I feel the dread stillness and torpor of our Sahara at Sandy Hill creeping into my veins," she noted. "It chills the marrow of my bones.... There is nothing but frizzle-frazzle talked in this house.... I would sleep on bare boards if I could once more be amidst the stir and excitement of a live world. These people have grown accustomed to dullness.... I feel abandoned of God and man here in this dismal swamp."[23]

But it was not just the loneliness and the routine that got into the bones of planter wives—it was the ridiculously petty details that were left to their capable care. Ordering the house, tables, garden, and children involved little of the éclat on which men rose and fell. A woman's sphere was smaller, and her cares were supposed to be smaller too. Some women, perhaps a majority, reveled in this sphere, finding in the rich rewards of farm and family a peace and pride of place they wouldn't have traded for the world. But even the happiest recognized the dark road down which women less fortunate were apt to go. Her head bowed down by trifling complaints and trivial duties, a woman could sometimes feel buried under a mountain of other people's needs. "I have many petty trials to which my temper gives way," noted Susan Cornwall. "It seems impossible to feel pleasant under a sarcastic remark, or patient when there are so many little ones to manage. The negroes are careless, the children out of sorts and something hinders the dinner or tea, the good man comes home hungry (and therefore savage) and away flies my pleasant face and I feel like wishing myself a huge pair of scissors to cut everything in my way." "I feel sometimes such an impatience of my life & its lot as I can hardly describe," echoed Cornelia Spencer. "I want to go & see & do something better than I have known.... I want to ... take wings & fly & leave these poor & sordid occupations [behind]." And Cornwall and Spencer still had their pluck. After enough "petty trials" and "sordid occupations" a woman could go altogether numb, the smallness of her world, like Anna King's, collapsing in on itself. "I look at [some of my women friends]," noted Sarah Morgan, "and wonder if God thought it worth while to give them souls to be crushed in that narrow little casket of the brain, which seems to die, and yet leave them living." For women like these, the consuming cares of farm and family offered not peace but torpidity. Whatever vibrancy had shone from them in their youth had been systematically dulled by the monotony of their lives. "We are very quiet, now, in this delectable little world of ours," Laura Cole explained, "and we have no better way of cheating ennui than to engage in all manner of housewifery, which employments are, doubtless, no less creditable than disagreeable." Slipping away to write a letter to a friend, Laura admitted that she was taking refuge from the other women of the household, who were caught up in "discussing the merits of a crimson, velvet riding-dress." But just as Laura had begun to slip into her epistolary reverie, one of the women came in to solicit her opinion. "Alas! alas! my fine structure is blown into air by a fair lady's breath," she noted, "Here is Miss——with her crimson, velvet riding-dress again. Oh, crimson, velvet riding-dress. You are ... odious to my ear."[24]

To be sure, antebellum women sought and found various releases for the nagging pressures of their lives. On their horses, for instance, women found a solution to their smallness and weakness; in the speed and exhilaration of the ride they found power, direction—and happiness. Riding on the beaches of Retreat plantation, Georgia King and her brother Mallery came across a porpoise, flailing in the shallows, obviously dying. Mallery went to the lighthouse to get a shotgun, returned and shot twice, putting the animal out of its misery. By the time the carcass had been dragged out into the ocean, a "storm was coming on grandly," and the two needed to hurry home. "Oh! How beautiful it was," Georgia noted. "We galloped home as fast as we could. It was very exciting, the black clouds, the driving wind, the lurid light of the storm-setting sun, & our horses foaming and racing on the open beach. I enjoyed it very much." In most of Georgia's letters, as in most of her mother's, death overshadowed life, dulling it like a heart swathed in cotton. In this letter death was controlled, dispensed, and somehow made to amplify life, to make the air saltier, the wind fiercer, the experience more exhilarating. Stuck in her parlor entertaining, Sarah Morgan indulged a similar idea of making her getaway on horseback. "So very interesting," she wrote in her diary, "to be reposing [here] in an arm chair looking 'pale' and 'spiritual' and playing with cords and tassles! Very nice, but I would rather be the observer, than the observed; or better still, I would rather be up and away, galloping over the hills with the pure air of heaven around me."[25]

But for the most part, the diversions available to women echoed the same inward turn as their duties and cares. "What a mysterious thing is music," noted an anonymous Selma diarist. "I know of nothing that can excite my thoughts as it does, if I were mistress of my time it would occupy the principal part of it.... [Music] drowns [my] thoughts, and is like a voice that speaks of things beyond this melancholy sphere." The production of music was no mean accomplishment in the mid-nineteenth century. With no Victrolas or radios about, an antebellum house was often a musicless one without the efforts of its women. "I suffer so much for the want of musick," William Elliott noted when his daughters left home. "I try to amuse myself by my own discords—and so open the piano—and strum my old favorite melodies, [but you] will think I am sure that my taste is on the mend when I assure you that I can no longer endure them." Stuck womanless on his new plantation, Tristram Skinner was, like Elliott, dumbfounded by the silence. "I wish ... very much to hear some of your fine music," he wrote his sweetheart, Eliza. "I never hear any here except that of the birds which, though very sweet, I would prefer if mixed with more art." But women could not escape the notion that in music, they poured out their emotions in a pretty performance for others. Their thoughts and feelings had always to be groomed, made safe and pleasant and pleasing to the ear. "I have been down stairs playing & singing for nearly an hour," noted Harriet Alexander. "Nobody in this house knows anything about music & it gives them pleasure to hear even the semblance of it, so I play for them & do it the more cheerfully because I hope that it is the last time in my life that I will ever have to play for anybody.... It would be good news to me to be told that I would never touch another piano." In this, women were like the birds they so often kept as pets, pressured to be charming and quaint, pretty to look at and listen to. "I had my mocking bird out in the yard to day, sitting on a table," noted a Selma diarist, "and while I was looking at it from the gallery another mocking bird came and danced upon the table all round the cage [and] my bird opened his wings and bill and screamed." She knew how the bird felt. "It [oft-times] makes me ... miserable," she said of her life. "I feel as one who has not even the liberty of its cage."[26]

In all of their trials, women turned often to diaries to record their frustrations. In the nineteenth century, a woman's diary was seen less as a record than as a confidante. When Elizabeth Ruffin found "no society within doors, tho' every room in the house filled," she settled into the comfortable society of her journal. Clara Solomon saw her diary as a "cherished friend" and told her book, "you have bound yourself so firmly around the tendrils of my heart that your existence now seems essential to my own." Frustrated by a lack of outlets for her private thoughts, Ella Thomas also sought solace in her journal. Thomas had an "irresistable inclination ... to confide in someone," but even Jesus, by his own maleness, was disqualified as a candidate. "There are some moments," she confessed, "when I must write— must speak or else the pent up emotions of an overcharged heart will *burst* or *break*." Thomas never felt wholly comfortable in her own diary—she wrote as if someone might be looking over her shoulder, straining to discover truths she was desperate to hide. But each time she protested that she would not write out her heart, she had already partly done so. Each entry in her journal became an exercise in losing and regaining control, a release of just enough pressure to prevent her from boiling over.[27]

In the absence of any evidence to the contrary, these women should be taken at their word that journalizing was crucial to their lives. But we should not necessarily take these journals at their word. In a rare moment Sarah Morgan admitted that she regularly lied in her diary. "As I look back [on my journal]," she noted, "I see nothing but Sarah, Sarah, as though there was no one living save myself." Her self-absorption, she claimed, could not be helped. "I am trying to persuade myself that Sarah is worth thinking of! ... In revenge for not being a favorite of the whole world, . . . [I] naturally take to petting [my]self, . . . to show[ing] [my]self off in the most amiable light." At first this seems absurd—lying in a diary is like cheating at solitaire. But people cheat at solitaire for a reason—they do it to feel better, to control a simple outcome, to compensate for bad luck. In her journal Sarah was someone she could understand, even like. She had craved since the age of twelve "for something beyond this present life [which] holds me down," and she finally found it not within her day-to-day living but in the life she crafted on the pages of her diary. Her journal, then, not only reveals a woman but helped constitute one. To Sarah, life outside her book was crushing, confining; within it she indulged a desire she could not define, a feeling which "sweeps over me . . . and I feel myself floating out, out, I know not where, except that it is to a higher Something . . . [a] something which I feel to be my right." Certainly, these were thoughts Sarah might have had without the journal. But like lovers who carve their names on a tree, Sarah was engaged in a kind of sympathetic magic. In writing out her imagination she captured it, made it real; and when she was done she had a transcript of her own liberation to read and reread—she had created a witness to the hidden life that safeguarded her dignity.[28]

Informal writing, then, became for these women part of the process by which they redrafted their lives to make them read a little better and reconciled the stories they dreamed with those that had been dreamed for them. These women, for example, were expected to have a marriage in their story; everything they heard from the time they were sensible prepared them for this climactic scene in their would-be lives. They were encouraged to build and rebuild the set, to cast and recast the characters, to script and rescript the dialogue. But they also understood how precious little control they had over the actual scene. Indeed, many felt that their control could be distilled to a single moment, a single yes or no. "[Woman] is born," noted an Alabama woman, "to suffer, and endure, and not complain, to foresee, to divine almost the results of doings which she has not power to avert or repel! She is made to live upon the breath of another, her very existence is depending on beings upon which she has no control, excepting the mockery submission of the hour when she is marked out by her tyrant for a still deeper slavery—and she knows it all, and still she will go on suffering, and yet smiling, cheering the spirit of the being who dooms her to this bondage, and cherishing the hand that plunges her into the abyss." Here it is clear that the great insult is not that women were subordinate to men, but that women were supposed to pretend not to notice. In making this declaration to her journal, the diarist has at least told someone that she does notice and doesn't much like it. This is a minuscule act of rebellion, a thing as harmless as any other thing made of paper. But for the diarist the process was critical because it was the silence that was unbearable. Any voice, even a small one, recorded for no one, made a difference. "Good night little journal," she wrote her book one evening, "you have been the source of more comfort that I should ever have imagined such an insignificant repository could have afforded." While most women were less vehement in their denunciation of women's place in the South, all had to, as any human being does, reconcile a lived and a wished-for life. Diaries were one of the places that this reconciliation was allowed, even encouraged, to take place.[29]

But again the female life, like Anna King's, spiraled always into itself. "I think this journal will be disadvantageous for me," wrote Mary Chesnut, "for I spend the time now like a spider, spinning [out] my own entrails." In the monotony of her rhythms, in the inward turn of her pastimes and cares, a woman led a dreamy sort of existence, always threatening to implode. "When we survey life," noted Sarah Wadley, "when we recollect how our short pilgrimage is full of fruitless cares and idle sorrows, life seems as a fitful dream, until it is again dignified by the thought that God has placed us here to prepare ourselves for heaven." And to be sure, in the contemplation of the hereafter, where the trivialities of life were cast off and the wages of goodness were meted out, a woman could take considerable comfort. But in the meantime there seemed always another day to face here on earth, replete with pettiness and sorrow, longing and confinement. Standing before her mirror one morning, Sarah Morgan found herself facing an existential crisis: "the thought . . . has occurred to me 'What, or who am I?' and it is so abrupt, so unanswerable, that a feeling of dreadful awe creeps over me at the sight of this curious, mysterious figure, so familiar, yet so unknown." Sarah tried to reassure herself that it was only her own reflection she saw, and she struggled to bring herself back into focus. Instead, the "unspeakable mystery" only grew "darker and darker": "though seeing myself, I lose all sense of my personal identity, and feel as though I stood face to face with the ghost of one who perished centuries ... ago." Almost bizarrely, Sarah Wadley had the same reaction to the gauzy dreaminess of her life. "Whenever I for a moment lose sight of the bible and of religion," she said, "my mind becomes involved in mazy labyrinths of doubt 'till I almost question the fact of my existence and wonder if I am not one of the fabled creations of ancient days." Many, of course, have had much to answer for in front of a mirror and many have felt themselves dissolving in the face of existential angst. But in the nineteenth century, men were less likely to dissolve. Identified as they were with their professions and their accomplishments and their last names that passed on from generation to generation, men had a clear sense of self, even in their self-loathing. Women, on the other hand, were linked only to self-sacrifice in a great chain of being that reached behind and before them for time immemorial.[30]

One evening while rummaging around, Meta Grimball found a cache of old letters exchanged by her mother and grandmother. Her husband wondered at her enjoyment of them, but for Meta they were fascinating. "It is the history of a whole family," she wrote her diary. "My Grandmother's style is very fine, so simple and so clever. . . . The tone of these letters, the gradual change from full happiness to the sad desolation of being nearly alone ... is very painful. . . . [but] I rejoice that such charming, elegant people belonged to me, and their memory and their lives, delight me." In these letters, Meta Grimball was connected to a vast womanly enterprise, which, while not composed of dramatic or grandiose lives, at least made sense of her own. In her diary, Meta fretted and stewed over the well-being and future of her family, hoping for better times but having little confidence in her own power to bring them about. In the letters of her female forebears, she found an echo of herself and her concerns, and it brought her comfort to know that she was not alone in the world and that her trials were not unique. Meta would be in the grave soon enough; she would join her mother and grandmother and her daughters would pick up where she left off. "Generation after generation [of women] have felt as we now feel," wrote Eliza Clitherall in her diary, "and their lives were as active as our own. They passed like a vapor, while nature wore the same aspect of beauty as when her Creator commanded her to be. The Heavens shall be as bright over our graves, as they now are over our paths. The world will have the same attractions for our offspring yet unborn, that she had once for our children. Yet a little while, all will have happened. The throbbing heart will be stilled, we shall be at rest. Our funeral will wind its way, and hymns sung, and prayers said and then we shall be left behind, in silence and darkness for the worm, and it may be for a short time we shall be spoken of, but the things of life will creep in, and our names will be soon forgotten. Days will continue to move on, and laughter and song will be heard in the room in which we died and the eye that then mourned for us will be dried and glisten again with joy; even our children will cease to think of us, and will not remember to lisp our names." Unlike their menfolk, whose imperial scheming held out the promise of immortality, women would never live forever. They passed their time in a world that grew ever smaller, until, quietly and simply, they faded away.[31]

<hr />

Men were not wholly insensitive to the hardships of a woman's life. Before they became husbands, men had been sons, watching with a child's intensity as their parents' emotional drama unfolded before them. In the theater of family, boys came to understand implicitly that father symbolized the family's ambition while mother symbolized its goodness. Father's ambition, of course, could be full of grand illusions and vanity, but for this he was to be excused, even loved. Mother's goodness, for its part, could be full of martyred carping and histrionics, but for this she was to be excused, even loved. Men and women, quite logically, had separate duties, separate excuses, separate burdens. Women were forced into subservient roles that occasionally hollowed them out and robbed them of life; men were forced into dominant roles that occasionally left them impoverished and humiliated.

Exactly what constituted a Civilization was a matter of debate, North and South, but all agreed that it was embodied by a woman. "A Winter in the South," *Harper's Weekly*, January 1858. North Carolina Collection, UNC.

As boys matured, the divisions between men and women became not merely a replication of notions absorbed in the family but an elaboration of lessons learned in school and in life. By the dictates of Civilizing manhood, women required protection—not merely because they were frail but also because they were good. White women, after all, were not just more refined than men; they were the most refined creatures on earth. As the sacred vessels that bore their Civilization's best instincts and aspirations, women were to subject themselves to male protection; this was their job, their contribution, their sacrifice, to the cause of Civilization itself. Men, too, had sacrifices to make. They had appointed themselves the protectors of women not merely because they were stronger but because they were expendable. If a man became sullied in the process of building a Civilization, so be it; if he died in the cause of defending a Civilization, so be it. The formula was as simple as it was clear: men were to build a Civilization; women were to embody it. And so the divide would remain and the attempts to close it would remain awkward, even terrible.

CHAPTER 4

PURITY AND DESIRE

One shade the more, one ray the less,
Had half impaired the nameless grace
Which waves in every raven tress,
Or softly lightens o'er her face;
Where thoughts serenely sweet express,
How pure, how dear their dwelling place.*

In the summer of 1855, William Elliott traveled to Paris to deliver an address before the Imperial Agricultural Society. Elliott was a South Carolina planter, a noted authority on the cultivation of cotton, and an enthusiastic hunter. He is remembered, if at all, for a series of hunting sketches of some sublimity entitled *Carolina Sports by Land and Water* (1859). "I think that if any thing I have written will live after me," Elliott correctly predicted, "it will be these 'Sports.' " On August 26, 1855, William Elliott was one of a throng of men and women gathered outside the Fine Arts Exhibition in Paris, hoping to catch a glimpse of Queen Victoria and her escort, the emperor of France. When Victoria's open barouche pulled up in front of the entrance to the Exhibition, Elliott found himself caught somewhat behind the coach as her majesty disembarked. Victoria was handed down by the emperor himself, but somehow forgot her train. "*That,*" Elliott noted, "remained in the Carriage while her majesty's feet were on the pavement." Thus it was that the back of Queen Victoria's legs were for the briefest of moments available to public scrutiny. "Of

* Lord Byron, "She Walks in Beauty."

course I looked," Elliott admitted, "and without flattery I saw two delicate *mince* feet, two ditto-ditto ankles, [and] two superb calves [of] royal George stock." "I think," he boasted, "I have seen more of her majesty than any man in France—except perhaps Prince Albert." Americans might claim to be uninterested in royalty, Elliott knew, but they remained fascinated despite themselves. If they had seen what he had seen, most of his countrymen would think the trip well worth it. "[My son]," Elliott noted, "if he hears this read will say, 'the old sportsman knew how to take a stand' but the truth is it was but a happy accident that placed me where I was, and I know that they who choose to open their eyes as they pass through the world can hardly help seeing some things worthy of being remembered."[1]

As Elliott's paean to the well-turned ankle attests, the South was a very Victorian place in the 1850s. Few in the twenty-first century, certainly, would find a foot sighting very memorable, however regal the personage to which it was attached. Incidents like this one have given the Victorians their prudish reputation; they are supposed to have been so repressed that the smallest patch of skin was a source of titillation or concern. The truth, though, is that Victorians were only starched about sexual expression in public; so long as private matters were kept private, men and women were allowed to practice a sexuality that was open-tempered, passionate, and playful.[2]

This makes the historian's job difficult, however. By their own admission, the Victorians built a wall around their private lives, a wall that says next to nothing about what went on behind it. Two factors further limit the evidence available to historians seeking to shed light on the antebellum Southern sex life. First, the letters surviving in present-day archives were culled and sifted by generations of family members before being released to the public. Second, the original letter writers understood correspondence to be a *semiprivate* medium and generally saved more salacious subjects for intimate conversation. Thus, when nineteen-year-old Ben Allston wrote his father from West Point of an "obstinate" penchant for masturbation, the father fired back a heated warning to be more circumspect in committing such thoughts to paper. "When you next have occasion to write to me so intimately of your private habits," the father wrote, "make use of a separate slip of paper. Your letters are read to or by all around. I am now by myself & your ... sheet is burnt." It is important to note that while the senior Allston objected to the medium of discussion, he did not object to the topic. By all appearances, Ben and his father had a relationship in which the subject of sex could be approached without embarrassment and treated as an issue of common concern—provided they employed separate slips of paper and burned them afterward. This affection for privacy, while understandable, is also unfortunate because it leaves historians with few records about a subject integral to Southern life.[3]

To say that little trace of antebellum Southern sexuality remains in archives, however, is not to say that there is none. In the case of the Allston correspondence, for instance, Ben's father was careful to burn Ben's original letter—but Ben was not so careful with his father's reply. "What you say of yourself and of an obstinate degrading habit gives me much concern," wrote the elder Allston to his son. "I would recommend ... the close observance of three cardinal rules, namely: 1) allow no license to your imagination, 2) occupy the mind constantly whilst awake, and 3) ... when you find the temptation too strong, sit over a bucket of cold water and use it freely until the passion is subdued." "Unless you acquire complete mastery over yourself," the father warned, "you will not be able to mingle with safety with either men or women and must become therefore a solitary misanthrope with solitary habits, constantly fearing exposure!"[4]

Even from such snippets as these, much can be deduced about antebellum Southern male sexuality. Though Ben's father certainly doesn't approve of his son's habit neither does he condemn it as sinful, abnormal, or unnatural. Rather the sexual urge is something Ben must learn to "subdue," "control," and "master." In this respect, male sexual desire was perfectly "natural" from the Victorian perspective—it was a part of the animal within that a man was expected to rise above, a psychic wilderness he was expected to tame. *Naturally*, then, men would have lapses, moments when passion broke free and reigned unbridled. So long as they were occasional and genuinely lamented, such lapses were forgivable; the important thing was that the struggle for self-mastery go on until death because it was the struggle that defined male goodness. "Every successful effort [to resist the sexual urge]," Ben's father had written, "renders the next one easier, provided there be no break or interruption to success. If there be, begin again. Never despair of success at last."[5]

The standards for female conduct were, of course, different. Women did not need to *struggle* to control their libido; their sexual urge, after all, was far weaker and their capacity to suppress such urges far stronger than a man's. Where a man was naturally inconstant, a woman was naturally faithful; her instinct for chastity was like her womb or her overtender heart—an intrinsic piece of her equipment, bequeathed to her by God. The loss of that instinct, regardless of fault or circumstance, could fairly be regarded as unfeminine, ungodly, and unnatural, and the faintest whisper of scandal could destroy a woman's good name forever. When it became public knowledge, for instance, that South Carolina governor James Henry Hammond had engaged in incestuous acts with his four young nieces, his reputation was sullied but not indelibly; he went on to the Senate and to immortality for his proclamation that "Cotton is King!" His nieces, however, in the common parlance, were "ruined," never marrying and never bearing children—never participating, in short, in the projects that defined a woman's identity and worth in the period.

Such double standards are so obviously deplorable that historians have rightly emphasized the degree to which women labored under their inequitable burdens. It is worth noting, however, that with male freedoms came concomitant responsibilities and pressures that, while never completely offsetting the enjoyment of those freedoms, nevertheless contributed to men's understanding of themselves. As in their professional lives, antebellum white men were far less conscious of the unequal opportunities they enjoyed than the unequal obligations they assumed in their unswerving protection of the fair sex.

As the last chapter laid bare, women required this protection not merely because they were frail but because they were good, the sacred vessels that bore their Civilization's best instincts and aspirations. What went unexamined in the last chapter, however, were the sexual consequences of such inequities. If women were sacred, could they also be sexual? If they were placed on a pedestal, could they be taken down without degrading them? Many men, perhaps most, answered such questions easily, seeing physical intimacy as yet another sacrament in the religion of romance. But for a substantial minority of

Southern men, the gulf between their baser urges and their belief in woman's unassailable purity proved a vexing, almost maddening problem.

The next sections, again, examine the lives of two very different antebellum Southern men. Had they ever met, Harry Dixon and David Outlaw would not have gotten along. They were of different ages and temperaments, with different concerns and ways of looking at the world. But they were each preoccupied with the subject of women. Staring longingly into the divide that separated the sexes, they struggled, each without success, to resolve a mounting tension between female purity and male desire.

David Outlaw: This Hollow Hearted Sodom

In January 1849, David Outlaw took his place in the U.S. House of Representatives. A new congressman from Edonton district, North Carolina, he had been chosen to represent the people during a grave political crisis. The war with Mexico was over, and a half million square miles of territory (not including Texas) added their generous portion equally to the United States and to the dilemma over the expansion of slavery. This subject, Outlaw admitted, constituted the "everlasting topic" of debate before the Assembly. "We dream of negroes, hear nothing else by the wayside or in the House [or] at our meals." The galleries were packed with gawkers; the representatives were packing pistols. Ultras on both sides postured and preened for their constituents and the crowds, "fan[ning] the flame and increas[ing] the excitement." To the hoopla and the harangues, the moderate Outlaw brought a rare moment of calm reflection. "Day after day the evils of slavery ... are paraded for our entertainment," he said, "by men who know nothing" of the South. But the Southern representatives are themselves barely above "braggadocio and abuse." "To expect men to agree that slavery is a blessing social, moral and political," Outlaw declared, when most Southerners "do not believe it and so far from believing it, believe exactly the reverse is absurd." "It is sufficient," he concluded, "to deal with [slavery] as an existing fact, one for which we are not responsible and which we must treat as practical men." This level-headed assessment was not part of any speech he made, however; sitting on the floor of the House, with the country crashing down around him, Outlaw had tuned out the Assembly and scribbled these words to his wife in his daily letter home.[6]

David Outlaw married Emily Turner Ryan on June 7, 1837. Though she was a widow and mother of two, David felt no remorse that he would not be "the object of [her] virgin affections." David was himself thirty-one, comparatively old for a first marriage, and he felt he had "none of those graces of manner" that attracted the opposite sex. Awkwardly tall, he stood a bony six-three, with red hair, fair skin, and thick glasses. "I am not a handsome man," he admitted to his wife, and "though blessed with ordinary sense, I am not a brilliant man in conversation or otherwise." Outlaw's nearsightedness made him aloof, more awkward; his world was the smaller one that lay within his immediate compass. Somehow, though, Outlaw transformed it all into a kind of cultivated coolness, a removed hauteur. "I do not think I am a very vain man," he summed it up precisely, "because I am too proud a man to be so." Given all his failings of physique and character, Outlaw found it a wonder that he should be loved at all—but he was, and by all appearances deeply. Ten years into their marriage, the Outlaws' letters still gushed with affection. When he was away from her, David wished he could "travel by telegraph" or, "like the genie in the lamp," be transported to her bedroom where Emily would awake to "find a man in bed with you, imprinting kisses on your mouth and neck & bosom." Emily was similarly smitten: "your love is to me," she assured him, "worth more than all the rest this earth contains."[7]

But the Outlaws' relationship, while emotionally close, was burdened by physical distance. David spent up to eight months of the year in Washington and another two as a circuit judge in North Carolina. This left him just two months to spend with wife and family, and those not usually in a row. While the Outlaws' love was undoubtedly genuine, absence threatened always to dull it, to abstract it into something less lived and felt than reflexively constructed in empty words. Emily found the loneliness particularly acute during

David Outlaw. From Pulaski Cowper, "Colonel David Outlaw," *Wake Forest Student,* 1896, 286.

her pregnancies, and when David did not come home as promised for the birth of their second child, she suffered bouts of deep despondency. She could not understand why he would willingly trade a life of domestic bliss, one which he claimed to prize above all else, for the hollow-hearted company of strangers. In time, however, fatigue and compromise guided even the long absences into a steady rhythm as much a part of the Outlaws' marriage as anything else. "I fear the time will never come for you to [return home]," Emily wrote her husband typically, "for I see plainly that you are to be a candidate next year. While I see no chance for us ever to live together again, I will never ask you again not to be a candidate & will pray for resignation to my lot in life." Complete resignation, of course, never came, and could not be expected. Emily's society, and indeed Emily herself, understood the worth of a woman as centered not only in her character but in that of her husband, her family, and her marriage.

David's absences were part of his eminence and thereby her eminence—but if extended too long or exercised too brazenly they could
easily become part of her humiliation. Trying to convince his wife
that his conduct was not unusual, David reminded her of several
representatives who *never* went home, hanging around Washington
during the intersessions or luxuriating at the latest spa. In her reply,
Emily used the example to make a more general case for the domestic
failings of politicians as a class, only barely excepting her husband
from the profile. As exasperated as she became, however, Emily always came at the problem obliquely, humorously. Partly she did so
because she recognized the limits of her power to change things—but
mostly she did so because she understood her love for her husband,
and his for her, as the most worthy and ennobling part of her life.
"You cannot know how eager I am to get your letters & how I read
them over & over again," she told him, "& you never can know, my
own dearest, how very precious your assurances of your love are to
me. They cheer me in sadness & afford me food for pleasant thought
in my loneliness. . . . Without [your love] I could not live."[8]

The feeling seems to have been quite mutual. Never fully engaging
Washington's social scene or even his own duties as representative,
David Outlaw threw himself into his correspondence home, composing
at least one long letter every day, often penning them right on the
floor of Congress. "Do you not think," he wrote Emily, "[that] you
were mistaken when you said [that] I should be [too] absorbed in
politics . . . to find time to write you? . . . I have almost persecuted you
with letters. . . . I venture to say without knowing how the fact is that
no man in Congress has written his wife so often as I have." More
amazing, though, than the prodigious quantity of David's output was
the energy he expended ensuring that in formulating and reformu-
lating his devotion to wife, home, and family, he never became for-
mulaic. Unlike other politician-correspondents, David Outlaw never
sought refuge in the vague and vainglorious language by which men
of the period justified their conduct; he never evaded requests from
home to help his wife build a love lived and felt, a love as effortless
and as involuntary as breathing. Indeed, though the couple's present
was filled with absence and longing, David was careful to write in
rich detail about his memories of the past and his hopes for the future,

making as concrete as mere words ever can feelings that might become abstracted over time and space. Temporarily housed in a hotel
room the Outlaws had shared on their honeymoon, David allowed his
pen to gambol through the pleasant recollections. "On such a night,"
he wrote his wife, "a person's thoughts wander back to when the
heart was fresher, the affections . . . less selfish than contact with the
world makes them. . . . [Tonight] I could almost fancy [that] you were
eighteen and that I was twenty-five." Fueled by such thoughts, he
claimed, "the romance and poetry of youth revive and burn [and], for
a short time at least," the Outlaws could fall in love all over again.
It was not just the past that gave their relationship its vibrancy, however. "Just think of it," David wrote Emily after they had been discussing their oldest daughter Harriet. "We shall soon have a grown
daughter . . . and you will be called the old lady and I the old gentleman. It almost makes me sad to think of it." Despite the long miles
that stretched between them, despite fouled and slow communications,
hurt feelings and occasional disagreements, the Outlaws compensated
for not having a present by crafting a love out of the memory of
being young and the hope of growing old together.[9]

The capital, however, was no place for a dedicated husband and
family man. Socially awkward among the rough company of men,
David spent most of his evenings alone in his boarding room "reading
documents and newspapers," writing letters and franking paperwork
to his constituents. Such tedium was made all the more unbearable
by the fact that when he finished "ten to one if some bore [who] is
prowling about" did not pop in on him. "You know it is not my forte
suddenly to contract intimacies and friendships," he told his wife. "I
cannot make a friend of every new unfledged acquaintance or give
my confidence to an acquaintance a day old. This is probably a misfortune, but I cannot help it." Washington, though, was a city that
thrived on ephemeral friendships and vapid posturing; it was a land
of boisterous make-believe in which alliances rose and fell in a stew
of self-interest and whim. Unable to function on this social level,
David had "scarcely an individual in Washington" whom he could
"look upon as a friend" and "not one to whom" he "could unbosom"
his "thoughts and feelings." Moreover, even if he had developed such
a friendship, he would not have been able to share the best of what

he understood himself to be, a devoted husband and loving father. "I should profane things sacred & holy," he told Emily, "were I to give vent to my feelings of love and devotion to you and ardent attachment to my children to men who might as soon as my back was turned make them the subject of jest and ridicule." In self-defense David had become the very thing he hated about Washington, a liar and a facade misrepresenting his heart in the close quarters of posturing men. His own participation in the sham, of course, only brought home the vapidity of political life and drew him stronger than ever to the honest talk and genuine society of the ersatz family he created in letters scribbled on the floor of Congress. "How I wish I could to night fold you in my arms," he wrote Emily, "and in your caresses forget the harassing cares of this feverish life." "You have been to me," he confessed, "a priceless jewel and the fact that I have you to share my joys and help me bear the ills to which all mortals are subject doubly heightens the first, my love, my friend, the truest, kindest, noblest and best whom I ever expect to find on earth."[10]

But if he found the company of his wife so enchanting, why did David spend so much time away from her? This, of course, was their marriage's nagging little question—it grieved Emily to ask it because asked and reasked it rang out plaintive and defeated—and it grieved David to answer it because while he found the question ludicrous and annoying, he also found it infuriatingly unanswerable, even to himself. Repeatedly, David assured his wife "how unsubstantial and unsatisfying . . . are all the excitements and even triumphs of public life when weighed against that domestic happiness which a man's wife and children bestow." But David must have recognized that his own conduct was difficult to square with these assurances of the primacy of home. Indeed, lacking a single satisfactory explanation, he combined myriad unsatisfactory ones in different proportions, never finding a mix he could throw his weight behind. Only once in his letters did David suggest that his absences were part of his duty to country, party, or district. "We all owe some duties to our country," he told his wife, "and we cannot from a feeling of selfishness shrink from the performance of them." For the most part, though, David treated his political career as something beyond his control, as if he had never made the choice to leave home for politics, and never having made

this decision he had no power to extricate himself from its consequences. His involvement in public life, he claimed, was a historical
accident. Local members of the Edonton Whig party had approached
him with the notion that he campaign for the district's House seat.
He was reluctant to run, but when he did and lost in a Whig district,
it was too galling to his pride not to try at the next election to avenge
the loss. And "after a man has once gotten into public life," he told
his wife, "it is not so easy to get out of it." He assured Emily that
he would never become a career politician, a man addicted to the
excitement and passions of politicking, but he was also not ready to
come home and not able to explain why. "We cannot always choose
our own pathway," he noted helplessly. "We are to some extent the
creatures of circumstances." But if he could not come home, why did
Emily never join him in Washington? Partly, of course, familial and
managerial duties kept her at home, particularly during her pregnancies. But a full answer requires a deeper understanding of David's
abhorrence of Washington.[11]

"The virtue which distinguished our revolutionary ancestors is gone,"
David wrote his wife. "Congress is filled not with patriots but with
mere politicians eager in the race of power and popularity." It is a
common refrain, uttered almost reflexively by every generation that
has succeeded the Founding Fathers. David Outlaw, though, brought
a special verve to his condemnation of life in the nation's capital.
Studying Gibbons's *Decline and Fall of the Roman Empire* during the
term, David believed that military men were taking over the country
and that the young American republic, like its Roman predecessor,
had developed a disquieting bloodlust and a strong addiction to military glory. "The ultimate consequences," he felt, were "likely to be
most disastrous." Already the American army was "large enough to
make itself powerfully felt in the Halls of legislation." "How long
will it be before rival chieftains" are marauding across the continent,
contending "for the glittering prize of empire with armed legions?"
In the deep tradition of twitchy small-r republicans, Outlaw eyed the
stuffed uniforms parading around Washington with the suspicion of

a man who believes he has been unjustifiably out-manned. "From a major general down to a lieutenant," he noted, every military man in Washington "thinks the eyes of all the nation are upon him and that he is destined to some high political distinction." But Outlaw was also astute enough to see in the new American fixation with militarism the fear of impotence which lurks in the small mind of the bully. Certainly it was galling that a man could be "brought forward and sustained" as a candidate "*alone* and if not so *principally* because he was a military man." Certainly it was a shame that a statesman like Henry Clay, who had "rendered [his country] more important and substantial service than all the military men of the present day" had to concede the political field to "men inexperienced and probably utterly unqualified" for office. But more disquieting was what the trend said about America more generally. Increased militarism, Outlaw discerned, was less a sign of America's confidence than its insecurity. "Courage is looked upon as the highest virtue" in this country, Outlaw noted, "and from the eagerness with which the populace run after it one would think we were a nation of cowards."[12]

Outlaw saw this same small-minded martial spirit operating in the halls of Congress. Never mind that factionalism had become so strident that Outlaw described his mess as composed not of "six democrats and five Whigs" but of "five Cass men, one Barnburner, four Taylor men and one Whig, to wit, your humble servant." Never mind that many congressmen slept in the chamber, talked through the speeches, or ran "into the house to vote and [were] out again as soon as their name [was] called." Never mind even that they cheated on their wives, gambled away their ill-gotten fortunes, or were regularly fall-down drunk *in the House*. All of this paled in comparison to the undercurrent of petty violence that ran through all the operations of government. "The present house contains an unusual number of large men," Outlaw noted humorously—"perhaps their constituents supposed there might be a general melee in which physical power might be as necessary as intellectual attainments." But of course, several melees did break out during Outlaw's term, and one of his close associates claimed to know seventy or eighty representatives who had pistols at the ready, concealed on their persons or in their desks. When Henry Foote of Mississippi drew a gun from beneath his cloak, cocked

the hammer, and strode to the center aisle of the Senate to confront
Colonel Benton, Outlaw, like most of his contemporaries, was cha-
grined but not particularly surprised. "Nothing short of murder," he
told his wife, "will arouse public indignation ... and prevent the halls
of legislation from being disgraced by scenes of outrage and violence."
And indeed this was Outlaw's central point—not only was the conduct
of the representatives deplorable, but so were the appetites of the
represented. In the crowds that thronged the legislature Outlaw discerned a kind of sadistic glee, as if they were actually hoping "to see
the Union dissolved by a general battle in the House." "We are I
fear," Outlaw wrote his wife, "running with fearful speed the race of
ruin of all previous republics."[13]

Obviously, Outlaw's gloomy perspective needs to be taken in context. Crusty republicans were not exactly a rare breed in the period,
nor were bespectacled curmudgeons bursting at the seams with lessons
overlearned from Roman history. The excesses of political life were
things Outlaw loved to despise, the decadence and the scandals of his
fellow representatives providing the perfect foil for his stiff moral
posturing. Like the preacher who is never so happy as when steeped
in sin, David's perennial grouchiness can sometimes be seen for what
it was—the smug satisfaction of a good man content with his place
in a bad world. But David's outlook cannot be dismissed as the typical
prickliness of the overstarched Whig. Though politically priggish in
somewhat familiar ways, Outlaw's perspective on Washington's "fashionable life" is both astute and revealing, involving deeply his complex notions of men and women, North and South.[14]

While David Outlaw was in Washington, the city's society was at
its zenith. Spare and decadent, frenetic and sleepy by turns, the little
village of Washington was, to judge from its infrastructure, ludicrously
underdeveloped. Its distances were "magnificent," its architectural
marvels abutted hovels and swampland. Pennsylvania Avenue cut a
huge swath through the city, providing "a perfect romping ground
for ... winds" that pestered the carefully coifed sightseer with a fiendish delight. Maintaining one's dignity, not to mention one's umbrella,
wig, top hat, or skirt, required the same studied balance of humor and
reserve as the custom of feigned indifference to the stench wafting in
from the sewage canals and shad fisheries. It was, as Outlaw noted, a

capital not rich enough to accommodate a European court, not sincere enough to be the seat of republican government, a sprawling splendor putting on airs in the middle of a marsh. But if the infrastructure was awkwardly immature, the social life was ripe if not more so. As Virginia Tunstall Clay, the notorious belle of the 1850s noted, "the capital was [at this time] synonymous with an unceasing, an augmenting round of dinners and dances, receptions and balls." "A hundred hostesses," she claimed, "renowned for their beauty and wit and vivacity vied with each other in evolving novel social relaxations." (One of Mrs. Clay's novel relaxations, it should be noted, was a box that rejuvenated her festive spirit by delivering her an acute electric shock.) Clay admitted there was a "reckless gaiety" to this Washington social scene and conceded that many of her closest friends were run "mad with rivalry and vanity"—but she never so much apologized for these facts as celebrated them.[15]

David Outlaw, as might be imagined, was not so gentle as Mrs. Clay in his estimation of Washington's reckless vanity. "Everything has a fair outside," David said of the city, "but it is in the language of Holy Writ a whited sepulcher.... It is all form, there is nothing real, nothing true about it.... We know not whom we can trust [or] upon whom rely." Part of David's problem was merely that he was lonely, an island of propriety in a sea of sin. He had no close associates and considered most of his fellow representatives selfish and corrupt. In the House he believed he bore witness to a "broad farce" where "scheme after scheme [was] offered to squander the public lands" and "dirty intrigues and maneuvers" attended "the miserable scramble for place." And in the wider Washington society Outlaw was, if possible, less comfortable. "The more I see of high-life or rather fashionable life," he wrote his wife, "the more am I disgusted with its hollow hypocrisy, its heartlessness and its deceit, and its utter selfishness." The "pander and pomp and ceremony" of the scenes Mrs. Clay so lovingly described were to Outlaw extravagant *and* petty, a "shabby gentility" that knew much of "mere decorums" but nothing of "real honor and nobleness of nature, chastity not merely of the person but of the mind and heart." Of course it was only more galling that Outlaw had to participate in the sham. Knowing that the city's dignitaries were meeting at the capitol, David sent a "servant in a

carriage, closely shut up" to leave his card "with all the foreign min-
isters and the members of the cabinet." "What miserable flummery
and farce," he grumbled, "and yet [this method] is a great conve-
nience to make visits to persons whom you never saw and never care
to see. . . . [My] visits will of course be returned in the same way."[16]

Then, too, the social pretenses of life at court offended Outlaw's
political as well as personal proprieties, undermining his faith in
America's republican experiment. He deemed the local papers, for
instance, "aristocratic monsters" for their indulgent descriptions of the
latest gala affairs. This "abominable fashion of putting in print the
dresses &c of the ladies," he noted, "of giving their names or initials
so that every body understands who is meant is copied from the Court
Journals of foreign monarchies." Outlaw's arch journalistic nemesis
was a Mrs. Royal, publisher of a particularly savage gossip sheet. Her
strategy, David said, was to search "out the members of Congress and
levy" what amounted to "black mail." He prided himself in the fact
that she had not yet caught up with him, but granted that most
representatives "take her paper to get rid of her for if they do not
she abuses them . . . and no falsehood is too atrocious for her to publish." Even the papers that eschewed the merely salacious had a tendency to engage in a kind of cult of personality quite at odds with
Outlaw's notion of a model republic. "It has become fashionable of
late," he wrote home, "to publish every thing in the public prints.
After a while I suppose whatever distinguished persons have for dinner, what time they go to bed, when they get up" will be the subject
of late-breaking news. The gossip sheets, of course, were not Washington's only court affectation—Europe also set the tone for the capital's fashions, manners, and amusements. As Virginia Clay observed,
"Foreign representatives and their suites formed a very important
element" in Washington society. They were "our critics, if not our
mentors," she noted, "and to be a favorite at the foreign legations
was equivalent to a certificate of accomplishment and social charms."
Outlaw, though, had little tolerance for such affectations. "Waltzing
is you know fashionable here," he wrote Emily, "as I fully believe it
would be to go naked if that were fashionable at foreign Courts. . . .
[These] miserably abortive attempts to imitate the style and fashions
of monarchical governments are to me perfectly disgusting."[17]

But it was not the aristocratic pretenses or sham civilities of the place that most often brought Outlaw's blood to a boil. At the heart of his blistering critique was sex. He admitted that he was prudish and somewhat behind the times in this "age of progress," but he also felt sure the age was progressing from "modesty and chastity" to "libertinism and licentiousness." Washington, he claimed, had become a "hollow hearted Sodom" in which "profligate men" and "abandoned women" gave themselves up to their animal urges. In his letters home he relayed several of the more lurid affairs in some detail. A Mrs. Jones, for instance, scandalized the city when she betrayed her breeding and a husband "devotedly attached to her" in a series of misadventures that ended with her fleeing to Baltimore and "taking laudanum very freely." Another scandal involved an unnamed senator who managed after one of his evening trysts to leave his love letters in a Washington hack. The affair was public information by breakfast. Still this indiscretion ended better than a love triangle broken only when the irate husband gunned down the offending paramour. And these examples, David promised his wife, were just some of the "many cases which occur here every session." "If all men who have cause to be jealous were to shoot a man in this city," he told her, "there would be a very considerable mortality here." Nor were the city socialites content to seek their sexual thrills behind closed doors. The city's museums, exhibition halls, and playhouses were often the purveyors of an astounding mélange of smut. Outlaw was particularly offended by an exhibition of model artists representing the world's most celebrated statues and paintings, some of them nudes. One of the exhibits, David noted, "represented an old man, gazing with intense interest upon a naked woman, and gazing at that part of her person which women most carefully conceal." The woman was "not actually in a state of nature," he noted, but was obscured only by "a slight drapery almost as thin as gauze ... thrown a round [her] waist." Such exhibitions, he said, only contributed to the "looseness of morals" that would make Washington as "dissolute as any European Court."[18]

But while Outlaw railed against "profligate men," it was the "abandoned women" who inspired his most passionate sermons. He claimed to have a "great reverence ... for virtuous women and [a] high appreciation of the influence which they exert on society." He believed that "female chastity and honor" constituted nothing less than the bedrock of all "public and private virtue" and felt that without a female influence "men would soon become savages." In Washington, however, the vast majority of women fell woefully below his standard. Old married ladies pranced about the capital, gallanted by "young coxcombs who have about as little brains in their heads as in their heels." They wasted all their time in making up their bodies and faces and tables and parlors and yet tended only to look ridiculous for all the effort. Outlaw admitted he had little knowledge of fashion but claimed he could spot "any thing outré in a lady's dress" and confessed to being "almost nervously sensitive to any thing like slovenliness." Mrs. Catron, for instance, seemed to be an intelligent woman but "dressed her head in a most ridiculous manner [with] curls enough to stuff a sofa." And an astounding number of ladies wore dresses so décolleté "[you] would not have had to make great changes to fit *them* for an exhibition of model artists." That these women treated Washington like a "fashionable place of resort for lounging and flirtations" was bad enough—that they involved themselves in politics was worse. "The practice is becoming very common here," he told his wife, "for ladies in person to solicit offices and favours of different kinds both from the Executive Departments and from the members of Congress." At this very "session of Congress," he told her, "a bill passed the House solely by the solicitations of a pretty woman. If it had been the case of a man it would not have received fifty votes." Such women were rarely content to peddle their influence in the lobbies. In some cases, he claimed, a congressman would be sent for, introduced into "a girl's bed room, she dressed in dishabille, and told if he would vote" a certain way "she could deny him nothing." One evening Outlaw himself was approached by a woman who "insisted upon my going up to her room." "Really," he told his wife, "I did not know but I should be ravished . . . and I positively declined to go."[19]

No doubt much of what Outlaw wrote was true—sex and politics, after all, have always made strange but inevitable bedfellows. Outlaw's extended commentary on the subject of women's sexuality, however, bordered on fixation, and one cannot but suspect that his Washington was oversexed in the same degree as he was repressed. For

A Kiss for a Vote.

Other contemporary critics shared David Outlaw's belief that mixing women and politics would lead to sexual depravity, abuse of power, and corruption of the republic. From *Southern Literary Messenger*, July 1860.

Outlaw, women's range of legitimate sexual expression was incredibly narrow. He despised alike women who appeared to have no sex and those who had any. One old woman disturbed him particularly because she did "not look like a woman." "I wish a person," he wrote crossly, "to be of one sex or another. One of these men-women or women-men are [equally] disgusting and disagreeable to me." But while he despised the he-women as having "the good traits of neither sex and what is revolting in both," he was more consistently disturbed by women who gave public space to the sexuality they did possess. Everywhere Outlaw looked he was presented with some unseemly press of bodies in which women indulged themselves in the rub of the crowd. He appears, in fact, to have been incapable of thinking about crowds without also thinking of women, and then in a sexual way, as if they were actually pressing in on him. "There is nothing of interest in our house," he wrote his wife, "and yet the galleries are crowded with ladies." Without "regard to decency or propriety," he claimed, they literally squeezed themselves into the mob of onlookers. "I imagine they cannot be squeezed enough at home or they would not have a fancy to be brought into such close contact with entire strangers." Outlaw also described a public appearance of Henry Clay where women nearly "kissed the old fellow to death" and the statesman had "to make his retreat . . . to get clear of suffocation." "Now I do not believe in such things," Outlaw wrote home, "kisses are tokens of affection which a woman ought to reserve for her husband, father, brother, or very near relations." He admitted he was prudish on the subject but refused to alter his opinion. "I regard the preservation of [female] purity," he said, "as so important to [women's] own just influence [on] society that I view with abhorrence, with an abhorrence which I can not express, every thing calculated to break down even the outposts of their modesty." Waltzes and polkas topped the list of David's offenders. "If I were a single man," he claimed, "and engaged to a woman, to see her waltz with another gentleman would be sufficient to break it off." Many people, he admitted, say there is nothing wrong with the dance. And "so there is not abstractly, nor is there any thing wrong in feeling a woman's bosom, or kissing her, provided there is no improper feeling. But do not these liberties tend to produce improper passions? Do they not tend to other and still greater liberties?" Later in the year Outlaw read in the paper of a new dance "introduced at Saratoga . . . far surpassing in indecency and lasciviousness the polka or the waltz." The concluding step involved the gentleman throwing his leg over the lady's shoulder. "Whether the lady follows the modest and delicate example," he noted, "we are not informed, [but] every woman who has a proper regard for the dignity and respectability of her sex ought to set her face resolutely against these things."[20]

With each of these frothy condemnations of female sexual excess, with each lovingly rendered and utterly gratuitous detail, Outlaw made it abundantly clear that he was not merely offended—he was titillated, tempted. At a crowded Washington exhibition, he found himself standing near a woman in a low-cut dress. At six-three Outlaw could peer right down the front of her gown and "see her bosom, nipples and all just as plainly as though she had never been dressed in her life." He of course decried the fashion as offensive to his "notions of propriety [and] good taste"—but he also looked, and probably more than once. When a newly married couple moved into a room adjoining his, he was, he claimed, "obliged to hear a great deal that passes between them." "I can hear their kisses," he told his wife, "and other marks of endearment." But was he obliged to listen? Or did he strain to do so? Himself unsure of the answer, he admitted the situation was "rather tantalizing, is it not?" And despite numerous diatribes against the evils of dance, Outlaw made it all but clear on one occasion that the great cruelty of the waltz was that he wasn't getting his turn on the floor. "I have a strong notion to go to a dancing school myself," he noted. "There is so much good hugging that I see no particular reason why I should not come in for my share. I dare say it would be quite pleasant to have a pretty girl in my arms, whirling around, with her eye voluptuously and languishingly looking into mine." While the great bulk of Outlaw's commentaries are categorical in their denunciation of open-tempered sexuality, there are these few occasions when his disapproval can be seen for what it was—the sour grapes of the disgruntled nonparticipant.[21]

But David did not blame himself for being tempted; indeed, as the crisis of union deepened in the 1850s he began to blame the North. Outlaw, it should be noted, was a unionist Whig. As a congressman he consistently voted for sectional compromise, even opposing the conquest of Mexican territory for fear it would destroy the country. But he was not blind to sectional differences. Washington, after all, was the front line between the North and South, and he was thrown into a society very different from the inhabitants of his hometown of Windsor, North Carolina. "There is an indescribable charm about home," he told Emily, "which no other place has, even though it be in a small village & mosquitoes do abound there. It has a holiness which appeals" to me, he said, because its people have "hearts which are not corrupted and hardened." Clearly, David believed that the people of Washington had been corrupted and hardened, partly from the excesses of capital life but also partly from their contact with the North. "Great crowds [of Southerners]," he told his wife, seem always "to be on their way North to spend their money." "That [Yankees] should be more prosperous than we are is not at all surprising. There is scarcely an article of necessity or luxury in the way of manufactured goods we do not buy from them. The very brooms with which we sweep our floors, the utensils in which we cook, the clothes we wear, the chairs we sit on, the carpets upon which we tread, the bedding on which we sleep, all come from [them]." But these Southern tourists came home with more than consumer goods and empty pockets. They "bring back Northern manners." As might be imagined, Outlaw was particularly concerned about the effects of such junkets on Southern women. "There is a boldness, [a] brazenfacedness about Northern city women," he claimed, "as well as a looseness of morals which I hope may never be introduced south." "Many of our women who go there," he noted, "when they come home are dissatisfied. There is not excitement enough, their ordinary routine of domestic employments are distasteful. They long for the ball-room, the theatre, the gay crowd." So far as Outlaw acknowledged, there were no sleepy Windsors in the North, no places where the people were genuine and the mosquitoes constituted the greatest moral challenge. The North was for him synonymous with the city, with the crowd and the press of bodies. There, he claimed, "crime and corruption of all kinds grow rank and luxuriant."[22]

⟫⟫◆⟪⟪

"It has often struck me as strange that any of us should wish to
continue in public life," David Outlaw wrote his wife typically, "when
we know from actual experience how unsatisfactory and unsubstantial
are the objects we pursue with so much zeal and avidity, how utterly
worthless they are compared with domestic enjoyment, with the love
of a wife and children." David was sure he was not alone in the
feeling. Beneath the pomp and the cheap thrills, he sensed in Washington an undercurrent of sadness, not of frustrated office-seekers or
spent sybarites, but of husbands and fathers who missed their homes.
"I have no doubt all public men have felt this at times," he told his
wife, "and deeply regretted they should have ever entered upon the
stormy career of politics." David, of course, had entered that career
and seemed unable to leave it. But considering that he was so lonely
and ill-suited to "fashionable life," why did he never invite Emily to
join him in Washington? An argument might be made that Outlaw
was concerned the city's corrupting influence would assail his wife's
treasured modesty—but it is clear he trusted her implicitly in this
regard. "It has often struck me," he wrote home, "how fortunate I
was in my selection of a wife.... My own temper is naturally high
and irascible. I am keenly sensible to [indecency and] I could not bear
that my wife's honor should be breathed on by the breath of suspicion.
Conceive then what I should have felt if I had been yoked to a woman
who was flirting with every body." Emily, though, was of a different
breed, a "noble-hearted, kind and affectionate woman" who devoted
"all her thoughts and endeavours to smooth [her husband's] rugged
path." I have "implicit confidence in your virtue and prudence, David
told her, and "unbounded confidence in [your] chastity." But it was
precisely this confidence, this purity that made it impossible for him
to feel comfortable bringing Emily to the capital. He had learned and
relearned in his nightly reading the greatest lesson history has to
teach—the things most worth preserving are invariably the most delicate. Everything Outlaw truly cared about, everything he believed
in—his wife, his family, Windsor, the republic—were, concomitant
to their very goodness, threatened by the corrupting influences ever
pressing in on the worthy. For reasons he did not exactly understand
he had ventured out into that press, into a world bent on running its
"race of ruin." He railed against those excesses, but it did not escape

his attention that his heart was not so pure, nor his character so
innocent, as they had been in youth. Emily was the part of him
incorruptible, unassailable; she was the hometown, the South, the republic he would return to when he shook free of the "ambitious men
[and] scheming women" slumming around his "hollow hearted
Sodom." Until then David Outlaw would keep his head down in the
House, scribble his daily letters home, dream of the simple joys of a
"stroll through a [Windsor] corn field," and dwell on "pleasures of
memory . . . almost equal to those of hope."[23]

Harry St. John Dixon: An Apple Before a Child

In the summer of 1860, seventeen-year-old Harry Dixon was growing
like a weed. Neighbors and friends commented on it regularly, surprised in that way adults can be when a child suddenly blooms beneath them. "Why Harry!" exclaimed one neighbor upon returning
from a trip, "I never saw any one grow as you do!" Harry's father
had noticed too, and late one evening he drafted a letter to an associate
in New Orleans requesting a "neat, level, serviceable, gold watch" for
his son. Harry understood the meaning of the gesture at once. His
boyhood, seemingly timeless, was drawing to a close. In the fall he
would leave "these rural pleasures, these home ties for the stern course
of College discipline, from that to a Law office, and whence, I know
not." The watch would be part of that new discipline; responsible for
its worth, accountable to its demands, Harry would carry in his pocket
a constant reminder that a man's time was a commodity valuable
enough to be measured precisely. The one problem, though, was that
Harry's father had not mentioned anything in the letter about a watch
chain. A new-money planter, Richard Dixon was not a highly cultured
man. At thirteen, he had quit school; at seventeen, he had quit his
Virginia home, setting off for Mississippi alone with $75, a horse, and
a loaf of gingerbread. More successful than he was refined, Richard
had overlooked the necessity of a watch chain, figuring that Harry
could weave one out of his mother's hair. For his part, Harry was
appalled, thinking hair chains gruesome, "horrible things." Ever
mindful of his father, however, he merely stammered out an obedient,
"yes, sir."[24]

A few days later, Harry was reading the paper to his mother when he came across an account of that "old hellcat John Brown." When Harry finished the article, his mother said, "there is not a negro in our quarter who" does not know all about John Brown and the raid on Harper's Ferry. Quickly seeing a way out of his watch chain dilemma, Harry responded, "Ma, will you bet me a gold watch chain and let me choose it in Memphis . . . if I find one [slave] who knows nothing about him?" Mrs. Dixon consented and that evening Harry went down to the quarter to make his inquiries. As one might expect, he did not find a single slave who would admit to knowing any particulars about the raid. Probably sensing that Harry was looking for negative responses, certainly understanding that it was better to appear to know less rather than more on such subjects, the slaves all stared at him blankly or made up wildly erroneous guesses. It seems never to have entered Harry's mind that the slaves were feigning ignorance; he had asked the most intelligent of them ("if I may so express myself") and they had answered. Harry Dixon did not question the essential probity of slavery, did not feel the slightest moral pang or qualm for its abuses; negros were dirty and dumb, worthy of the work they were doing, beholden to the whites who allowed them to lead such simple, happy lives. Earlier in the summer, Harry's father and a slave named Edmund had gotten into an argument in the front yard. Richard was attempting to scold Edmund for some oversight, but Edmund kept interrupting him. After repeatedly ordering Edmund to shut up, Richard threw a chair at the slave and told him to go back to the quarter. When Edmund instead made a move to go through the front gate toward town, Richard grabbed up a handy brickbat and, advancing on the man, grabbed him by the collar and "jerked him about and pushing him on before him, made him go to the quarter." When Edmund continued blathering and again made a move to run off, Richard picked up a hoe handle and threatened to beat him with it. The general commotion brought the entire family to the front porch, including Harry, who looked on laughing. Horrified, one of his little brothers asked him, "Harry, haven't you got any feeling; I don't see anything to laugh at." "Nevertheless," Harry noted in his diary, "it was funny to me." To Harry Dixon's mind, slaves were too dumb to be wounded by such treatment; their intellect, like their humanity, was stunted and grotesque, making them fitter objects for ridicule than for pity. And so when none of the slaves in the quarter had heard of John Brown, Harry accepted their ignorance readily and returned to his home without giving them (or John Brown, for that matter) a second thought. His watch chain after all "had been got easily" and certainly that was luck enough for one day.[25]

≡▸◈◂≡

The Dixon household consisted of firstborn Harry, his father Richard and mother Julia, six brothers, one sister, one uncle, and at least two cousins. Julia Dixon is a pitiable figure in Harry's diary. Constantly pregnant, forever grieving the loss of something or someone, she was a woman so preoccupied with birth and death she had little energy left for life. In March 1860, most of her sister's family was poisoned in New Orleans; a household slave had chosen an important dinner party as the occasion for seasoning the main course with arsenic. In April, her brother Hadley died of unknown causes; in December, her youngest son died of pneumonia; the following February, another brother died of another unspecified disease. Julia's losses for 1860–1861 totaled two brothers, one sister, one son, one niece, and one nephew, not to mention the loss of a close neighbor. With each death, she leaped suddenly to the front of Harry's diary as the whole household strove to contain her grief. When Uncle Hadley died, Julia spent much of her time lying on a couch, Mr. Dixon rubbing her hands and a slave nurse rubbing her feet. The mass poisoning in New Orleans required more elaborate damage control. Newspapers became suddenly scarce as Harry and his father moved to cut Julia off from any reports of the grim tidings. While Julia Dixon undoubtedly performed a variety of mundane, daily chores on the Dixon plantation, she is in Harry's diary an ephemeral figure—a moral model whose example is more adored than followed, a wilted matriarch whose weakness for grief oddly strengthened the family that united to coddle her.[26]

Harry's father, on the other hand, is a stronger presence. As might be expected of a man who turned $75 and a loaf of gingerbread into a profitable plantation, Richard Dixon was a stern man, forbearing and fair but also structured and systematic. Harry accepted his father's authority completely—it was but a small part of an interdependent system of hierarchies (father/son, man/woman, master/slave) whose basic legitimacy he did not question. "I am nominally your slave until I am of age," Harry told his father typically. "But I glory in having you as my master and every day shows me how infinitely I am bound to love and obey you outside my duty to you as my father." Harry and Richard did have their differences, however. Harry, for instance, was devoted to poetry and tended to lose himself for hours in its pages. "All day Thomson lead me through his flowery labyrinths," Harry noted one evening, "while at many ambrosial springs . . . I drank sweet draughts which made my soul and heart feel light and untrammeled from all external things." Richard, however, thought that poetry "seduced one from the substance of life, answered no good end," and was, in fact, "utter trash." "Show me a poet and I will show you a worthless man," he told his son, "useless to himself and every one else." The fact that his son read poetry was particularly alarming as it signified a "romantic disposition" and a head too fanciful to be productive. Dixon was not the only one to get an earful of his father's opinions on the subject. While dining at the Dixons' one evening, Mr. Herbert, a teacher, was informed that "the supremacy of Latin and Greek" in a classical education was ridiculous and that teaching was "a hang-dog life" better suited to women than men. "In his plain, downright way," Harry wrote in his diary, "[Pa] spoke of his contempt for a man who gave himself up to idleness" and his belief that true "men should lead . . . out-door" lives. "The old parson was stung," Harry noted, "for I could see it."[27]

The Dixons lived on a large plantation near Deer Creek, a tiny town outside of Greenville, Mississippi. According to Harry, Deer Creek was a close community, "more like one family than neighbors." If ladies ran low on a particular provision, they were free to borrow. If an accident befell any household, they could count on their neighbors to pick them up and dust them off. In 1857, the Dixons' house burned down—women twenty miles distant sent clothes and food until temporary cabins were established. In 1860 a tornado demolished the slave quarters at the Percy plantation—every free hand was sent to aid in the repairs. "I do believe the world could be searched and a more brotherly and sisterly neighborhood could not be found," Harry told his diary.[28]

With most of the neighborhood boys, Harry attended classes at the Deer Creek Select School. Because buildings were scarce in Deer Creek, the town's schoolhouse doubled as the Methodist church, which annoyed the boys who had to rearrange the pews on Monday mornings. The combination made a certain sense, however, because the town's teacher and preacher were the same man, Mr. Herbert, who traveled Deer Creek in both capacities, raising money to reroof his all-purpose edifice. Harry was the best student at the school, mostly because his affection for writing made him the only boy who regularly turned in his compositions. Harry committed his share of mischief, however. One morning Mr. Herbert found the schoolhouse locked and the key missing. Harry and his friend Taylor were playing marbles nearby, and Mr. Herbert asked after the key. Harry pretended to know everything about the theft but refused to give his teacher any information. After a while Mr. Herbert "became angry" and hauled Harry and Taylor out to "the school house shed." Mr. Herbert then submitted the problem to a vote—the students were "unanimous in favor of not opening [the door] by violence." Helpless, Mr. Herbert dismissed the boys, and Harry and his friends spent the rest of the afternoon throwing dirt clods at each other. Less than a week later, Harry and his friend Hal got in a spitting fight—Harry used water, which had a higher douse factor, and Hal used tobacco juice, which had a better range. Harry admitted to his diary that this was all fairly routine, that he had received from Mr. Herbert only "a typical day's worth of demerits." Harry was, by his own admission, "a scamp." His mother had once told him that her greatest hope was to see her sons grow to be good and righteous men. Harry replied that it was the "hardest task she could have imposed upon herself." "I am conscious that the sentiment she expressed was a most noble one," he wrote in his diary, "and as natural as could be, but, at the same time, I never had the least hope to be as she wished, 'good and righteous.' " Harry's personal motto was *dum vivimus, vivamus*—while we live, let us live.[29]

After school, Harry usually "knocked around until dark," swimming, picking strawberries, playing with friends, supping at the house

nearest him when the sun got low. Sometimes he would go out hunting with his dog Sam ("who goes with me everywhere"), shooting at
soft-shelled turtles down by the creek bed or at wild turkeys across
Judge Rucks's field. Sometimes he would go out riding, usually bump-
ing into friends along the way. One night they all met under "a gum
tree where we halted and had a good time of it, singing, dancing,
laughing, and talking." "Our songs were not of the most refined quality," he admitted, but were "such as boys of our age generally like
best." In the fall of 1859, a celebrated trial was taking place in nearby
Greenville, and Harry and his friends traveled to the courthouse to
hear the arguments. The accused had beaten one slave to death and
hung another; his lawyer's closing statement reminded the jury that
his client would be in hell soon enough but should in the meantime
be spared to his mother. The jury agreed and acquitted him. The trial
did not interrupt the rhythm of Dixon's boyhood; it was like all his
diversions—something he picked up for a while and put down when
he tired of it.[30]

One diversion, of course, he never tired of—women. "I did a little
thing during my walk this evening," he wrote in his diary, "which I
will not overlook as it is clearly indicative of my inordinate and un-
governable I-don't-know-what towards the soft sex." Harry had been
returning from a walk when he saw two ladies, one in mourning,
coming up the path behind him. His curiosity was "immediately kin-
dled," and he "slipped down the bank" of the creek bed, where he
"stood observing but not observed." "I will do anything to get a peep
at a woman," he admitted. "Who won't?" There were, of course, easier
ways to get a "peep." Harry's neighborhood was close-knit, assembling
often for fish frys, candy-pullings, dinners, and dances. Much like
Harry's own boyish rhythms, the town could be quiet for a few weeks,
then suddenly erupt with activity. "When this old Creek does get
started at frolicking," Harry noted in his diary, "it goes like wildfire."
Harry liked to attend such fetes, though he could be brutal in his
criticisms. The women all "bundled in the present clumsy fashion of
the ladies" and the young coxcombs blathering about their apparel
was "supremely disgusting" to him, and he despised being caught on
the sofa with a particularly vacuous woman, "doing what a fellow is
obliged to do with the pretty little things—talk all sorts of trash to

them as if it would make a woman disgusted with one if he talked
common sense." But when the company was good, the "pretty eyes
rivalled the brilliancy of diamonds," the "smiles and witticisms were
copious," and "vivacity prevailed among both sexes." In these moments, Harry was at his happiest and would "float around, poking
[his] bill in here and there, making engagements ... chattering, dancing, and feasting." But while the pretty eyes and the witticisms had
their charm, it was the dancing that most interested him, and he
admitted to his diary to being "in it more for the hug than the dance."
"It is enough to make a boy of sixteen feel curious," he wrote, "to
have his arm around a pretty woman's waist, her left hand on his
shoulder and her right in his left (and in some cases, their bosom on
his) and in the later instance to feel the gentle undulations of it." By
curious, of course, Harry meant *pleasurable*, and he was no tentative
dance partner. "My arm does not go half way or touch them lightly,"
he explained, "but goes as far around as it can and holds them close
and firm while my left as I have before said squeezes their right. Isn't
it a blessing to be a boy? It is, it is! To feel ankles, squeeze hands,
and clasp waists!" While the physical contact did not go beyond ankles, hands, and waists, Harry was occasionally thrown "into ecsta-
cies," inflaming his imagination and indulging his "fancies (*naughty
ones*) too far." Such indulgence, of course, had its frustrations. One
evening Harry had engaged to dance the ninth set with a girl "as
pretty as a speckled pup." When the ninth set did not come around,
Harry "went home mad and woke up mad ... and was mad all [the
next] day."[31]

The only unique thing about such fancies, of course, was that Harry
wrote them down. It was, after all, a very dog-eared copy of *The
Lustful Turk* that Harry devoured one June evening before passing it
on to Taylor. And, certainly, it was a well-thumbed series of "colored
cuts ... more tempting and beautiful than decent" that Harry dis-
creetly took into his possession at a dinner party in September. As
Harry himself said, "Who will blame me and point out a single youth
of 17 who would not gaze at them as I did?" The problem, though,
was not the impulses themselves but the way they contradicted his
extreme reverence for female virtue. "One who ... read this [diary],"
Harry noted, "might think I am rude to women." "To these secret

pages I will confess that to me they seem more like Gods, combining
all good qualities within humans. So sweet, so gentle, so lovely in
appearance, and as to purity of heart, they are unexceptionable—all
virtue, purity, and chastity." Their chastity was in fact one of Harry's
favorite subjects—he dwelt on it lovingly, longingly, indulgently in
his diary. He acknowledged that he had "a peculiar fascination about
maidens" and that he found their innocence "intoxicating." They
seemed to him somehow unlike the rest of the world, "not polluted
... imbued in degradation [or] stirred by impious and vicious inchast-
ity but ... fresh and blooming from the hands of God." Dancing or
conversing with a virgin, Harry would look into her eyes and see
something that he did not find in other women, something that made
his "heart bow in reverence—a bright holiness" which he had "no
words to convey an idea of, something insoluble and inexplicable!"
He allowed that any woman could be virtuous, but only the "blushing
maiden who knows no carnality, whose person is as God has made it,
not as man has changed it" could inspire him: "Give me the fair lily
which knows not the wiltering sun of noontide, but whose soft folds
have known only the gentle breezes of a vernal morn! This is what
I look forward to; this is what [motivates] me, what leads me into
toil; this is the bright jewel I hope to fold to my bosom to protect, to
cherish and to love that it may shine for me, for me only." It enraged
Harry that "99 times out of 100" this sweet innocence was sacrificed
to drunken and debauched scoundrels. Sitting on the schoolhouse steps
with Mr. Herbert, Harry worked himself into a lather decrying the
men who with seductive words and pretty promises separated women
from their virtue. There was no punishment harsh enough for such
wretches, he told Mr. Herbert. And still worse were the dissolute
husbands who came home late from the "houses of the ... polluted,"
"belch[ing] forth volumes of oaths" and treating their wives with
indifference, brutality, and vulgarity. "That their tender arms must
embrace this, that their luscious lips must kiss this, that their most
gentle caresses are to be profusely lavished upon this" was almost
more than Harry could bear.[32]

While Harry abhorred the degradation of women, his descriptions
of their defilement tend to be loaded, like the one above, with sexually
indulgent language, betraying the fact that even as he condemned

the defilers he wished to join them. Visiting his Uncle Findlay in Abingden, Harry was introduced to "a pretty little damsel with long raven curls floating over her snowy neck, with a dimpled pair of downy cheeks who looked like they had stolen their color from the roses, with large, dreamy eyes, as black as they were sparkling, and to crown the enchantment . . . a pair of coral, little lips." One afternoon, Harry took her out for a stroll, and as she leaned on his arm he plied her "unmercifully" with "protestations of devotion [and] love." "I never thought she would believe the first word of it," Harry admitted to his diary. "My tongue knew no bounds; my mouth was filled with flattery deceptions. . . . At last in my excitement and intoxication caused by her ravishing beauty and voluptuousness, I pressed [her] hand to my beardless lips—next I put my arm around her waist—I imprinted on that downy cheek a kiss—she lent over on my bosom and our lips were sealed—kiss after kiss as burning and as voluptuous as blissful followed each other. . . . My sensations at that moment baffle description." "Intoxicated" and "giddy," Harry was struggling to restrain his desire when "the soft whisperings of conscience" stayed his hand: "Will you dishonor this poor girl whom you have led on . . . ? Will you condemn her to a life of misery, dishonor and degradation . . . for the gratification of a licentious and evil passion you yourself have aroused by improper liberties taken with this inexperienced and unsuspecting virgin whom you have beguiled by the machinations of your oily tongue?" Gradually, Harry pulled away from her and led her back to the house. He walked with a light heart, happy that his conscience had won out over the promptings of his "evil genius," but he admitted that the contest had been a close one.[33]

This tension came out even more clearly in his wet dreams. "A night or two ago (I can't help it)," Harry wrote one morning, "I dreamed of a perfect legion of women. . . . It seems as though my brain at night is wholly wrapped up in [them]." In one such dream, Harry and a girl from the neighborhood were walking along a forest path when they came to a stream that could only be crossed by wading. "She wade?" Harry said, "I'd die first"; ever the gentleman, Harry moved to carry the girl across the stream. But as soon as he picked her up Harry's disposition became less than gentlemanly. "Oh I have no words to express how I felt," he confessed to his diary, "I felt her arms, saw those nectared lips. I pressed her still closer to my throbbing heart—my cup of bliss was filled to overflowing!" In this dream, there is a definite tension between a desire to revere women and to ravish them. Harry's initially gallant impulse is undermined by baser urges almost as soon as he takes the girl into his care. In another dream, Harry was propelled by "lechery" to devise an elaborate means of entrapping "a pale little woman," but his "hellish designs failed after many maneuvers" and he came very near being exposed. ("The Mitchell girls [neighborhood friends] seemed to rise up against me but I escaped uninjured.") Frustrated in his attempt to lure a stranger, Harry suddenly noticed that a close acquaintance, Ella Brown, had appeared beside him, looking "as blooming as she ever did." The two walked together as twilight fell, and Harry felt "yet happy in my innocence." As they walked on, however, their shoulders touched, sending an electric shock through Harry's body. "Could I shake off that terrible excitement even if I had tried?" Harry asked his diary. "Its grip was like iron.... Her surpassing beauty made me mad; all reason was gone. I saw nothing but her, her sparkling eyes turned to me in ... fear and apprehension.... I knew but one thing—I in my madness had but one object: I knew I possessed her charms ... [my] object was fiendish beyond thought. My soul was on fire, my brain was dizzy with excitement; I was strangely enthralled and my feelings defy words." Harry went on to describe in sexually explicit detail his "illicit" encounter with Ella, after which the two fell asleep. When they awoke, the full gravity of what had happened hit them both. Ella sobbed over her lost virginity and Harry, heartsick and ashamed, tried to console her. Mrs. Dixon suddenly appeared, and Harry ran off, his mother pursuing him furiously until the end of the dream. This sex dream is a relatively pedestrian one for an adolescent boy. There is, however, a considerable amount of anxiety sown into this scenario. Harry does not condone his conduct, nor does he enjoy the experience; rather it is as if his own monstrous urges, barely kept in check while awake, are raging across Deer Creek in his sleep. Harry here is a sexual predator, unable to control his voracious appetite as he stalks the members of his own neighborhood. Ella fears him, the Mitchell girls suspect him, his mother finds him out and casts him from the community. While such analysis can be carried too far, it is clear that this is a dream of anxiety as well—Harry's sexual desire is something he does not fully control or understand, something which, if exposed to his friends and family, might result in his banishment. Harry's own reverence for female chastity has made it impossible for him to imagine consensual sex, even in the perfect freedom of dreams.[34]

In reality, Harry's relations with women were much more respectable. Harry was a cheeky flirt, to be sure; his brains and his brass tended to make him a mischievous conversationalist, but he knew the difference between putting some color in a girl's cheek and actually embarrassing her. In the spring of 1859, Harry and his friends developed simultaneous crushes on three women staying with Judge Rucks. "Hal, Nat, and myself are in love (even at our age)," seventeen-year-old Harry confessed. "Miss Wingate is Hal's lady love, Miss Smith, Nat's, and Miss Ella R. Scott is mine." He described Ella as a lady a little over the medium height, with a form and disposition "void of fault." "She is not pretty," he admitted, "but when one has become acquainted with her, he utterly forgets all the allurements of beauty and only sees her mental charms." Harry became particularly fond of Ella when she stitched together a flag for his little boat, the Pandora, which he happily rechristened the "Ella R. Scott." The two grew even closer during a local fish fry when Ella pulled thirty brim out of the river in an hour while Harry managed only one. He hooked it while Ella was away, tending to the picnic they had left to the mercy of some wild pigs. Late one evening, Hal, Nat, and Harry decided to serenade their sweethearts and stole the melodeon from the church for accompaniment. The instrument was incredibly unwieldy, and Judge Rucks's home was a fair distance from the church, but the boys were richly rewarded. The girls threw a note down from their window when the serenade was over thanking them for the wonderful concert. Harry returned home to document his success in his diary: "and now I will retire hoping that I may have pleasant dreams of *my lady love*. Ha! Ha! Am I not a happy youth?" Eventually, of course, Ella, with her companions, left Deer Creek, but Harry was not devastated by her departure. He played at losing her as buoyantly as he had played at winning her in the first place. Romantic experience is incomplete without a sense of loss, and Harry

Harry St. John Dixon used a substitution code he called hieroglyphics to encrypt his saucier entries. In this passage, he describes his "illicit" sexual encounter with Miss Ella Brown. Harry St. John Dixon Diary, Southern Historical Collection, UNC.

was happy to have "loved as a boy of sixteen can love only—without foresight, without anything but love."[35]

And indeed, whatever Harry lost in Ella, he quickly found elsewhere. Two months after Ella's departure, he fell for someone else, a woman he met on a trip to the Virginia spas. The tour began with a Methodist camp meeting, a sort of divine bracer before descending into the den of iniquity. The Methodists worked Harry over so thoroughly he "shed tears of regret" and "prayed fervent to God to forgive" him his many sins. God, however, could not compete with the spas, and Harry quickly abandoned himself to the dizzying whirl. "The seriousness lasted a few days," he confessed to his diary, "but on account of the circumstances it soon wore off." While at the spas Harry rose at 11:00, flirted until dinner, napped until dusk, danced until midnight, serenaded until 2:00, then retired to dream of his many "loves." "This is the way my time was occupied the whole time I remained at the Springs," he confessed to his diary. On one occasion, Harry was lying on a bench, holding the hand of a "pretty little gall" from Wytheville, while she combed his hair. Harry's mother caught a glimpse of the spectacle and sprang back into her cabin. "Do look at Harry!" she exclaimed, blanching at the thought that her daughter should ever be so situated. "If she had seen me on some other occasions," Harry promised his diary, "she would not have blushed at that." "I don't mean . . . that I did any thing towards dishonoring any one of them," he added, "but I mean that I was somewhat *more pleasantly situated*." Particularly pleasant were the long walks he took with one young "Virginia gall" who granted him as many kisses as he asked for. She was such a good sport that Harry asked her to marry him and was accepted. Harry did not tell his parents of the engagement but felt sure he could free himself of this little "love scrape." After returning home, Harry neglected the girl's letters mercilessly until she took the hint.[36]

Despite the fun and frivolities of a spring with Ella and a summer at the spas, there was an idea in the back of Harry's head that gradually lodged itself in the front—it was time for him to grow up. Others of his friends had already left the Deer Creek School—some for college, others for better preparatory schools. Suddenly when Harry took his evening rides he did not meet Hal or Nat or Taylor but their younger brothers and sisters. When he went down to the watering hole, he did less swimming than reminiscing. Asked to prepare a composition for Mr. Herbert, Harry deviated from the given subject and wrote a treatise on why he should be allowed to go to the University of Virginia in the fall. His parents' objections, he knew, were not that he lacked the necessary learning but that he lacked the necessary discipline and would be "led off by bad examples and by the allurements of vice and debauchery." "You shall never see me intoxicated," Harry pleaded. "I know too well the miseries of drunkenness and intemperance. I repeat it; you shall never see me intoxicated; no! never, never!" Harry's father read the document over dinner and, after some discussion, relented. "Now," Harry wrote in his diary that evening, "I will go to college to return . . . a man!"[37]

This latter was a subject of some soreness with Harry, and he found himself unusually sensitive to the respect (or lack of it) accorded by those around him. "Perplexities seem to have attacked me lately," he confessed, "or I have lost some of my hardly-gained control over my rebellious temper." The littlest things set him off. He took it personally, for instance, when a servant forgot to send up the cream for his strawberries and again when he left the room and returned to find another man reading his newspaper. On another occasion Harry's uncle and cousin rode by his window, as they often did, asking him to break into his father's liquor cabinet and pass out the whiskey. Harry could not contain his anger and replied facetiously, "Now it does look nice that I must 'trapse' up and down a flight of stairs like a negro to wait on two great, lazy men that do nothing but drink liquor, sleep, and go to see women." "I considered it beneath my station to be *Mr. Anybody's butt*," Harry explained to his diary, and he would be damned if he would "gallop around the house drawing whiskey for any one!" "But this is not the thing," Harry admitted—the problem was larger than any one incident. "It is this d——d slight," he wrote, "this way people lately have got of overlooking me." One evening William Percy was over visiting Harry's father; Harry sat in the same room with them but was never acknowledged. "Have I offended them?" he wondered, "Or have I committed some monstrous misdemeanor? Is it because I am a *boy*? Because I have no hair on my chin and have not been to college? If this be the cause . . . why within one week I am subjected to such humiliating indignities, I consider them too far below me, too much of 'lick-spittles' to even deserve my contempt." Still running red-hot, Harry brought up the incident at the dinner table. His eyes swollen and a knot tightening in his throat, he said, "People these days don't seem to think it worth while to speak to me; Dr. Percy this evening took no more notice of me than if I had been negro." His father tried to explain that some men spoke to boys while others did not and that Harry was too sensitive. "I tried to answer," Harry noted, "and stammered out a few words about being treated with contempt but that knot was in my throat. I could say no more, I was too mad." Excusing himself from dinner, Harry found he was too distracted to study. "I could not study my music lesson for thinking of it," he wrote his diary. "I've been thinking of it ever since; am still thinking of it; and this won't be the last time I will think of it." Harry had always been a bristling, confident youth. His father reprimanded him often for his pride and was particularly concerned that Harry be more deferential to his elders. In the summer of 1860, Harry's tolerance for such deference had worn thin. While always respectful of his father, Harry had enough regard for his own intelligence to believe his opinions as valuable as anyone else's. While he loved his neighbors, his uncle, and his father, they did not seem to understand that Harry was changing, had changed, had become bigger than Deer Creek; going away to college would help Harry prove it. "I do not expect to live a fast life," Harry wrote in his diary, "but I do not intend to bury myself in such a place as Deer Creek."[38]

Harry's last summer at home was filled with mixed emotions. He continued to chafe under slights real and imagined, and his younger brothers had never seemed so annoying. Mr. Herbert took longer and longer with the example problems, feebly masking the fact that he was no longer equipped to direct Harry's studies. Even Hal and Nat began to get on Harry's nerves with their foppish habit of fawning over shoes and cravats. But knowing he would soon leave Deer Creek, Harry grew sentimental about the place and its familiarities. The town's aggravations seemed suddenly quaint by comparison to the monumental challenges that awaited him in the wider world, and his anticipation of collegiate manhood was tempered by a nostalgia for his happy youth. Mrs. Dixon noted the change in her son, telling

Harry that he seemed to have "stopped all [his] boyish ways and acted like a settled person much older" than himself. Harry did not dispute the point; "as soon as I am left to my own thoughts," he confessed in his diary, "I feel an oppression and seriousness which is by no means pleasant. Formerly . . . I had a light heart, whistled all the time and built castles in the air. . . . Such boyish pleasantries and daydreaming I fear have vanished and that sterner things impend over my youthful head." Wandering through the house one day, Harry spied an old copy of Cooper's *Prairie* on the mantel. Leafing through its pages, he was temporarily returned to the "continuous day-dreams" of his youth. Then, he said, "my only ambition was to be a man, to have my camp, my dog, my rifle and my pony. To be far on the border of the prairies towards the setting of the sun. To live among the fallen red men and be their friend, to fight their battles against my race [and take] a wife, an Indian princess, radiant [in her] fascinating simplicity." Such simplicities held their charm for him still, Harry granted, but the time had come for him to put away childish things, and he returned the book to the mantel. "I must in a short time launch myself into a world, cold and heartless," he noted in his diary, "among strangers and men of corruption, men whose sins far out-balance those I have committed and God knows they are many. . . . But I will not flinch."[39]

Harry spent his final afternoon packing and repacking his trunks to his father's satisfaction; finally Mr. Dixon took over the packing altogether. Harry's mother had spent most of the summer denying that Harry was really going. In the final week she became withdrawn and depressed and Harry felt a "peculiar embarrassment" when discussing his departure with her. He tried to be lively, but too much was awkward and unspoken. "I feel sorrier to leave Ma than any other," Harry noted, "because I think she loves me more and will miss me more sincerely than others of the family. As the time has approached my ardor has diminished. I do not feel a reluctance to go, but I cannot leave all that I have been raised with without pain." In the evening, Hal, Nat, and Harry said their good-byes. Nat told Harry not to worry, that he would probably make plenty of new friends in the university pubs. "Nat," Harry shot back, "do you make your friends that way?" It was a biting comment, considering Nat had recently been dismissed from his academy for "brick-batting" and "getting tight." "He is so vain," Harry admitted, "I like to do him so." That night, after everyone had gone to sleep, Harry sat up with his dog Sam, writing in his journal. He had worked feverishly all day but did not feel tired. "I am not wearied," he wrote, "not wearied of looking on the stillness, the solitude and silence of this night . . . nor am I wearied of my wooly pet, my dog who lies asleep at my feet under the table while I write." Sam would have no master now, Harry lamented, no one to feed and pet and love him as he had done. "The affectionate thing seems to know I am going to leave," he wrote. "He has staid closer to me the last two or three days than ever before. . . . I must say I hate to leave him. Is it strange? Is it uncommon? Astray again!"[40]

The following morning, Harry worked deliberately on his mother's mood and finally cheered her some. The trunks were once again a source of concern and Harry spent an hour or so packing another with last-minute necessaries. "The time at last came," he wrote. "All was ready and the dreaded parting took place. The first tears ever shed for *me* came from the eyes of my mother today. She wept." Harry restrained his emotions until his father had guided the buggy down the road a pace; then he could not help it. "Looking back I saw all the family standing in the gallery watching the buggy as Pa drove." he noted, "I could not force the tears back, they would come." Harry's father traveled with him as far as Memphis, giving Harry considerably less advice than he had expected. "Dusk was closing in when I left Memphis and my loved father," Harry noted. "We parted with firm hearts, as a father and son should part."[41]

On September 26, 1860, Harry Dixon began a new journal to commemorate his arrival at the University of Virginia. He believed that college was the most formative period of a boy's life, that it would determine, in most cases, the "manners, habits, pursuits, views and opinions" of the man. He knew, too, that strong temptations would be held out by some of the university's more "dissipated and notorious children," and he prayed for the strength to avoid the worst of them. Harry had arrived earlier than most students and had taken up a single room in a boardinghouse outside Charlottesville. His first evening, he admitted, he "felt alone, unloved, and dependent on myself alone, among strangers and strange things." The next morning he heard a clunking on the stairs outside his room. A Mr. Smith was moving into a single near Harry's; the two boys sized each other up and, both vouching for their studious dispositions, they decided to room together. Harry would not write another homesick letter (though he did pester his family to have an daguerreotype taken of Sam); instead, he was drawn quickly into a collegial social whirl.[42]

Harry's principal friends at the college were Mr. Smith, Mr. Cline-bel, and Mr. Ewing. Mr. Smith proved to be something of an annoy-ance as a roommate; Harry found him "effeminate," "fainthearted," and lacking in that "hardihood" that would "keep him from ever being independent upon some one for guidance and support." Harry, of course, became that someone. Mr. Clinebel was a roaring, senseless egotist who disgusted Harry at first, then tickled his sense of the ridiculous, then became a (still laughable) friend. Clinebel was a mess mate at the boardinghouse and always took a seat next to Smith, who quailed under Clinebel's "rough remarks, loud laughing . . . and spreading elbows." Harry claimed to know just how to handle such braggarts and promised to exchange places with Smith and take Cline-bel "through a 'course of sprints.'" Gradually, though, Harry became accustomed to Clinebel's pomposity and took a certain pity on him. "[Mr. Clinebel] is very poor and a state student," Harry wrote home, "and having learned what he knows by himself and among his ig-norant kindred they have thought from this that he is what he thinks he is, and have puffed him up thus, merely about his having had application enough to learn a little." Clinebel, though, was good for laughs, which was always good for Harry. Walking home one day, he fell into a puddle of water, throwing Harry into hysterics: "Just like him after getting out he ran to his room as though he was certain to get the Pneumonia." In Mr. Ewing, on the other hand, Harry had a friend he could not laugh at or take care of; quick to find the weak-nesses in people, Harry could not find any in Ewing and, as was his way, he ungrudgingly accepted his friend's superiority. "I wish we could live together always, never to part," Harry confessed to his diary. "There are few men I've met with who in my estimation can compare with him. He has a heart as big as a mountain."[43]

There was nothing particularly unusual about Harry's education at

UVA. He attended his classes regularly but not religiously; he prepared his lessons adequately and was satisfied at that. In the evenings,
he hung around his room with the others who hung around his room,
occasionally lamenting that his friends preferred the floor to the spittoon. On Sundays, he and his friends went to church, or rather, went
to stand outside the church and watch the women file out. On one
occasion, the Episcopal church was late dismissing its parishioners,
and the boys went over to the Baptist Institute for a gawk at the "soft
'uns." "They walked to the gate through a double file of staring eyes
for the whole college seemed to be there," Harry noted. "It must be
right trying to them. One put a handkerchief over her face; I was
told that she was not pretty by any means!" To be sure, there were
breaks in these routines. One evening a shot was heard from a nearby
boardinghouse. Two men of "merry mood" had determined to play-
fully shoot at each other with a revolver; on the second shot one of
the boys was struck on the knee. Harry described the incident as
"something upon the Don Quixote order, and, we are happy to say,
not more serious than some of that gallant knight's exploits." A week
later a brawl erupted during a lecture, overturning desks and spatter-
ing blood on the floor. "The last brilliant glimmerings of the chiv-
alrous flame have not yet expired," Harry wrote facetiously to his
father, "some of the University's sons yet love to show the world that
they have brave hearts, and in the absence of an immediate enemy
turn—not their rapiers—but their fists against each other . . . these
brave sons of the South." But even the outbursts had a certain rhythm
to them, and Harry adapted to it all easily. He wrote home every
Sunday, assuring his parents that he would never darken the doors of
the Charlottesville bars and billiard rooms. His mother wrote back
plaintively every other week: "My dear boy you have raised hopes
and expectations that if blasted would be a blow I could never recover
from"; and his father wrote more sternly on the weeks in-between:
"You may be fully assured that all admonition . . . is for your good,
no matter how the words may sound at first." For Harry's part, he
was happy to have settled in with new friends. Within two months
he felt comfortable enough to sit in the parlor of his boardinghouse,
with his feet propped up on the mantel, and tell "loose anecdotes with

[his] jolly college fellows." "So," he wrote in his diary, goes "college life at the U. of Va."[44]

By late fall, however, the loose anecdotes of jolly college fellows had to give way. First the election, then secession, and finally the question of war dominated discussions, "carr[ying] every other idea before [them]." To judge by Harry's diary, slavery played little role in the coming of the conflict. He mentions the "ruinous tarriff" as often as abolition, slavery, or any euphemism for the same (Southern institutions or ways of life); more often the cause is put to some ill-defined Northern "aggression" or "rascality." But on slavery and race, Harry was unreflective, unrepentant. In Virginia, he picked up comfortably where he had left off in Mississippi, seeing blacks as essentially subhuman. "Smith and I have just had a great deal of fun out of an old negro who has sold us some lightwood," Harry noted one evening. The boys made the man run around the room with his wood tongs and a bayonet, speaking words he did not understand. Upon leaving, Harry noted, the man "forgot the steps in the Hall and in the dark fell down them at which we laughed outrageously." Harry accepted easily the hierarchy that made such scenes possible. As he put it, "There's always a plus and a minus in affairs of life as well as [in] Algebra." Only once did he seem even to have an inkling of blacks' humanity. One afternoon while gamboling about campus, he and a group of boys stumbled into the dissecting room where they saw "three revolting sights—three dead negro women, shriveled and decaying with the skin scraped off in many places. The teeth were visible and the dust and dirt on them, combined with their blue, sunken, half-opened eyes made them disgusting sights." Harry was the first of the boys to crack a joke, and he kept them all laughing over the corpses for some time. "But still my reflections were on my leaving the place quite different," he confessed to his diary. "It looked a little like a degradation of humanity, although the subjects were negroes. It is sad to think that every one, let him be as beautiful as he may, let him have the fairest proportions God can give them, still is not exempt from death and revolting putrification—all, all alike must die and must decay." To Harry's mind, though, the tragedy was not that the Negroes had to die, but that the beautiful people, white people, God's people, would have to die deaths better fit for the ugly and the black.[45]

Regardless of their views on race, however, an overwhelming number of students favored immediate secession of the individual Southern states and the formation of a separate government for the South. "This is a secession college," Harry wrote simply in December, "students, officers, & professors." The basic rhythm at the college was exactly as it was throughout the South. At first it was secession cockades, then secession flag-raising ceremonies, then volunteer companies and volunteer company uniforms. In April war was declared and Virginia seceded. The news reached Charlottesville around ten in the morning and was met with "huzzahs and shouts." The military companies hastily fell out for drills and general revelry; Harry's friends began leaving by every train. In the ensuing weeks, many of the faculty left to find posts in the government or army; those who remained announced they would be offering a class on military tactics next semester, hoping to boost sagging attendance. Just as the students were leaving, young men began to pour through Charlottesville from the western states on their way to muster into the Confederate army. "Fifteen hundred Kentuckians, armed only with hatchets, passed here en route for Richmond a day or two since," Harry told his father. "These are the men for any emergency." Harry wanted desperately to go too; he argued patriotism, he argued duty, but his father insisted that he remain in school. "I have already said I will call you as soon as needed," Richard wrote of his son's repeated entreaties. "Be patient, be assured that it is not yet necessary that you should make this sacrifice of your education." But the truth was that his education was exactly what Harry wanted to sacrifice. His days at UVA had convinced him of something he had suspected before arriving: "My walk in this life must be a lowly one," he confessed to his diary, "I am not, as [Ewing] says, 'born to lead.' I'd rather follow such a man as Jeff Davis, *anywhere*." After exhausting all other lines of argument with his father, Harry finally tried honesty. The letter has the tone of a man who is too fatigued to continue to delude himself or others. In it, Harry told his father that he liked poetry, that he believed it expressed the "noblest thoughts of human nature and of human mind" and that he would continue to read it regardless of his father's opinion; he told his father that he did not disagree with those at home who saw him as "a light-headed and *vain* boy." "I am a boy," he claimed, "and subject to a boy's infirmaties"; he told his father that he had not the slightest thought that he would "win distinction in this world," and that his path would undoubtedly "be humble and quiet in life's drama"; in short, Harry told his father, he was not a boy to be groomed at a high-powered university but a boy who should be allowed to follow such a man as Jeff Davis anywhere. Harry had a little part to play, and his father should let him play it. For the first time, Harry had disagreed with his father and said so. "I have contented myself—so to speak—with the idea of remaining at the Univ'ty," he wrote. "That it is against my wishes . . . I won't deny." "I have been a thousand times tempted to go at all hazzards."[46]

Three things stayed Harry from joining the army: his scrupulous obedience to his father, his concern for his fragile mother, and a secret he had kept from them both. "Today I have to record that which is forever to be a stain upon my character," Harry noted in his diary. "No one but myself shall ever see this page of my journal for the act which I am about to record on it is blacker that the ink I write it in." In all his Sunday letters home, Harry had trumpeted his virtues, had proudly proclaimed his perfect abstention from liquor, tobacco, and gambling. His diary provides no evidence to dispute these points. But Harry had a "constitutional failing" that he did not document in those letters: an affection for women that went beyond gawking. Harry had been in Charlottesville less than a fortnight when he went to see a concert; the singer was "one of the most lovely little creatures" Harry had ever seen. As he watched her, as he watched the "expression of her fair countenance and the deep swellings and heavings of her fairer bosom," he felt an urge to run and hug her. "Such is my disposition," he confessed to his diary, "such is my *vile* love for any woman who thus fills my eye of wickedness." Harry wished he could discard such thoughts and feelings, but the woman "made the cold chills roll down" his back and "the corners of [his] mouth salty." "Could I help it?" Harry asked his diary, "Place an apple before a child and will he not wish to bite it?" Two months later, on Christmas Day, Harry came closer to biting. He had planned on visiting one of his instructor's homes, but he passed the professor on the street and said nothing. "I saw some boosy fellows around some night-burning tar barrels," Harry noted in his diary. "What I did, or what I would have done had I had money, I am ashamed to write and only refer to my memory for what occurred."[47]

Though he does not document it, Harry must have gone back with some money on at least one occasion—in the spring of 1861, as his friends scrambled to defend the South, Harry lay in bed struggling to recover from a venereal disease. Smith's effeminacy proved to be an asset after all; Harry confessed his secret and Smith became his unofficial nurse. For two weeks Harry lolled in bed under the influence of heavy opiates. His dreams were haunted by images of his dead brother, of returning home to find his family dead or dying. In one vision, he found his mother alive but too vacant to recognize him. Harry put his arms around her and repeatedly said, "Ma, Ma, don't you recognize me?" but she did not regain her wits. In the sex dream examined earlier, Mrs. Dixon represented the conscience that banished Harry from the community; in this dream she is the part of his conscience that will never recover from his act of youthful indiscretion. "My heart is not stone," he confessed to his diary. "I feel this most heartily. Let me once get well and there will not be a harder student at the University. . . . This is now the turning point of my life; I know it." On April 26, Harry raised himself from his bed to see Ewing off at the Charlottesville depot. He was returning home to Nashville to join the army of the South. "I truly hated to see him go," Harry noted. "He has been indeed the warmest friend I have had at the University." Harry went a little way with him on the cars, until they started to pick up a little speed. "He heartily wrung my hand as I stepped off the platform. . . . I raised and waved a hat at him as a last adieu as the train slowly carried him off. Poor fellow. I hated to part with him. He loved me most." Ewing was off finally to become a man; Harry was left behind and limped gloomily back to the sickbed he had made for himself.[48]

Conclusion

Once again, these character studies are drawn from the lives of very different men. Harry Dixon was the quintessential Young American, content to run wide open, operating always under the general credo that while he lived, he would live. David Outlaw was older and more reserved. His wife and children preoccupied him, even in Washington, even as his dear republic ran the last leg in its race of ruin. Dixon was remorseless about slavery; Outlaw had his doubts. Dixon was open-tempered and vain; Outlaw was stoical and sad. But on the subject of women the two men were in firm agreement. As Victor Hugo had said in 1822, "A woman has only to belong to the public in one way, for that public to believe she belongs to it entirely." Dixon and Outlaw, with much of their society, concurred completely. Dixon's fixation on virgins and Outlaw's fixation on his wife's virtues were part of the same Victorian preoccupation with storing the values they hoped to remain inviolate in the frail vessel of a woman.

The consequences for women of such a storage system has been the subject of much study. But there were consequences, too, for the men who are supposed to have controlled the system in the first place. To Harry Dixon, white women were almost unbearably magnificent. "To these secret pages I will confess that to me they seem more like Gods," he wrote in his diary, "combining all good qualities within humans." But even while revering women's unassailable purity, he had obsessively impure thoughts, resulting in an almost maddening tension. Having made gods of women, he also made a demon of his own desire for physical intimacy, a demon that stalked his beloved neighborhood in his sleep. Unable to consider his own sexual urge as anything other than polluted, Harry turned to whores. When he returned from his first trip to a brothel with a venereal disease, he bore it easily as the necessary consequence of physical passion. David Outlaw suffered similarly from the effort to place women above the sullied world of which he was himself an unfortunate part. Lonely and estranged, unable to bear the idea of Emily coming to cheer him, Outlaw let his republic go, hoping thereby to quarantine from degeneracy his South, his hometown, his family, and, through these, the little that remained of his own decency.

Finally, both men resented their society's failure to take the proper measure of their masculinity. Outlaw's virtue and self-restraint, once the emblems of republican manhood, were now the markers of weakness and effeminacy, and it grieved him to think that the blowhards bullying their way around Washington were reckoned real men. Harry Dixon was similarly aggrieved. No rite of passage, it seemed, had worked the necessary magic. Turning seventeen hadn't made him a man. Going to college hadn't made him a man. Taking a woman to bed hadn't made him a man, either. In the spring of 1861, of course, another passage to manhood had opened, erected on the ruins of Outlaw's republic, and Harry, with thousands of others, was desperate to take it.

PART III

MEN AND WAR

CHAPTER 5

A FOUNTAIN OF WATERS

Oh! that my heart was a fountain of waters
that I might weep it away for this my ruined country.*

For most antebellum Americans, disunion was, to use one of their favorite metaphors, a dark cloud brooding endlessly on the horizon, a storm ever building, never breaking. To be sure, a few eyed it greedily, imagining its power to reorder lives and circumstances. But far more viewed it as a peripheral grimness. The cloud had been there every day of their national existence, and, while they did not like the look of it, they had had ample time to get used to it. When finally it crashed about their heads, they might have reacted with a weary fatalism. But the surprising thing is how surprised they were—how suddenly and powerfully secession gripped them and shook them. In the early fall of 1860, there was in most Southerners' correspondence a stunning *lack* of attention paid to the election or its possible consequences. By December the subject was omnipresent, inescapable. "Nothing was talked of but secession," remembered one Southerner, "in every company, at every street corner, whenever two people met that was the subject discussed." How could Southerners not have seen secession coming, especially as they were, taken as a group, its

*Amanda McDowell Diary, June 15, 1861, in Joan Cashin, ed., *Our Common Affairs*, 285.

architects? They did see it coming, of course. They voted and acted
in ways that made it a likely, then an inevitable, then an accomplished
fact. But they did not, could not, have foretold how it would feel.[1]

And how did it feel? In diary after diary, letter after letter, Southerners describe themselves as being in a state of what might be termed
political shock. The particulars and timing, of course, vary from state
to state, family to family, person to person—but the trajectory goes
something like this. Passing references to political affairs begin to
lengthen, deepen, and become more personal; the abstract busy-ness
of everyday life takes on direction and then energy, surging, swirling,
and building, until the writers find themselves at the epicenter of
something mammoth and unknown to them. It is a curious feeling,
so immediate and strong, so much larger than the little bodies that
seek to apprehend it, direct it, join it. Eventually, when political affairs
have achieved sufficient gravity, time begins to warp. The months
that stretch out between the election and Sumter become a hurtling
calm, a furious wait. Finally, the wait—timeless and brief, exhilarating and terrifying—is over. It will be War. The mammoth something
has swallowed up all the little writers, leaving of each only a dis-
embodied narrative voice to comment distantly on the life it has surrendered to the rush.

This was an aspect of the secession crisis white Southerners shared
regardless of political stripe. They were, all of them, at the center of
the furious calm, safe for the moment but watching nervously as a
storm raged about them, beyond their power and their ken. Men who
had dedicated their whole lives to Southern independence pinched
themselves as events they had set in motion took on a life of their
own—and then slipped quietly out of their control. Others more removed from politics were altogether thunderstruck, exhilarated and
dazed by turns. In diary after diary, unionist and disunionist alike
document a reaction that seems a lot like shock. "Things seem to
progress in a slow but certain way," Meta Grimball marveled from
her South Carolina plantation. "Everything goes on as usual, the
planting, the negroes, all just the same; and a great Empire tumbling
to pieces about us." North Carolinian William Bingham compared the
feeling to that of being drugged. "I am in a sort of stupor as to the
political state of things," he noted, "and am waiting patiently for evils

that are surely coming." Virginian Judith McGuire felt equally helpless: "Can it be that our country is to be carried on and on to the
horrors of civil war? . . . I shut my eyes and hold my breath when the
thought of what may come upon us obtrudes itself; and yet I cannot
believe it." William Russell, a visiting Englishman, preferred a me-
teorological metaphor, claiming he'd been caught in the eye of a
hurricane. "The chaos of opinions into which I was at once plunged
over head & ears," he noted, "was all so opposite & so violent that
like opposing forces they produced at the unhappy centre to which
they directed their course complete absence of all motion." Here, in
a freak calm within a funnel of whirling wind, Russell wrote, men
gave themselves over to the storm, surrendering their destinies to the
march of events. "Every man is an atom in a gale," he explained,
"overwhelmed & controlled by the force which has set it and its
fellows in motion & can of itself effect nothing or go beyond the blind
submission to chance." Tellingly, these observers situated themselves
at the quiet center of something inescapable and immense—Mrs.
Grimball within a tumbling empire, Mr. Bingham at the patient forehead of evil, Mrs. McGuire before an unwatchable unknown, Mr.
Russell within an atomizing gale—yet somehow their own centrality
has the paradoxical effect of distancing them from the action—Mrs.
Grimball potters about the empire's ruin, Mr. Bingham blinks heavily
through his stupor, Mrs. McGuire's eyes are closed, and Mr. Russell
can of himself "effect nothing." In each case, the writer does not even
touch upon politics. What has captured them is not a particular position or ideology but a feeling, a sort of political vertigo. Events have
rushed far ahead, leaving their witnesses disoriented in the wake.[2]

    Without question, political persuasion and economic interest played
the largest roles in determining whether a person supported secession.
Personality and the psychology of the individual, however, determined
the *style* of that support. Those who took to disunion with a sort of
devotional enthusiasm tended to believe in romantic risk generally.
They were comfortable with long odds, reckless posturing, and
doomed causes, at their happiest and best when cavalier. Pessimistic
and risk-averse Southerners, by contrast, knew in their bones that
nothing good ever came of destruction. They were comfortable with
compromise, steady living, and the status quo, at their happiest and

best when worrying—and in the coming of war they had worries aplenty. These differences in emotional style are critical to understanding secession as an experience. As each would-be Confederate state seceded, the Southerners within it had to secede too.

Secession, then, was a mosaic of a million American unbecomings, each with its own peculiar dynamics. To Dolly Lunt and Louisiana Burge, disunion offered an opportunity to feel and speak in ways altogether new to them. The girls were cousins and playmates situated on opposite sides of the Mason-Dixon line. In the winter of 1860–1861 they exchanged a series of bitter letters, seizing, as they put it, the "chance for vehement language." They wrote as if their opposing views of secession were "final and unshakable," as if their former love for each other meant nothing amid the chaos of the times. "It was bombast on both sides," remembered Dolly Lunt. "We flew to trample and intimidate . . . to ride roughshod, and crush underfoot by trenchant sarcastic bluster." Partly, of course, they argued because they were ideologically opposed to each other's position. But the way they argued was an indulgence; they were drunk on rhetoric, tight with politics, delighting in damning the proprieties of the well-mannered lady in their epistolary howlings. And, as Dolly later admitted, they had imperiled their love for each other not because it meant nothing, but because it meant something, as all true sacrifices must. In these girls' secession psychodrama, their love for each other was the most important prop—in dashing it they made real their claim to have turned their backs on an entire section of the country they knew less well than they despised it.[5]

Secession was a particular godsend for the South's adolescent boys. This is not to say that most were fire eaters; they weren't. But for anyone waiting for something dramatic to happen—and this would include most of the young men of any period—the wait was over. "We did not think; we were not capable of it," Samuel Clemens remembered. "As for myself, I was full of unreasoning joy to be done with turning out of bed at midnight and four in the morning . . . grateful to have a change, new scenes, new occupations, a new interest. In my thoughts that was as far as I went; I did not go into the details; as a rule [a young man] doesn't." Ill suited or ill disposed to their schoolwork and their clerkships, most of the South's young men, like

Clemens, put aside the mundane drudgery of building a career and took up indulgent visions of adventure and fame. "Every man," remembered George Eggleston, "was a hero in immediate prospect." War had not yet come—it might never come; and in the posturing and bravado of arguing the secession line there was a sort of bristling manliness that better comported with their sense of who it was they wanted to be in the eyes of others. Southern prep schools and colleges, particularly, became hotbeds of secessionism. Buoyed by the spirit of student rebellion endemic in any age, Southern schoolboys happily poured their adolescent angst into a newly legitimated political form. Away at the West Military Institute in Nashville, C. O. Bailey wrote home that the town and the university were practically at war over a secession flag the boys had raised over the school. Bailey and his friends eventually took the flag down, but they published an article in the local paper taunting the townies and challenging them to a brawl. "The challenge has not been answered yet," noted a disappointed Bailey, but if it ever was he promised the boys would be ready. John Henderson was equally determined to take his stand against the establishment. Barely fifteen, Henderson was a student at the Alexander Wilson academy in Melville, North Carolina. "This evening I wore my [secession] *cockade* in to supper," he wrote his parents, "which offended young Dr. Wilson so much that he told me to take it off." Henderson refused, explaining to the headmaster that he had not intended to give offense and was merely expressing his own opinion. Dr. Wilson informed the boy that he had given offense and intimated that only men knew enough of themselves and the issues to wear such things. Needless to say, Henderson's cockade remained right where it was, and, raging, he marched out of the dining room. Still livid the next day, Henderson consoled himself with the fact that his friends had been so impressed by his stand that they had all determined to wear cockades. In the spring of 1861, boys like Clemens, Henderson, and Bailey flooded into hastily organized drilling companies, blithely leaving parents and sisters to worry for their welfare. "I am I own loth to see him engage in [such things]," wrote Amanda McDowell about her brother Fayette's joining up, "[but] I know it is hard . . . for a young man with any spirit to stay away now they make so much noise." Thus it was that across the South an army of children dropped their dusty books and took up the only role they knew to be worthy of men—fighters for freedom—and they knew it to be worthy because their books had taught them so. For any still curious as to why young men fought in the Civil War, they need look no farther than this—they fought because they were young. "It was such a 'Crossing of the Rubicon' as rarely happens at so early an age," remembered Randolph Shotwell. "It was more than the mere giving up of school, acquaintances, property, comfort; it was the complete cutting loose from boyhood to assume the responsibilities and perils of manhood; both magnified by youth's inexperience."[4]

Middle-aged men were by no means unaffected by this heady spirit. When Laurence Keitt received the telegram that South Carolina had seceded, he leaped into the air and waved the paper about, trumpeting that he felt "like a boy let out from school." Many of the South's thirty-somethings felt the same way. Their youth slipping away from them, their ambitions faded and dulled, secession was a chance to go through the male rite of passage again and this time get it right. When Georgia-born Lordy King set off for Harvard in 1848, he promised his father that he would be the pride of the family. "It may sound ridiculous to say so now," he claimed, "but I hope or rather *think* that I *will* be one of these days or years a *great* man, whether a Washington or a Napoleon, a Bishop or a Tom Paine." On his twenty-ninth birthday in 1860, after twelve years of billiards, whist, drinking, smoking, whoring, and carousing, and after three years of hapless studying for the bar, Lordy woke to an awful truth. "How little have I done to be proud of," noted the would-be Napoleon, "how much to be sorry for." Needless to say, Lordy King took to secession like a drowning man to driftwood. For Edward Butler it was not a birthday but a New Year's that triggered this personal stock checking. "These annual summings up are unpleasant enough to those who are prosperous and happy," he wrote a friend in 1860, "but to those who are the reverse, who are discontented with themselves, and find their youth passing away with nothing done, no victory gained in the great battle of Life, surely the reflection can bring nothing but remorse and bitterness." By year's end Edward was in uniform. "I joined the Army," he admitted, "because I found I was good for nothing else." Daniel Hamilton didn't need a holiday to tell him he was on the

wrong track. "It will be but a few days more and my connection with
Government will cease," he wrote his son. "I am heartily glad for it
has been a galling service, and I pant for the disenthralment of the
South." The ease with which Daniel conjoins his own independence
to that of the South is, of course, revealing. One wonders which was
more important to him—the disenthralment of the South or the disenthralment of Daniel Hamilton. It need hardly have mattered, of
course—they were, for the moment at least, one and the same.[5]

In late November 1860, Virginian William Thomson wrote his son,
William Jr., in Tennessee, decrying the foul work of the fire eaters.
The peace and business of the country, he claimed, were being threatened with destruction by madmen, and he begged his son to "keep
cool and unexcited amidst the wrath." In his response, William Jr.
told his father not to worry—"those . . . in favor of disunion are mostly
a lawless set," the son agreed, stirred up by "bustling politicians" hell-
bent on rule or ruin. Having secured a sympathetic ear, the father
then fired back another antisecession harangue. "I begin to think
there is almost as much fanatic sentiment in the South as in the
North," he claimed. "The nigger question and the everlasting nigger
is about to drive many crazy and turn our country into a huge insane
hospital." But William Jr.'s sympathetic ear suddenly turned deaf.
Every day, he wrote his father, the locals were becoming "more and
more embittered against the north, until at last they have come out
for secession *openly*." William Jr. had himself converted to secessionism while participating in a debate over the question, "Has any state
a right to secede from the Union?" There were five or six speakers
scheduled to answer the question in the negative and only two or
three in the affirmative, so he had taken the affirmative. When all
the other speakers had taken their turn, there were, William Jr.
claimed, "loud cries for 'Thomson' so I took the stand, and spoke,
until I was from the bottom of my heart a secessionist, and I guess
you are too." He guessed wrong. "Well, you say you are for secession,"
William Sr. wrote dejectedly. "I am not at all."[6]

Throughout the winter of 1860–1861, the Thomsons exchanged
long letters, attempting to win each other over. The son's letters are
a veritable laundry list of secession's typical tones and phrases: Cotton
was King, the South was unconquerable before its hearthstones, the

Northern masses were about to rise up, and civil war was preferable
to the alternative—seeing "the dusky sons of Ham leading the fair
daughters of the South to the altar." Young Thomson even took "Better death than dishonor" as his personal motto. William Sr.'s arguments were more personal; he was fighting not for the union but for
his son. It was as if the boy had joined some kind of cult and had,
with the standard-issue secession kit, set about building airy castles
on borrowed rhetoric. "The young and sanguine are rapidly carried
away into dreamy fields and flawed visions," the father warned. "Let
yourself down to earth; don't take pictures for realities. . . . Cotton is
not King, it is a vulgar error; by its frequent repitition the cotton
states have come to look upon the *words* as *facts*. . . . Calm down!
Down! Don't by the plaudits of the thoughtless carry yourself or permit yourself to lose sight of ancient and holy remembrances." But
William Sr. understood that "ancient and holy remembrances" were
fusty nothings to a young man full of pluck and that the real draw
of secession was not what it was but what it was not—the humdrum
everydayness of William Jr.'s new profession. William Jr. had gone
west to Tennessee to become a schoolteacher, but several of his students were as old as he was, and their parents were annoyingly intractable on questions of discipline and curriculum. "My scholars are
over me too much," William Jr. admitted in one letter. "Some of
them will come to school with no lessons at all, and if I say a word
to them, they will insult me; and if I attempt to carry out any rules
the parents get angry and if they don't learn they are angry." Re-
sponding to such complaints, William Sr. folded career counseling into
his antisecession argument, understanding that secession and schoolteaching were competing professions in the young man's mind. If he
could make schoolteaching sound suitably dramatic, he seemed to
think, secession might lose its allure. "The icebergs and rough seas
[young men] encounter," he told his son, give them "often a greater
staunchness and sagacity in navigating unexplored regions than those
who are accustomed to smooth waters and close to shore sailing. . . .
Lay yourself down to the work of acquiring greater endurance and
double determination and you will rise equal to all difficulties that
present themselves for your conquest." But most important, William
Sr. advised, "Don't be hurried by the plausable appeal of young or

old and artful secessionists . . . into placing your hopes of advancement and gratification of ambition on anything that may be offered in this destruction."[7]

Exchanges like the Thomsons' were rife in the winter of 1860–1861. "John has resigned and gone to town to offer his services to the Governor," Meta Grimball grumbled of her son in December. "He is very much enchanted at getting rid of a profession his heart was *not* very much interested in." James Petigru thought he discerned the same impulse animating his nephew Johnston. He has given "into the general sentiment," Petigru wrote of the young man, "and being put the head of a regiment of Volunteers is no longer a pale inmate of the obscure building in St. Michael's Alley, where he used to pore over dusty books in a foreign tongue; but bestrides a gallant steed, with gay trappings, long spurs and bright shoulder knots." While such grumblings undoubtedly contain more than a grain of truth, their tone suggests that parents sometimes underestimated the depth of their sons' predicament—and their resolve. "You must not take up the erroneous idea that all this is a mere freak," Virginia-born Richard Corbin wrote his mother on running off to join the Confederacy. "My future happiness depends upon this step [for] if I don't shake off this dull sloth, my life will for evermore be embittered by the most galling and humiliating regrets. . . . Just think that if you have now any affection for your idle, useless son, how much more that affection will be enhanced if it is mingled with a little pride at his manliness."[8]

Men's enthusiastic embrace of soldiering, then, is easy to understand. Unlike their prewar professions, the war combined with a felicity too perfect to be possible the twin drives of the masculine enterprise. To be sure, men joined the army to fight for cause, comrades, and country, and they gave fealty to these motives in their public remarks. But privately they were fighting, as they always had, for women and for eminence, and they confused the two as liberally as ever. "I always thought that you deserved something better," boasted William Pender to his wife on receiving a colonelcy. "I would like to be a great man for your sake." Their prewar professions had demanded discipline and patience and offered only sluggish prospects for advancement. The war, by contrast, demanded only an assent (I will join) and offered the possibility of a meteoric rise to distinction.

Where antebellum society had condemned Southern men for their drinking, sloth, sin, and miscegenation, the war would reward them for the open-tempered expression of masculinity's most basic impulses to conquer and kill. And, most important, their drive for distinction and their role as women's protectors would be synonymous in a way they had never known. "I shall fight [the Yankees] as if they were entering your dwelling or ready to give the deadly blow to my dear wife and child," promised one Georgia recruit in a letter to his beloved. "I tell you, I shall feel like I am fighting for home, sweet home."[9]

So it was that across the South, each county seat became a muster ground, ostensibly dedicated to drilling but more particularly to a celebration of the opportunity God occasionally gave a man to rise and be counted. The Confederate army would eventually become quite good at the grit and the grimness of war, maiming and killing as effectively as any that had come before it. But in the spring of 1861, this transformation lay well in the future. For now men were content to pose as soldiers rather than kill like them, standing more fixedly, more splendidly, before the daguerreotypist than ever they would before the enemy. Decked out in uniforms hand-tailored by their sisters and sweethearts, sporting "epaulets of gorgeousness rarely equaled except in portraits of field-marshals," they stared into the future with that rare certainty—they were, for the moment at least, exactly where they wanted to be. And why not? Marching and maneuvering was, after all, a blithe respite from their books and their professions, and they obeyed the commands of the drillmaster "not so much by reason of its being proper to obey a command," George Eggleston remembered, "as because obedience was in that case necessary to the successful issue of a pretty performance in which [we] were interested." In the evenings, the married men threw themselves into their letters home with all the fire of their early courtship, loving all the more intensely for the fact that their wives were some distance away. "Sitting down to write you a love letter carries me back to old times," James Williams told his wife. "You ought to be delighted at my occasionally leaving you," noted William Pender in a letter to his beloved, "for it shows me more plainly than anything else that you are my wife indeed." Reconfirmed in their patriotism, their manhood, and their marriages, the Penders and Williamses could then sit back to enjoy their cigars, tug at their hipflasks, chat with their fellows, or avail themselves of the camp's many sporting women. The times were festive, death loomed just close enough to make life taste the sweeter, and all indiscretions could be explained away as the wages of patriotism. "Henry and I, after dinner, started off to hunt a good bathing place," Edgeworth Bird informed his wife from camp. "After steering over country, passing a few farm houses, a sick camp, or so, a great many fine views from high hill tops, and sundry well-opened chinkapin bushes, we found ourselves by a clear, cool branch, some 3 miles from camp." Stripping to the "natural man," Edgeworth and Henry plunged into the river and "by dint of soap and violent manipulation . . . became new creatures." Washed of their camp dirt and clad in clean garments, the men picked out a clover patch and sat down to enjoy some teacakes and "a little rye juice from a flask accidentally found in a pocket." They lit up their meerschaums and had begun to drift off to sleep when it began to rain. "Before we dreamed of it, so comfortably were we lolling and puffing away, the rain was upon us," Edgeworth noted. "Through rain and slush we tramped it to camp, forgetful that we had turned out pleasure seeking and thoroughly impressed with the belief that we were two flaming lights on the altar of patriotism, breasting the storm and fatiguing forced march for our country's good." So it was with most would-be Confederates. Forgetful that they had turned out pleasure seeking, they strutted about in their uniforms content in a world that made sense, a world where men did the fighting and women did the worrying.[10]

What they were ill-prepared for, however, was the world of dying they had unwittingly embraced. The political ideology of the average Confederate could be—and often was—boiled down to a simple phrase: death before dishonor. As the war ground on, however, many Confederates discovered a fatal contradiction in this simple sentiment—death, in and of itself, could dishonor a man. How much nobility is there in dying of dysentery? How much grandeur in a gurgling gut shot? As their fellows and friends were shot to pieces next to them, the soldiers left standing were forced to admit, even through their grief, that a dead man's sacrifice was not pretty when viewed up close. In the maimed, mangled, and decomposing patriots left to rot on the field, there was a sort of dishonor to the body that ate into the honor one gained in dying for cause and country. "This fight beggars description," James Edmonston wrote home after Shiloh and the Seven Days Campaign, "I have never before witnessed anything to compare to it and I pray God that I may never witness anything like it again. On the battlefield men are lying in great piles dead [and] mangled horribly in every way [and] decomposition has gone on so far that it is almost if not impossible to go upon the fields." It was not the prospect of dying, per se, that had shaken Edmonston; it was the fact that, heedless of the cause for which a man might fall, death remained intractably corporeal. "A death upon the battle field would lose half of its horrors to me," he noted, "were it not for the fact that I have no very near relatives here who would or could attend to me, and the probability is that I would lie rotting upon the battle field unburied." Even if a soldier could steel himself against the corporeality of death, however, there was the matter of its indiscriminacy, impersonality, and randomness. For many Confederate soldiers, death came suddenly and unceremoniously, catching them unaware, picking them out of a crowd with a sniper's bullet, a rogue shell, a ricochet, or friendly fire. In more than a few cases, a man was killed while chatting amiably with friends who could only stare on in wonder as he fell. Intelligence or decency could not guarantee a man's survival; bravery and mettle could not guarantee a good death. Ordered to drop back behind a tree line, Joshua Callaway and most of the Twenty-Eighth Alabama did as they were told. One member of the company, however, decided to contradict the order, not wishing to be seen fleeing before the enemy. "One of our boys told him if he did not get behind a tree he would be shot," Callaway noted, but he just "smiled & replied, 'I am not afraid of them.' " A minute later a ball struck the man in the privates, putting an end to his defiant gesture and unmanning him rather completely. Needless to say, this was not what most men had in mind when they proclaimed their willingness to pour out their all on the altar of patriotism.[11]

The indignities of random, impersonal, and gory death were not the only ones a soldier had to bear. Smaller, daily indignities added their share of miseries as well. The life of a soldier, William Nugent noted, consisted mostly of "mud, filth, rain; every imaginable species of vermin crawling all around you; little sleep, hard work & fed like a race horse; constantly annoyed with stray bullets, whizzing shells & pattering grape; dirty clothes and not a change along; little or no time to wash your face and hands and very little soap when the opportunity offers." Nugent was even plagued by his government-issue underwear. "I have three pair of drawers purchased from Government," he noted, "which have become all unsewed and hang very loosely about my person. They are about 2 sizes too large and are *perfectly* loose." Edwin Fay had the same reaction to his Confederate undergarments. "If you have an opportunity of sending me you had better send me a pair of drawers," he wrote home. "Those I drew from the Government would not fit any body in the world." These might seem petty concerns for soldiers under fire, but it was a little difficult for a man to screw himself up to an honorable death with his underwear down around his ankles.[12]

If death and soldiering did not look good up close, neither did the army itself. Victorian Americans were not a cynical people; they tended to confuse easily at the notion that moral ends could be achieved by immoral means, and an army was undoubtedly an immoral instrument. Confederate soldiers were horrified, for instance, at the effect their own armies had on the countryside they were supposed to protect. "A country could hardly have a worse curse or plague than to have a large army march through it," Joshua Callaway wrote home. "We completely eat it out as we go. The locusts of Egypt were not more destructive." Other Confederates agreed. "Amanda, I never knew how mean the army could do in a country," noted one Georgia recruit. "I believe our troops are doing as much harm in this country as the Yankees would do.... Where this army goes the people is ruined." Another Louisiana recruit described the damage inflicted by the army on its own supporting populace as "scarcely inferior" to any the poor farmers might fly to. This was particularly troubling given the fact that many of the soldiers had themselves been simple farmers before they volunteered. Then, too, like any bureaucracy, the Confederate army was plagued by imbeciles and their concomitant nonsensities. Generals were often drunken and foolish, politicians were often wrangling and petty, and soldiers were often left to be governed by policies that defied common sense, a subject on which every man considered himself an expert. Edwin Fay described a typical army catch-22: A sick man, he said, could not be discharged unless he was on his deathbed. By then he was too sick to move and would be sent to a hospital where he could not be discharged until he got better. Once better, he would be put back on active duty until he got sick again. Governed by policies like these, soldiers were left to wonder if they would be discharged when they died or if they would still be required to muster for reveille. "I believe that after I am done being a solider," noted James Williams testily, "I'll be a philosopher!" After all, he figured, "I have learned to submit my will and my personal comfort even—to men who are fools."[13]

Civil War armies were composed of amateur soldiers—men who kissed their wives, slung their rifles over their shoulders, and headed out to scare some Yankees. Most of their soldiering experience was limited to spotty militia service and desultory reading in the romances of Sir Walter Scott and the epics of Homer, books whose heroes rose in valorous rage, slaying at will and single-handedly carrying the field. Confederate soldiers were not fools, however. Such festivals of gore might make for compelling reading, but even the schoolboys knew that the Romans provided the best model for an army. In the Roman scheme, each soldier was an interchangeable part of a larger unit; victory was more important than heroism, the army was more important than the man. European tactics had codified the system, but this was the basic philosophy behind Civil War armies. Drilling was about stamina, obedience, discipline, and, within these, the subsuming of the self. The cadences of drum, voice, and march were designed to facilitate this process, to play and replay the same tired rhythm until the individual did not act or react but was simply carried along in the hypnotic motion of the multitude. Thus it was that a collective collapsed into a singularity—*a* regiment, *a* division, *an* army.[14]

Discipline, of course, was not something grown Southern men were accustomed to receiving, especially at the hands of other men. The most convenient model for such a relationship—one man directing the labor of another—was slavery, which undoubtedly rubbed some Confederates the wrong way. "It grinds me to think that I am *compelled* to stay here," Joshua Callaway remarked typically. "I've got a dozen masters, who order me about like a negro." The twenty-first-century sensibility seizes on such vocabulary instantly—an Old Southerner comparing himself to a negro!—but the truth is Southerners compared themselves to slaves all the time. The least little chore—toting a bucket, roofing a house, digging a ditch—was apt to invite the comparison. In fact, given a sufficiency of ill humor and a moment's reflection, every white bucket toter in the South probably indulged the idea that such things were unworthy of his whiteness. As an index to disgruntlement, then, such language is easily overread. Callaway himself followed up the comment about his dozen masters with, "But I talk very plain to them occasionally"—something slaves rarely did with impunity. "To all this [discipline]," he noted in another letter, "[the soldier] soon becomes accustomed and, if naturally ambitious and resolute, he is jolly at all times and under all circumstances." So, if it *was* slavery, it didn't really chafe all that much. An army did not work without discipline—Joshua Callaway understood this; following orders was not submissive and the directives of a superior officer were not *personal* affronts (the sticky point in the South). Discipline, moreover, went both ways—from the top down, certainly, but also from the bottom up. "An officer has to be very careful of his reputation for courage," William Nugent informed his wife, "for upon that in a great measure depends his efficiency & ability to command the soldiers under him. When once the troops lose confidence in the bravery of their Commanders they necessarily have an utter contempt for him, and will not cheerfully obey his orders. I know I would dislike to have a cowardly Captain over me, and I presume my *Subs* are pretty much like me in disposition." So long as they were devoted to a common cause (whatever that might be), most Confederate soldiers were willing to accept army discipline.[15]

But if soldiers accepted the discipline, they resisted the loss of themselves. The notion that men were interchangeable flew directly in the face of Southerners' self-beliefs. Depersoning was supposed to be a Yankee phenomenon, like soulless machines, soulless men, and the cult of interchangeable parts. In the South, a man was supposed to be able to find his own way, claiming for himself all that his decency and his dignity demanded. But to their frustration, soldiers found that the loss of self was an impersonal enemy; try as they might, they could not locate its source in the actions of a man who could be challenged or knocked down. Rather, it seemed a part of the air they breathed or the dirt they slept in, elemental, an inalienable part of the project itself.

Lafayette McLaws's dissolution of self began almost instantly. In June 1861, he boarded a Virginia-bound train with 116 volunteers from Lowndes County, Georgia. Sweltering in the hot cars, the boys removed their shirts, then their shoes, then whatever they chose. The resulting odor, McLaws noted, was "tremendous," and the fact that the boys sang and cheered most of the way only contributed to the all-out assault on his senses. Disoriented by the bellowing yells and the stifling smells, McLaws began to lose himself in the general press of humanity; a tangle of limbs, a stew of sweat, a symphony of patriotic huzzahs, the occupants of the train car were one man, singing with one voice, stinking with one stink. "From that time," McLaws noted, "there was an end of all individuality." From then on men marched and ate and died just the same. The abstracting process was so irresistible that some men even began to forget what they looked like. "I have no opportunity of judging of my appearance," James Williams complained to his wife. He had seen "the reflection of a dirty dust begrimed face once or twice in a glass," but could he even be sure that it was his own face he saw? "You can hardly tell one man from another," Joshua Callaway noted. "Everybody's hair, whiskers, skin and clothes are the same color." Eating, drinking, sitting, sleeping, living, and dying in dirt, men finally just seemed to become dirt, vacant golems with pretty dreams. The whole experience convinced Edwin Fay that Moses had been right—men were composed of the dust to which they would surely return. In the case of soldiers, however, God had added a generous portion of some more substantial element. "I think the 'dust' of which soldiers . . . were made must have been comminuted atoms of iron," Fay told his wife. "No man whose sinews are not of triple steel and whose frame is not of Brass can stand a 3 yrs. Campaign if I judge from my experience." Fay had been physically toughened by the war. He could make daylong marches without food or break, then throw himself down and sleep soundly on the ground. But did the war stop there? If it was making steel of his sinews and brass of his frame, what was it making of his softer organs? Collapsed on the ground, Fay had ample time to consider what he had become. "I am not worthy to live," he wrote his wife helplessly, "I am unfit to die. My heart has become harder than the nether Mill Stone. I have no love for anything save you and my child." But did he not also fear that he had become too hard even for this last love? A metallicized Fay might survive the war, might even find his way home, but of what use was a metal man to a wife of flesh and blood? Was such a man worthy of her affections, her touch, her bed? "If I come home," Fay told his beloved, "I think I shall bivouac for the future in your flower yard." Perhaps that was as close as a golem dared dream of being to something so much softer than himself.[16]

Across the South, the war remade men in its unforgiving image. "War is fast becoming the thing natural, tho' abhorrent to my feelings," noted William Nugent. "I go at it just as I used to go at lawsuits. Still I am not by any manner or means fond of the profession. The idea of being continually employed in the destruction of human life is revolting in the extreme. Necessity imperious and exacting, forces us along and we hurry through the dreadful task apparently unconscious of its demoralizing influences and destructive effects both upon . . . nation[s] & individuals." In distancing themselves from the death they caused and witnessed, men found themselves also at a disconcerting distance from their own decency, and it was a gap they wondered if they should ever close. "[We are] hardly allowed to sigh at the fall of our friends and relatives," noted Joshua Callaway, "and if we do happen to shed a tear secretly, it is soon dried up to make room for one for some one else. We never will have time to contemplate and comprehend the horrors of this war until sweet, delightful peace is restored to us, & we can take a retrospective view."[17]

It has long been maintained that such demoralization was mitigated by the fact that Civil War soldiers volunteered, fought, and died alongside kinsmen and townsmen. A unit was composed not of strangers but of friends and relations who had known each other all their lives. The privates were all schoolmates; their captain was the local grocer, planter, lawyer, or alderman. They had joined up together; they would see it through together; they were comrades. Yet, in reading soldiers' correspondence, one is struck not by the deep familiarity

A crude sketch from a soldier's pocket diary. In panel 1, three soldiers are engaged in a pitched battle: one of them has been shot while trying to fire, and another has crawled behind a tree to die. Panel 2 depicts a tombstone and a fresh grave, presumably the artist's, as the date of death has been left blank. In panel 3 the soldiers have returned from battle and contentedly amuse themselves with a louse race. Forced by circumstance to adapt themselves to vermin and death, soldiers like this artist recognized, at least unconsciously, that their new world consisted of more grimness than glory. Harry St. John Dixon Diary, May 19, 1864, Southern Historical Collection, UNC.

but by the deep dysfunctionality of such all-male ensembles. Camp living was, for the most part, womanless living, which drew its expected share of complaints. "Occasionally a *woman* passes camp and it is three days wonder," noted Edwin Fay. Tally Simpson echoed the sentiment: "There is not a woman that passes camp but there are a hundred men, more or less, huddled together, gazing with all their eyes." When Willie Bryant was finally transferred to a post in a town, he shuddered to think of going back to camp life: "*For 10 months I had not held half an hours conversation with a woman,* not two conversations with the same woman; that alone shows that I must have been unfortunately and unhappily situated." But if the unrelieved womanlessness was a problem so was the unrelieved maleness. Men smelled bad; they drank too much, talked too much, cursed too much, played too hard, couldn't cook, couldn't wash a dish, didn't respect property, and tended to spit on the floor. This was all an accepted, even a celebrated, aspect of male/male society, but when taken to extremes it began to compromise the project itself.[18]

To be sure, plenty of younger men enjoyed the mud fights and wrestling matches that were an inevitable part of camp life. But for the vast majority, some combination of age, natural reserve, and social standing made such pastimes seem a trifle undignified. Men kept each other at a distance; that was the point—the distance was the measure of the other man's respect, and in consequence the measure of one's own self-respect. Normally, of course, women were available to fill in these emotional distances and help mediate men's relations with each other. But in a womanless camp, all this distant self-respecting made for a very lonely life. "In contact with men I am philosophic, to a certain extent stoical and self possessed," William Nugent wrote his wife Nellie, "with you I am swayed by an impulsive affection, and the simple story of love." None of this is to say that men were never impulsive or affectionate with each other, but most preferred not to do so for prolonged periods. "I would be the gladdest person in the world to see you all and talk with you a while," Benjamin Jackson wrote his wife, Martha, "for I see nobody here but men and they appear to be very sorry company for me."[19]

Isolated within themselves, touchy and standoffish, men stewed in their self-imposed distances, deploring from afar their touchy and

standoffish comrades. These men were sharing, as Oliver Wendell
Holmes would later put it, "the incommunicable experience of war,"
an experience most of them would remember and celebrate the rest
of their lives. But while they were sharing it, they were not much
inclined to share with each other; however mammoth the experience
that bound them up together, each man felt dependent on himself
alone. "In these times the best motto is take care of Number One,"
argued John Fort. "Generosity has ceased to be a virtue, for you can
lend or give anything away and have nothing yourself." "I have never
seen so selfish a place as a camp," Edwin Fay reluctantly agreed. "No
one seems to care much for any one else." Some of this selfishness,
certainly, originated in the nature of war itself. So much misery and
deprivation, indignity and death, throws each man back on himself
alone, severing the ties that bind him both to individual men and to
humanity generally. Isolation becomes the soul's best defense against
the corrupting influences of the world around it. "There is so little of
that human nature which makes the whole world kin, nowadays,"
William Nugent explained, "that we cannot rely upon any one with
certainty. The distress everywhere prevailing ... [has] thrown every
individual upon his own resources for a support and have had the
effect to isolate, it seems, every human being." Other men, though,
were less willing to excuse such selfishness as a product of the extreme
circumstances of war. They believed they discerned within it a familiar pattern, a pattern that had dogged them in their professions
and in their schools, a pattern that lurked not in war or in humanity
generally, but in the hearts of men specifically. "I tell you, it is awful
to think of the wickedness and corruption attending an army," noted
William Dickey. "I sometimes think there is not enough goodness to
save us from being destroyed. I believe if the country is ever saved,
it will be from the many prayers of the good women of our country.
Don't understand me to say there is no good men. But there is comparatively speaking, so few."[20]

The remedy for all of the common consequences of war—the brutality of death, the depersoning of soldiers, the selfishness of men—
was simple: a man needed to find his way back to his sweetheart, to
the decency she symbolized and the succor she provided. At the be-

ginning of the war, each man had planted his patriotism in the sturdier soil of his love of woman. It was for her that he was fighting; it was for her that he would suffer and die. Let the men spit and the politicians wrangle; let the generals drink while the soldiers fought— it was all endurable while she could make sense of it. Rejecting a subordinate's request to visit his dying spouse, Stonewall Jackson famously put it to the anxious officer that a man's devotion to his country was more important than his devotion to his wife. From all indications, Jackson was one of the few Confederates who felt this way. "A man's family is dearer to him than anything in the world," noted Edwin Fay, "at least mine is & 40 Confederacies may go to the devil if I am to be kept away from all I hold dear during the rest of my life." William Nugent concurred: "May the remembrance that I have so gentle and noble a creature for my life companion," noted Nugent, "ever buoy me up amid the many trials through which I am called to pass and nerve my arm in the dread hour of a battle. Dear is my country to me, yet dearer far is [the] treasure [I have] in [my] little woman." Indeed, for most Confederate soldiers choosing between wife and country was impossible, ridiculous. Their woman was their country and their cause, the reason for which they fought and killed. Choosing between them was like choosing between female virtue and manly honor—silly on the face of it because they were mutually reinforcing. "What would poor man do," asked Walter Taylor, "what would he be worth but for the softening, purifying, all powerful influence of his most precious gift, his highest treasure—woman!?" Taylor worked as an adjutant on General Lee's staff, and his duties could be petty, pesky, and often beneath him. But Bettie made them all sufferable, gave them a larger, more tangible purpose that he could grasp and hold on to. "Whenever I am harassed by an accumulation of miserable paper calling for my attention," he wrote his sweetheart, "or annoyed by any imaginary unreasonableness or ill temper on the part of my Chief, how much it adds to my patience and stimulates me to greater efforts to perform my duty manfully with a single eye to the good of our cause, when I imagine your face looking over my shoulder with its encouraging smile and an approving look in those dark fathomless eyes, so pure, so irresistible in their expression? Ah!

My good angel, it is a sweet and yet a sad reflection to me, to think of the unlimited control exercised over my whole life, my every act, by my intense desire to win and be worthy of you."[21]

In woman, then, a man could rejuvenate himself and his cause, finding in his love of her the grounds for his love of country. The key to this process of romantic renewal was letter writing. In the exchange of letters between swain and sweetheart, a man was given a chance to rekindle his enthusiasm—for love, for life, for dying in defense of them both. In writing to his beloved, a man poured out his heart, damning those who deserved damning, rewarding those who deserved rewarding, remembering, as the words and phrases tumbled onto the page, that there was individuality and dignity within him yet, and that there was at home something to live for, fight for. Composing a letter, however, was no mean feat. Pens were as apt to cut the paper as to ink it. Ink was as apt to smear or trail off invisibly as to render a smooth stroke. In winter, pens froze to hands so numb they could barely be forced into operation. "It is cold enough this morning to freeze the hair off a cast Iron dog," one soldier remarked acerbically, "my ink is ice and fingers here in the open are not far short of it." In summer soldiers had the opposite problem—papers were soaked with sweat and pens were slippery as men baked their brains in stifling tents or browned their skins under a merciless sun. "The weather, Lizzy," noted a member of the Twenty-First Alabama, "demands a 'mere-mention' to-day, as having attained [a] degree ... compatible with [the] existence [of no] one but a Salamander or the Fire King." Rain and snow, of course, added their own miseries, particularly for those in leaky or nonexistent tents.[22]

Regardless of shortfalls and heedless of inconveniences, however, soldiers and their sweethearts persisted in writing—on anything, with anything. Men who had foresworn scavenging among the Yankee dead made an exception for writing materials. Others crushed strawberries for ink and sharpened sticks for pens. One soldier promised his wife that if they had to take pencils to corn shucks they would always write to each other. "O you have no idea how it helps me to get a letter from you," Joshua Callaway wrote his wife. "Really it is all my solace." George Peddy felt the same way: "You cannot tell how well I like to read [your letters]," he told his beloved Zerlina.

"The lines you write look like they are written with gold & the words seem to mean volumes to me." Letters were all-important; nothing took precedence. One soldier told his wife to let their farm go to seed rather than shorten her letters: "Letters are to be attended to before work," he commanded. "Work can be put off." Another soldier consumed a letter rather than his dinner, though he admitted he was half starved. "Although I was very hungry and had eaten but one mouthful," he wrote his wife, "I rushed to a smouldering oak fire to devour the contents of the long looked for epistle." One man even went so far as to claim that if he received a letter *during battle*, he would not hesitate to stop, drop, and read. It did not particularly matter what the letter said. The letter was important even as a thing. It had mass, though little, dimension, though unimpressive, and substance, though frail; but, most important to the soldier, it had a point of origin—a world away. This frail little something came from somewhere else, proving thereby the existence of a place beyond the trenches and the minié balls, a place delicate and undefiled, capable still of making such wonderful things out of paper.[23]

But the attempt to find one's way home by mail was fraught with problems beyond material shortages and inconveniences. The Confederate mail service was slow and unreliable, and, particularly late in the war, a man might go a month without hearing from anyone. In the long stretches between letters, Tally Simpson remembered, a man's mind could go dormant, as if in some kind of hibernation. "Inactivity, indolence, and various other things," he wrote home, "have very nearly reduced me to the lamentable state of a nontalkative Quaker. I lay my back upon my pole bed, lost to every thing around me like a snake in winter time, and am only aroused from my stupor by a call to dinner (if a few biscuits & a little rank bacon gravy can be called dinner) or the tap of the drum to roll call. But I must confess that the reception of a letter from old P [his hometown] moves my spirit, and Quaker-like I must up and speak for myself." Then, too, the war had a way of disrupting the letter-writing process, and with it the metaphysical journey home. Seated in his tent, Winston Stephens was just beginning a letter to his young bride when he became aware of a man at the door. "Through courtesy I invited him [in]," Winston noted, but "he came in with his pipe in mouth and then Gabe Priest came among and in he walked with his pipe in his mouth." Pretty soon it seemed to Winston as if the men had chosen his tent for some kind of smoke-off, making it impossible for him to lose himself in a letter to his beloved. Edgeworth Bird was also deeply offended at the intrusions of men upon his epistolary reveries. "As lovely a Sabbath day beams upon us this morning, my darling, as is ever the good fortune of mortals to witness. It is bright, cool, and bracing. Of late, we've had fine rains, there is no dust and the fields are putting on a fresh suit of velvet green." One can almost picture Edgeworth, settling into this pastoral rhythm, preparing himself for a long, letter-sponsored daydream of home. His own words begin to lift him, transport him to some spring meadow near his house in Hancock County, itself resplendent in a suit of velvet green. He puts his back against a familiar tree . . . he laces his fingers behind his head . . . and soon . . . he is drifting . . . drifting . . . And then, just like the man in the meadow, Edgeworth is suddenly startled from his rev- erie—the wind has shifted over the meadow, bringing with it the telltale odor of some nearby cow pasture. "The strong passions of men sweep like a desolating sirocco over all this . . . beauty," he wrote his wife peevishly, "and there is no pleasure, no peace." For James Wil- liams, it was not pipe smoke or a "desolating sirocco" that cramped his epistolary pleasure but the constant teasing at the hands of his "comrades." "They make so much fun of me for writing so often to you," he wrote his wife, "that I sometimes do it almost on the sly: taking time when Col. Cayce is absent, or spreading out some report before me, that I might appear to be copying."[24]

Even if time and materials could be found, a man needed someone to write to. Letters to and from fathers and mothers, sisters and broth- ers were important, but it was the exchanges with a sweetheart that fired a man's self-belief. His love for her was the foundation on which he could build and rebuild his love of country; his all-consuming belief in her provided the sacred space in which he could surrender and reclaim his soul, remembering himself and the reasons for which he fought. But what could a man do if he had no sweetheart? How could he fire his patriotism and steady his arm if he had no woman to anchor and make meaningful his many sacrifices? The case of John Floyd King (known by his middle name) and Lin Caperton illustrates the lengths to which a man would go to find a female focus for his war effort. Floyd met Lin while attending school in Virginia. Their courtship was perfectly typical up to a point, progressing easily along a trajectory that had launched many a successful Victorian marriage. Floyd requested permission from Lin's father to write to her, didn't exactly get it, but wrote her anyway; they exchanged photographs; and finally Floyd confessed his love for her in the parlor of the Caperton's Elmswood plantation. The problem, though, was that Lin was quite young, had grown to know Floyd as a family friend, was somewhat confused when his affections turned so grave, and would probably have agreed with her father when he noted that she was too young even to know her own head aright.[25]

It was at this point, while Lin did not know her own head aright, that Floyd was swept into the army. There Lin became the center of his world. "The severities of the service softened by your influence are by no means unpleasant now," he wrote in one of his weekly letters, "and my duties no matter how irksome, when I think of you pass off as lightly as possible." "You and you alone engage my thoughts and the tenderest of my heart's joys," he noted in another. "Of you and you only . . . can I think, and dream, and live." Lin's letters to Floyd were more cautious, tepid. She could not return his love, she said, but she did appreciate it. "I know myself too well not at least to respect the love of your very generous heart," she told him. Even while respecting his heart, however, she sought to deflate it a little, as if it was some beautiful balloon, risen to dizzying heights on nothing but air. "'Tis your own goodness . . . that can ascribe to me qualities which I regret sadly not to possess," she informed him, "but I will say nothing more upon this subject tho' I do feel so deeply."[26]

Lin's demure responses only complicated an already confusing situation for Floyd. Floyd claimed that his affection for Lin was perfectly "celestial." Undoubtedly it was. But his missives also contain some rather earthy overtones. "I shudder! lest my love, in the innocence of its nudity, may press too much upon you," he wrote Lin in one letter. "I cannot resist making [confessions of love] whenever I commence writing you," he told her in another. "My pent-up emotions, always pressing to be relieved, rush to my pen, the moment I give them the slightest opportunity." Floyd was not aware of these overtones, of course. He would himself have been rather shocked at the nudity rushing in on his celestial Lin. His was a torrential prose style; the words came in an ecstatic surge, undisciplined and unself-conscious. What was this thing that had seized him? He seemed powerless to stop it, powerless to explain it. Even when he tried, he seemed only able to pair his own inconsistencies with the word *yet.* "My heart is so full I do not know what to say, yet I am urged by a resistless desire to express myself." "How tiresome my confessions must be to you! ... I feel it, yet I cannot resist." "I cannot see why I had any hope of your returning my affections and yet I would think you cruel if you did not." "I would do all, yet I dare not know what to do to win your heart. Can you not tell me?" But Lin could not tell him. There was after all nothing to tell. She did not love him. And yet ... How could this be? She had become everything to Floyd. "Through vicissitudes and through grief," he wrote her, "through the din of cities and through the pleasures of home; through the changes of traveling by land and by sea; through the duties of garrisons and the long fatigue of marches; through the rain and cold of the midnight watch, through the camp and through disease, and through death I have ever loved you constantly, and with my whole heart!" The Confederacy could not warm him in the snow; slavery could not give him a reason to march; honor could not explain disease or death. Lin explained the war to Floyd; she made sense of it. He was fighting for her. "My devotion to you is based upon my love of country," he confessed, "for were it to be conquered, and disgraced, with what power, or with what conscience could I come forward to claim your hand? A degraded soldier I would seek obscurity in some distant hemisphere, never forgetting you, and, ever holding you dearest in my heart, I should live in the unhappy knowledge that you and my country had been taken from me by the force of arms alone." Lin sustained Floyd's war effort, through rain and snow, disease and death, until finally—after enough rain and snow, disease and death—she simply became his war effort.[27]

And it was at this point that Lin's head righted itself, and she requested that Floyd not correspond with her anymore. Floyd was incredulous, furious—even though he had on occasion described his love for her as unrequited. "Dearest Miss Lin, my beloved, what can you mean? Have you raised me to Heaven merely to cast me out again?... Surely, surely you love me still. Oh!, I am too embittered to speak, yet I must write on." Floyd begged her to reconsider, or to at least postpone her decision. He needed from her only a shred to hope on, but he needed that shred. "Tomorrow, our Generals say we will have a battle here," he noted, shameless now. "What do you think will be my feelings when riding down the lines of action to be conscious that I have been discarded and disgraced for no reason by the one I love & whose honor I am fighting for?... Should some considerate ball find my heart, remember thro' life how I have loved you." But did he love her? Certainly he loved the opportunity she gave him to love himself, to know himself, to feel himself. And he loved the meaning she gave the war. But somewhere within his torrential prose lurked the truth. "At times when I have shut out all others save yourself from my mind," Floyd wrote his beloved, "I wonder whether I am laboring under a mental aberration or whether my dreams are real." Floyd did not want Lin; he wanted a dream; he wanted the version of her that helped him through the snow. What's more, he expected her to give it to him. "I desire only to understand you," Floyd lied, "yet I would rather remain in darkness than to be enlightened as to any conclusion of yours that would be disastrous to myself!! You see selfishness rules me still. I want you to tell me *all*, yet only that which is to render me happy! Oh, Miss Lin, what would life be without you? Surely it would be a day without a sun."[28]

Floyd King sustained himself on a romance he in part invented. Tally Simpson, a soldier in the Third South Carolina Volunteers, sustained himself on a romance he *wholly* invented. Tally had been excited early in the war by the attentions paid him by women, attentions that formed no little part of his enthusiasm for the war itself. "Ladies at little stations, and even in towns and cities," he wrote his sister of his trip to Richmond, "go up to the soldiers, any and every one, and converse with them as familiarly as old friends." Shortly thereafter, however, Tally's regiment settled into camp and suddenly there were no women at all, at least no available or respectable ones. His sense of womanlessness was further aggravated in 1862 when his brother and fellow volunteer Dick Simpson married and was discharged from the army due to ill health. Now trudging through the war alone, Tally became all the more envious of the married men around him, but he was himself without prospects, and camp was no place to look for a wife. "I am entirely without a gal," he lamented. "My future is a blank, but if my life be spared and I reach home safely after peace has been declared, that blank shall be filled if there is any gal in all this big world fool enough to say y-e-s." Tally spent some time fantasizing about this as yet faceless fool, but he needed some more fixed point on which to focus his imagination. Rained on and shot at did not mean much without a woman, and if Tally died before he found one, for what, for whom, would his life have been sacrificed?[29]

Finally, it was Tally's aunt who dispelled his ennui, writing richly embroidered missives about a young woman she felt would be perfect for him if ever they met. Tally was beside himself. "Your description of Miss Fannie is truly charming," he wrote his aunt gratefully, "and my feelings have already been enlisted in her favor. Tho you say it is impossible for me as any young man to fall in love with a girl without seeing her first ... I place implicit confidence in what you say and [your letters] have created curious as well as pleasant feelings in my heart." After a few more of his aunt's letters, Tally owned that he had completely fallen for Fannie, a woman he had never met and never corresponded with, a woman who quite possibly didn't know his name and quite definitely didn't know the depths of his feelings for her. Tally's sisters apprised him of the impropriety of loving a woman to whom he had not been introduced and questioned whether he could know her character well enough to consider bringing her into the family. None of this mattered to Tally. "I picked up a pamphlet some time ago and found a portrait of a most magnificent looking lady," he wrote a cousin, "[and] I showed it to Harry, and he declared that it looked exactly like Miss F. I looked at it hard and studied it well. Then I cut it out and put it carefully away to look at it every now and then for my own gratification. It is before me now, and I imagine I see Miss F in all her glory." Tally did not need an actual woman; all her quirks and faults might even have gotten in the way. What he needed was a focal point on which to specify his love for women generally—and through them his love for life. Miss Fannie suited this purpose admirably. Precisely because he did not know her, she became Everywoman, a divine amalgam of woman's best traits. Yet precisely because she did exist, out there, somewhere, drawing her beautiful breath from a place he longed to be, she helped to anchor his dreams of outliving the war. In flying to her, he flew home, a way he could not find so easily without her. Miss Fannie was Tally's life wish, drawing *its* breath from that place beyond the camps and the killing. And *that* was a place worth defending. "Tis woman's influence that chastens the orator's eloquence," noted Tally, warming to his favorite subject, "that increases and exalts the statesman's patriotism and compels him to exert his great intellectual powers for the promotion of the nation's welfare. Tis her influence that nerves the arm and emboldens the heart of the warrior and causes him to give full utterance to the noble expression, 'Dulce et decorum est pro patria mori,' [It is sweet and seemly to die for one's country]."[30]

Southern soldiers began the war with a sense of simple synonymity between their love of woman and their love of country. They were encouraged in this by period propaganda, but it was a conflation they made easily, routinely, well before the war. As this study has suggested, antebellum men were accustomed to seeing women as an essential part of the masculine enterprise; women were witnesses to male becoming, sponsors who allowed a man to feel that his acts of self-love were acts of self-sacrifice, thus bolstering his self-belief. The Civil War amplified these basic dynamics, borrowing against the enormity of death to transform Love, Sacrifice, and Belief from the merest platitudes into the constituting elements of a man's life. The distracting mundanities of the antebellum period melted away and masculinity's twin drives—a love to fill the heart and a bid to live forever— were renewed, reenergized, and felt, perhaps for the first time, in all their purity and power.

A Confederate's patriotism, then, was planted in sturdy soil; his love of country was anchored in his love of woman, which was his love of self in part. Even early in the war, this cozy arrangement proved susceptible to certain pressures. Instead of facing Death, Confederates faced Inconvenience, Unpleasantness, and Discomfort,

adversaries hardly more appropriate as a test of manhood than the
ones they had faced in their prewar professions. As important, their
comrades fortified their *will* to die (in maddened charges on en-
trenched enemies) but could not give them a *reason* to die. Only a
woman could do this. To be sure, men understood themselves to be
dying for some ideology or other, and so they were. But the meaning
of that sacrifice, their emotional experience of it, was, like all men's
sacrifices, only possible because a woman bore it witness. So long as
a man could see himself through the idealized eyes of a woman, he
would continue to fight. If ever he could not, romance and patriotism,
love of woman and love of country, might become disaggregated, and
then he would be forced to choose between them.

CHAPTER 6

LOOKING HOMEWARD

And here at length is somewhat of revenge,
For men's most golden dreams of pride and power,
Are vain as any woman's dream of love;
Both end in weary brow, and withered heart,
And the grave closes over those whose hopes
Have lain there long before.*

The South began the war confidently, believing the Yankees would fight a war of aggression with only their flawed isms to steady their arms. The Confederates would wage a defensive war for their fields and firesides. As the Yankees began to occupy those fields and warm themselves before those fires, however, this defensive posture began to feel very vulnerable to many Confederates. Their sisters, mothers, and sweethearts were being occupied, after all, the people in whom they had vouchsafed the best of themselves and for whom (they were convinced) they were fighting in the first place. In the long stretches between battles, men helplessly far from home had all the time in the world to imagine the worst. "I wish you to keep [a] pistol loaded and capped," Edwin Fay instructed his wife precisely, "and if the Yankees come to Minden to wear it on your person, never be without it and the first one that dares insult you blow his brains out. This you must do or you are not the woman I married." Winston Stephens had the same concerns for his beloved Tivie: "One thing I do hope and ask of you don't let [the Yankees] get near enough to

---

* Selma Diary, December 16, 1835, in Michael O'Brien, *An Evening When Alone*, 129.

In *Tracks of the Armies* (1863), Adalbert Volck drew on the fear, common among Southern soldiers, that Yankees intended to ruin farms and families. Here a Confederate soldier is depicted returning to his tumbled-down house. His wife lies dead amid the rubble, nude to the waist and clutching some strands of hair, presumably those of her rapist and murderer. Among the ruins are the carcasses of a dog and a mouse, underlining Volck's (far-fetched) point that the Yankees systematically slaughtered everything in their path. Etching, ⅝ x 7½ in. Louis A. Warren Lincoln Library and Museum.

insult you—for my sake go from home back in the Country when they come. I had rather lose every thing in this world than to have you in their power."[1]

If the image of Yankees possessing their wives was disturbing, so too was the almost inexpressible fear that their wives might want to be possessed. "Already," remarked William Nugent, "there have occurred instances of nice young girls marrying Yankee officers ... and in N.E. Miss. there are numberous cases [too] of illegitimacy among the wives ... of soldiers who have been gallantly fighting in Virginia

for two years." Illegitimacy is a concern in any war. Nothing is more
harrowing to the soldier than to discover that while he is fighting to
protect his wife's virtue another man has taken her to bed. But the
fear that the *enemy* might be sleeping with her has a psychological
dimension all its own. Certainly the sense of betrayal is more acute.
The wife has committed not merely adultery but, in giving aid and
succor to the enemy, she has committed the marital equivalent of
treason. But is there not also, buried deep in the self-doubting psyche
of the soldier, a horrible fear that the enemy better deserves his wife's
bed? Particularly for those soldiers whose homes have been occupied
or are threatened with occupation, an important psychological battle
has already been lost, no matter the outcome of the war. Each man
has failed in his most basic function—protecting his family. Even if
his house still stands and his wife is safely lodged with a relative, he
experiences a kind of helplessness he has probably never known.
Forced by circumstance to watch from afar as his home is disgraced,
he feels a kind of self-loathing—did he really do his all to ensure
that his wife was safe?—and in his self-loathing he may lead a Yankee to his wife's bed and force himself to watch this disgrace as well.
"I often think what would become of you and Rosa if I should get
killed," Winston Stephens wrote his wife, "for you would have nothing left you for a support as the Yankees would take your negroes
from you leaving you nothing but a small peace of land in Marion
and perhaps they would confiscate that. Then I think perhaps your
Father might live through it and would perhaps take care of you, but
then another thought pops in my brain and that is that you might
be taken north and in a few years marry some Yankee that had been
instrumental in destroying me! I want you to promise that no matter
what befalls me that you will never marry a yankee, no matter what
his calling or position." What is Stephens talking about? Why does
he torture himself with this? Surely he knows that his wife wouldn't
let a Yankee in the door, much less into her bed. And yet he can't
seem to help it. The idea just, as he put it, popped into his brain.
And this, of course, is Winston Stephens's death wish. For being unworthy of his wife and manhood, this is how he must pay—dying
with the knowledge that his wife, his life, his all, will take a Yankee
lover.[2]

The decision to join the Confederate army, it has been suggested, was like a conversion experience—soldiers had only to give their assent, and they were reborn, re-Christened as defenders of the Confederate faith. Beginning in 1864, Confederate males began en masse to experience a sort of unconversion experience—they registered their varied dissents and reclaimed the project that was themselves from the project that was the Confederacy. As in their conversions, men bound women up in their unconversions, using them to explain to themselves why they wanted no longer to be soldiers.

This process was highly individual, of course. The next two biographical sketches give a sense of the compelling variety in men's war experiences—and a sense of the continuity within those experiences. Both Nathaniel Dawson and Theodorick Montfort installed women at the center of their war efforts. Both wrote, imagined, and dreamed of home to have their faith restored in the cause for which they were prepared to give their lives. And both began to doubt that cause when it interposed itself between them and their sweethearts.

Nathaniel Dawson: The Unstudied Language of the Heart

The man and the hour were officially met at 1:00 P.M. on February 18, 1861, when Jefferson Davis turned his back on the Union (literally) and inaugurated a new country. Thousands of spectators thronged the state capitol building in Montgomery, straining to catch a glimpse of a president they had never voted for. In even tones and measured phrases, Davis made clear that the Confederacy intended a peaceful removal from the Union; he made more clear, however, that any resistance to that removal would be met with force of arms. Though not a moving or particularly eloquent address, it had one unequivocal virtue—its meaning was lost on no one. "A Government is formed for the South," noted one observer, "and no idea of reconstruction is entertained." The inaugural exercises complete, men and women returned to their homes and hotels to prepare themselves for the Confederacy's first gala event, a levee to be held in Davis's honor at Estelle Hall. Tiffany & Company of New York had shipped $30,000 worth of jewelry to Montgomery in the days preceding the levee; Confederate belles would celebrate their independence in Federal

chokers and chains. By dusk, "every house, little and big, was illu-
minated from the Capitol to the Exchange," and rockets and bengal
lights were being thrown steadily across the width of the street. The
receiving line formed at about eight o'clock and quickly bunched up
behind the voluminous skirts of the carefully coifed ladies. In the
press of bodies, the temperature in the hall rose steadily toward the
unbearable, and by ten o'clock the crowds began to disperse, the weary
for their beds, the stalwart for a dance being organized at nearby
Concert Hall. There the festivities continued until dawn, closing what
one observer called "the greatest day in the annals of Montgomery."
It is possible that many new romances were inaugurated in this heady
moment of Confederate becoming. History records only one, that of
Elodie Todd and Nathaniel Dawson.[5]

Born in Charleston on February 14, 1829, Nathaniel Henry Rhodes
Dawson was a quiet and sensitive youth. While his sister resembled
their father—outgoing and lively—Dawson was bookish and reclu-
sive, apt to miss meals while lying out in the gardens that surrounded
his family's mansion. There, he would later remember, he spent many
of the happiest hours of his childhood, playing in the woods or walking with his "loved mother . . . look[ing] up into her face as she re-
counted the deeds of Robin Hood and his men." Introspective by
nature, Dawson developed an early affection for "domestic scenes"
that did not leave him when he learned to conceal it behind a "reserved exterior." In 1842, the family relocated to Carlowville, a Dallas
County, Alabama, outpost for Charleston bluebloods. Dawson attended
local schools until he was old enough to be sent to St. Joseph's College
in Mobile. He returned home in 1848 to study law under his father,
but the sickly old man died just before Christmas, and Dawson was
forced to move to Cahaba to study with George R. Evans. He was
admitted to the state bar in 1851 at about the time his beloved mother
died.[4]

In 1852, he married Anne Mathews, the daughter of a Selma cotton
mill owner. The union produced only one child, Lizzie, before Anne
died in October 1854. To forget his grief, Dawson threw himself into

politics, losing a close race as a "Know-Nothing" and subsequently stumping for the Democratic party. In 1857, he married his second wife, Mary Tarver, who gave birth to a daughter of the same name in 1858. By that year, Dawson had become a prominent Selmian; his name and his inheritance from his father, as well as his legal practice and his investments with his father-in-law, provided him a firm foundation in the planter class. His property included fifty-one slaves and 2,129 acres outside the town and a house and law office within it; his net worth was $133,984. With this wealth and social standing came political opportunities. In 1860, Dawson was selected to attend the Democratic convention in Charleston and was with William Yancey when the Alabama delegation stormed out in protest of the Douglas nomination. Waiting for him at his hotel was a note urging him to return to Selma. His second wife was dying, and he made it home in time to say good-bye. By the time Lincoln was elected, Nathaniel Dawson was thirty-one; he had lost both parents and two wives in a little over a decade. The truth, though, was that he was getting better at grieving. Each time he lost a loved one he tightened his grip on his Episcopal faith and added an anniversary to his sacred calendar. "Tho the reflections caused by the yearly return [of these dates] are melancholy," he noted, "I love to dwell on them. They are mile posts on the road which reminds us of our progress on the journey of life." Death, as he had come to understand, was simply part of the process by which God "wean[s] us from this world."[5]

In early April 1861, Jefferson Davis called for three thousand volunteers from the state of Alabama to be organized and mustered into the Confederate army. Dawson had been leading a small group of men in military drills for a month and asked them if they wished to offer their services. The vote was taken "without a dissenting voice," and the men hastily prepared their kits. "Tho' the step is one that will call for some sacrifices," Dawson wrote a friend, "I hope it will give me that entire, constant employment that seems so much to relieve the troubles of this life." Still grieving Mary's loss, Nathaniel had little to draw him to Selma, and the army offered an escape. "My own home is so dark & desolate," he noted, "that I will hardly miss its absence and I can expect no trials that can equal those of the past

year. I would fly from them if I could." Selma did have one attraction
for Dawson, however—one that had been growing on him steadily.[6]

Nathaniel Dawson first caught sight of Elodie Todd in the fall of
1858 on the streets of Selma; she was peering in the window of Mr.
Clark's bookstore and Dawson sized her up in a brisk walk by. Her
bouncing black curls, then the essence of female fashion, made a
particularly strong impression on him and he made the customarily
discreet inquiries as to her identity. Elodie, he learned, was the sister
of Martha Todd, now Martha White, a Selmian and an acquaintance
of Dawson's. Their brother-in-law, of course, was Abraham Lincoln,
the Republican making a name for himself in the North but not yet
so famous that Elodie's visit to Selma would receive much coverage
in the press. When she returned in November 1860, however, things
were different. Elodie was now a sister-in-law of the president of the
United States and a walking propaganda coup for the Confederacy.
At the inaugural reception in Montgomery, Martha and Elodie were
the cynosure of the affair and were repeatedly toasted for their patriotism. It was during that reception, Dawson would later recall, that
"I made up my mind to endeavor to make the star mine in whose
beams I had wandered." When they returned to Selma, Dawson began
his courtship in earnest. Under the pretense of lending books or sending flowers, he attached short notes that gradually revealed his feelings. By early April, just as he was preparing to leave for the Confederate army, he had become determined, and on April 19, he asked
Elodie for her hand. Dawson understood that some might question
the move, coming so soon after his second wife's death, but he claimed
that he could no longer bear "the want of that sympathy & friendship
which a wife only can give." Elodie had not anticipated the question
and knew her mother would be displeased. "Ever since I can remember," she noted, "I have been looked upon and called the 'old maid'
of the family and Mother seemed to think I was to be depended on
to take care of her when all the rest of her *handsomer daughters* had
left her." Elodie, though, had her own ideas. They may "think I am
committing a sin to give a thought to any other than the arrangements they have made for me," she contended, "but as this is the age
when Secession, Freedom, and rights are asserted, I am claiming

mine." So Elodie said yes and Dawson sped off with his Magnolia
Cadets, now part of the Fourth Alabama Infantry Regiment, to his
new post just outside of Washington and his soon-to-be brother-in-
law.[7]

Elodie Breck Todd was born on April Fool's Day 1841, a fact that she
felt gave her a special license to commit mischief. She was a confident
young woman, and, while not a staggering beauty, was easygoing
about her appearance. "I am just as they say in K[entucky]," she
noted, "the ugliest of my Mother's handsome daughters and simply
plain Dee Todd. I am used to being called so and I do not feel it at
all." She had a natural wiliness that made her mature for her age
and a wit that edged toward the sarcastic. Her mother had "always
predicted" that her "temper and tongue would get [her] into trouble,"
but Elodie was prepared to "stand up to whatever it utters." She was,
above all, she told her friends, a Todd, a member of a family "noted
for [its] determination or as *malicious people* would say, *obstinacy*."
Her worst trait, then, was one she would never apologize for, an
unforgiving heart that once angered could "never again be reconciled
to the offender altho' that person may have been my dearest friend."
Fierce in her hating, she could be fierce in her loving as well, particularly when it came to her family or her Kentucky roots.[8]

Beginning in the spring of 1861, it often came to both. The Todds
were arguably the most bitterly divided family of the war; in their
sprawling saga the fratricidal conflict seems less tragic or glorious than
wrenching and bizarre. "Surely there is no other family in the land
placed in the exact situation of ours," Elodie noted, "and I hope will
never be [another] so unfortunate as to be surrounded by trials so
numerous." Elodie's father, Robert Todd, married his first wife, Eliza
Parker, in 1812. Eliza bore seven children before her death in 1825—
including the future Mrs. Lincoln. After Eliza's death, Robert Todd
remained a widower for a scandalously short six months before proposing to Elizabeth "Betsey" Humphries. Betsey bore him nine children before he succumbed to the cholera epidemic of 1849—of whom
Elodie was the second youngest.[9]

Despite a fundamental disagreement over the worth of Betsey Humphries as a mother, the Parker Todds and Humphries Todds shared a father and, for the most part, fond recollections of each other as children. When their father died, the three male Humphries Todds—Samuel, David, and Alexander—moved to New Orleans, where a rich uncle owned a sugar plantation. Each joined the Confederate army; each was killed in its service. Samuel was shot in the temple by a sharpshooter's bullet while leading a charge at Shiloh. David took up a command at a Richmond prison camp where he was scandalized by reports of torture and desecration; he died from wounds sustained at the battle of Vicksburg. Little Aleck, remembered fondly by all family members for his red-headed innocence, was killed during a skirmish outside Baton Rouge. Though notoriously unsympathetic to her Confederate relatives, Mary Lincoln was brought to tears by Alexander's death. "Oh little Aleck," she cried on hearing the news, "why had you to die?" Still more bizarre, Elodie's sister and Mary's half sister Emile married a West Point graduate, Benjamin Helm, to whom Lincoln offered the position of paymaster of the U.S. Army. Helm's conscience pulled him southward, however, where he rose to the rank of brigadier general before being killed at Chickamauga. Of the fourteen children of Robert Todd who survived to adulthood, five were Unionists, nine were Confederates, five were either casualties of war or had husbands who were, if we count Lincoln in that number.[10]

In 1861, of course, most of these grim developments awaited the future. For both Elodie Todd and Mary Todd Lincoln, however, there was even at the war's outset a sense of foreboding, of pressing sadness, for their family's condition. They would each deny it, often fiercely; they would each support their respective sections, often fiercely. But the steady rhythm of their family's tragedy hammered at them remorselessly, often becoming more than they could deny or bear. Elodie was only a year old when her half sister married Abraham Lincoln, and Mary did not return to Lexington often. Still, Mary had a maternal instinct toward her younger half sisters, perhaps because she never had a daughter of her own. Emilie and Elodie were particular favorites in this regard; vivacious and talkative, they seem to have lightened Mary's often brooding spirit. While in fundamental disagreement on political questions, Elodie and Mary were placed in

oddly similar circumstances by the war. For the first month, Elodie's
fiancé and Mary's husband slept twenty miles from each other, the
Potomac River rolling gently between them. The Confederate flag
that so galled Lincoln by its proximity to Washington flew over Dawson's division, and it is not impossible that the president spied his
would-be brother-in-law in his telescope while surveying enemy
positions.

Both Elodie and Mary were unwavering in their loyalty to their
respective sections, yet both faced considerable suspicion for their ties
to the enemy. Much has been written of how the Washington press
and public hounded Mary Lincoln for her Confederate connections.
Elodie was similarly mistrusted in Selma. "The inhabitants of this
little town think because Kentucky is *not on a Cotton Plantation* that
there is no difference between me and a *Northerner*," she wrote Dawson. "I sometimes let them know of their mistake ... for when I am
at home we Kentuckians think ourselves as much Southerners as anybody." While incensed at the suspicions of their fellow countrymen,
both sisters attempted to compensate by occasionally denying any
emotional commitment to their step-siblings. When David Todd
joined the Confederacy, a piqued Mary Lincoln declared that "by no
word or act of hers would he escape punishment for his treason against
her husband's government." Elodie was irate when she read the comment in the papers. "I do not believe she ever said it," she noted,
"and if she did and meant it, she is no longer a sister of mine nor
deserves to be called a woman of nobleness and truth.... What would
she do to me, do you suppose? I have as much to answer for." But
like Mary's, Elodie's indignation often belied her pain, her fits of
temper could only partly conceal her real concern. "You see I am
sad today," she confessed to Dawson, "and you may be right in thinking I take the cares and troubles [of my family] to heart too much,
but I have tried in every way to drive them from me and I cannot.
Tho' I employ every moment & take no time for thought, yet they
find their way to me." While her principal anxiety was for her full
brothers in the field, her sympathy extended across the lines of battle
and all the way to the White House. To be sure, Elodie disapproved
of Lincoln's policies, but she would not allow him to be personally
insulted in her presence. "That is a privilege I allow myself exclu-

sively," she explained, "to abuse my relations as much as I desire—but *no one* can do the same before me."[11]

Elodie's stand on this issue did not play well in the Selma ladies' circle and infused a local society already divided and volatile. Throughout the spring of 1861, the town was uneasily grouped into two camps, one associated with the men of the Selma Blues regiment, the other associated with the men of the Magnolia Cadets. The Cadets had left Selma in such a rush that the women of the town did not have time to organize a proper send-off. The Blues, by contrast, hung around for weeks after they were organized, parading in their uniforms and indulging in local hospitalities. The disparity was too much for Cadet partisans, who chided the Blues for being too dainty to eat army rations and too comfortable to ever leave Selma. The Blues departed eventually, but the divisions remained an essential part of the town's social calculus. "It seems strange to me that so few are together and all helping for the one and the same cause," Elodie noted, "that they *cannot work together* cheerfully and happily in place of actually working against each other and throwing as many obstacles in their way as possible." "I do not know of anything that has been tried," she claimed, "that has not been opposed by another party." The divisions played themselves out most viciously at the tableaux, the fund-raising soirees organized by the Selma ladies' circle. Every month or so, the women of the town put together a program of charades, skits, dancing, and musical entertainments designed to solicit donations from the remaining local gentlemen. These donations, of course, had to be distributed between the Blues and the Cadets, a process that became so bitter Dawson threatened to return the money sent to his men. The social politicking became even more rancorous when it was decided to hold separate tableaux for the two regiments, and it was Elodie's touchiness on the Lincoln issue that cemented the antagonisms for the remainder of the war. Fond of singing, Elodie had participated in several of the earlier soirees and had been present when an organizing committee suggested a skit that ridiculed Abraham Lincoln. Incensed, Elodie made clear she took personal offense at the suggestion and threatened to remove herself from the program. The committee relented, and the Lincoln scene did not appear at the tableaux. A few months later, however, Elodie received the program

for the first soiree organized for the exclusive benefit of the Blues:
the skit was on the evening's agenda. Elodie was irate. "I must confess
that I have never been more hurt or indignant in my life," she wrote
Dawson. "What have we ever done to deserve this attempt to personally insult and wound our feelings in so public a manner?" With this
incident, the loose division in the Selma social circle became a deep
rift. "Society [here] has undergone a change," Elodie explained, "and
is now divided into two distinct classes." The first class, calling itself
the Anti-Whites, contained the Weavers, Weedows, Fourniers, Mor-
rises, Mrs. Steele, the Perkinsons, the Watts, Miss Echols, and the
Misses Sikes and Carroley. The second class, calling itself the Whites,
was composed of Elodie, her sister Martha, Mrs. Mabry, and the
Misses Goodwin, Elsberry, Ferguson, and Bell. "The rest of the inhabitants," Elodie noted, "have been allowed the privilege of placing
their own positions." With everyone clear on the sides, women who
had insulted each other only obliquely heretofore came straight to the
point. "There has been a *war here in words*," Elodie reported, "and
the *Victory* is not yet awarded."[12]

Dawson was sympathetic to Elodie's predicament. He conceded that
Selma could be a disagreeable town and that no family's loyalty had
been more tried than the Todds. But he also seems to have found
Elodie's tales of social unpleasantness an unfortunate intrusion into
his reverie and routine. He assured her she would come to like Selma,
or, failing that, she could so throw herself into her duties as a wife
that it would not matter. Counseling her on her familial problems,
he waxed poetic and vague, suggesting she "cheer up [and] take a
brighter view of the matter. Look beyond the clouds and see in the
distance arching the heavens the bow of hope assuring you that there
are pleasures in the future for you, that happiness may yet crown your
life with its greenest bays and laurels will be the reward of those who
love so well." He was not being insensitive per se but was distracted
by his own difficulties and by a domestic imagination that needed to
see Elodie as someone beyond petty trials, as "an imaginary being . . .
as perfect as humanity can become."[13]

After rousing scenes at various train stations between Selma and
northern Virginia, the life of a Magnolia Cadet settled into a dull
routine. They were raised at 4:30 in the morning by reveille and

drilled until breakfast at 7:00. They had a general inspection at 8:00, further drilling from 9:00 until 12:00, recess from 12:00 to 12:30, more drilling until 5:30, then supper and lights out by 9:30. Playing whist, reading novels, and writing letters filled out the interstices, particularly on rainy days. For Dawson, Elodie was a fundamental part of that routine. He wrote her a letter a day, sometimes two. He kept her miniature attached to his watch fob, creating a somewhat embarrassing situation when anyone asked him the time. Every evening at nine o'clock, he left his tent for a secluded spot where he might gaze at the moon, imagining the life that awaited his return to Selma. Elodie, he knew, was on her porch, musing on the same subject, staring at the same moon, just as they had agreed before his departure. Hundreds of miles separated them; they could not talk and letters took a week or more to exchange. They were connected, however, by the shared reality of the moon, and its magnitude, its permanence, seemed somehow reassuring. But while Elodie was a part of Dawson's daily routine, she also embodied his hopes for a life beyond such routine. Amid the monotony of days and the deprivations of camp life, Dawson could only believe there to be something more in him than these, something Elodie came to symbolize.[14]

Partly this was a simple function of Dawson's isolation. He had few male friends, either in camp or out of it, and he seems to have preferred it that way. He had spent most of his boyhood daydreaming and had quickly lost touch with his college acquaintances. Politics, too, had soured his opinion of his own sex, leaving him with the opinion that "men are friendly only to be benefitted." Dawson's disaffection for men, however, went beyond the imputation of selfish motives. He tended, for instance, to be disturbed when another man attempted to get close to him, either physically or emotionally. James Averitt, a fellow Selmian and Episcopal preacher, for example, believed that he and Dawson were dear friends, a "second Damon and Pythias." Dawson, though, found Averitt "too loving. He puts his hands on me and is guilty of many such to me unpleasant ways as I do not think become the conduct of a gentleman." In part, Averitt was effusive by nature, a trait that clashed with Dawson's emotional restraint. Ebullient and fun loving, conditioned by his profession to be comfortable with touch, Averitt tended to be physical in his affections, demonstrative in his emotions. In his mind, his friendship with Dawson was marked by complete confidence and high regard; their physical familiarity was easy and natural. Dawson recognized this and counseled himself to excuse Averitt's excesses. "I like him," Dawson wrote, "he is a very innocent man. All his geese are swans [and] he will speak in the most rapturous terms of a hot roll or a fried chicken." But at other times, Dawson found Averitt's physical attention more troubling. He described it as the behavior of "a *very affectionate wife* to her husband" and took comfort in the fact that Averitt was "very much in love with some lady." Clearly, Dawson was disturbed not only by Averitt's effervescent homosociality but by his potential homosexuality, an observation he could never make categorically, but one that filters through his language of awkward obfuscation and confession. One cannot know, of course, whether Averitt's attentions had any sexual import, but it seems highly unlikely, and, indeed, there is evidence that it was Dawson, not Averitt, who tended to probe the sexual significance of homosocial relationships. Dawson's friendship with a Lieutenant Shertridge, for instance, soured when the man over-indulged in toasts to the Confederacy and "in a fit of intoxication" drew his knife and "insulted [Dawson] most wantonly." The two had known each other for years; Shertridge had read law in Dawson's office and had been an enthusiastic supporter of Dawson's captaincy. Shertridge, however, was under the impression that Dawson "liked Lieut. McCraw better than himself" and had determined in his stupor to avenge his wounded pride. "Did you ever hear of such infatuation?" Dawson noted after the incident. "It may become a jealous lover but not a man." It is possible, of course, that Shertridge had a deep emotional attachment to Dawson, but again it is unlikely. Rather, it seems that Dawson had positioned himself as the object of the lieutenant's desire, if only rhetorically, if only to condemn his actions as ridiculous. Dawson chose this same rhetorical position when Elodie suggested that had he not proposed when he did, Averitt might have been a rival for her attention. In his next letter Dawson set the love triangle straight—Elodie was "the *rival* that [had] supplanted" Averitt in his own confidence. None of this is to suggest that Dawson had homosexual tendencies, only that he was unusually attuned to the sexual dimension of all human dynamics and that his homosocial relations were characterized by an awkward distance he was careful to maintain. Sensitive and introverted, Dawson found other men incomprehensible at a distance, off-putting up close, and the result was a slight alienation from the rest of his sex. Unable to express the feeling any other way, he confessed to Elodie, "I frequently think that I was intended for a woman."[15]

Dawson was most comfortable at home in his library. There emotion was dispensed in clean, discrete units that never pawed or pressed but stole courteously and quietly into his receptive mind. Roasting his feet by the fire in winter, propped in front of an open window in summer, Dawson indulged an appetite for Bulwer and Collins, Shakespeare and Pomfret, Addison and Madame DeStaël. Reading, he claimed, was "an amusement that can never be taken from you," and in moments of unhappiness he turned to books "with the avidity of an opium eater." "I [have] derived more relief" from reading, he noted, "than from the society of friends." The library, though, could be a lonely place, and the rich imaginings of the mind were nothing without someone with whom he could share them. Elodie, he hoped, would one day join him in this sanctuary, and the room provided the setting for many of his domestic fantasies. "I love to create a picture," Dawson told his beloved, "where you are enthroned [there] as the principal personage. I love to see myself seated at your feet, listening to your sweet voice as it discourses of love and home."[16]

Trapped in a "tent hardly 8 by 10 feet, the ground wet, not even straw to place on the ground with the rain beating in at the door," Dawson's mind turned naturally to the warmth of hearth and home. He believed, though, that he had from his "earliest boyhood yearned for the comforting love of woman" and felt they possessed a singular ability to soothe his "troubled and wounded spirit." His mother was his model in this regard. She had been, he claimed, a woman of remarkable virtue, and he lamented that he had ever been forced to wake from his happy childhood to "the stern realities of life." When his mother died, Dawson acknowledged, he had "felt all alone and yearned for the love of someone to supply her place." His wives had filled this "gaping void of companionship," and Dawson recognized that "the deep love I have always had in my nature for domestic scenes" made it impossible for him ever to live long unmarried.[17]

Dawson's courtship of Elodie Todd, however, went beyond a quest for domestic companionship. With much of his society, he believed women to be unique repositories of divine grace, and he saw Elodie as a kind of personal intercessor in his relationship with God. "I sometimes reproach myself that I have not as much love of sacred things as I have for you," Dawson confessed to her, "but I hope you will pardon me for loving you as I do for I can love Him through you." God had made woman that she might teach man "the love he should bear his creator," and Dawson did not believe that "men could have received the revelations of the gospel without the inspiring faith of the gentler sex." "All of the virtuous impulses I ever feel," he noted, "are [to be] attributed to the teachings of my sainted mother and the influence of [the female] sex. Without these I would have been a barbarian." Content with this indirect pipeline to the Almighty, Dawson set about the rituals of courtship with a devotional enthusiasm. He gave up smoking and drinking for Elodie's sake and found himself able to resist the other vices of campaign life as well. Her love, he noted, had made him a better man, and the desire to do nothing that she would disapprove of exercised a "very healthy control" over his conduct. "It is in some degree the feeling which actuates the Christian in all his dealings," he noted, "and I hope for my own good that I will never be relieved from the 'bonds' of my love for you." Letter writing became a religious exercise, a chronicle of his devotion, confession, and spiritual struggles. Often he would admit that he had opted to write to Elodie rather than read the Bible, regarding the two rituals as roughly equivalent from a spiritual perspective. The coincidence was not lost on him that he knelt while writing and that "like the penitent Christian ... commun[ing] with a Superior being," he felt "a *better and purer man*" when the ceremony was over. It did not seem to matter to Dawson that Elodie was by her own admission not an Episcopalian but "a stubborn, hardheaded Presbyterian," that she was "ignorant ... on religious matters," that she had never been confirmed and was not prepared to take the step, or that "far from being able to assist" Dawson in his duty, she would require assistance from him. Dawson glossed over these facts easily. Elodie was a woman, "an angel of goodness," "a messenger of Peace and Love from above, sent to brighten and cheer" him in the path of life.[18]

Interestingly, while Dawson's formal religion, Episcopalianism, tended to be somewhat stiff in its presentation, his devotion to Elodie freed him from such proprieties and allowed him to indulge a more mystical, even totemic, sentiment. He worshiped her, he claimed, with a kind of "Eastern idolatry" and he regularly turned toward Selma and kissed the miniature attached to his watch fob. He felt best when his love took material forms, and he often sent personal objects folded into the pages of his letters—pressed flowers, leaves, pebbles, scraps of material, a lock of his hair, a bit of gold lace from his sword belt. When Elodie requested that her letters be burned after he read them, Dawson refused, telling her they were "sacred writings" and had to be preserved. He took considerable trouble to make sure the letters were returned to her for safekeeping, though he kept two of them on his person at all times. When he had no new letters to fire his domestic fantasies, he took long walks across the flattened grasses of camp to some secluded spot to be inspired by his own sentimentality. "I am disposed to be romantic," he explained to Elodie: "Scenery and circumstances by which I am surrounded always affect my disposition." At Quantico Creek he sat on a hillock picking violets, staring bemusedly at a Union gunboat on the river. "I can see the men aboard plainly," he noted, "and sometimes fear the sorry little wretches will throw a shell at me." At Harper's Ferry he chose a vantage overlooking the confluence of the Shenandoah and the Potomac. "You have [from here] a lovely view of the surrounding country, fields and farms," he noted, "while, just at your feet, the waters of the two noble streams ... mingle together in friendly sympathy.... In the distant fields one sees flocks of sheep and herds of cattle, browsing upon the rich clover and luxuriant blue grass [under] a blue and broadening horizon." From such a scenic lookout, the war and the monotony of camp life seemed far away—the distance between him and Elodie began to close. "I see your image in the beautiful morning," he told her, "and in the beautiful country around me. You *color* everything." Commemorating the moment, Dawson carved Elodie's initials into a rock. "If fortune favors our love," he told her, "and we live, I will bring you here that you may see for yourself."[19]

No place, however, provided a better setting for Dawson's reveries than the local cemetery. At each new camp, he sought out graveyards and markers, sometimes strolling the grounds for hours, musing on

Elodie and the nature of man. "You know I am fond of such places," he wrote his beloved. "They teach us of the uncertainty of life and always carry to me a touching lesson of our mortality." At the Lord Fairfax plantation he came across the marker of a Williamme Herris, a British soldier who died in America during the Glorious Revolution. Dawson made detailed comments on the stone's design, a slab of free-stone supported by four pedestals with deep reliefs of a griffin and an hourglass at the top and a sword insignia at the bottom. At Fredericksburg, Dawson chipped a piece of granite from the tomb of George Washington's mother and sent it to Elodie. "Is it not singular," he asked her, "that the American Union did not last to see the Washington monument completed?" Dawson was particularly impressed by a cemetery near Dumfries, where "umbrageous oaks...flourished upon the elements of man." "This is one of the laws of matter," he noted, "that nothing perishes, and here it is beautifully exemplified." He was seeking, he told Elodie, "an acquaintance with the living through the silent instruction" of the dead—but what he indulged was an appetite for melancholy, for emotions strong enough to carry him back to Selma. Squatting and bedraggled in his tent, death could seem faceless, pointless, without memory or remorse; in the cemetery, death was cultivated and courtly, polite and dignified, its magnitude was not terrifying but epic. Here Dawson could borrow against its enormity to drive his emotional commitment to life, to romance, to Elodie.[20]

Dawson also sought romantic inspiration in literature, particularly when the rain or the cold made a scenic stroll impossible. He had a strong taste for sentimental novels and tended to hold them up as models of how emotion should be felt and prose written. In his letters to Elodie, Dawson frequently managed a well-turned phrase of his own: "You are the first subject of my thoughts in the morning," he told his beloved, "and when sleep closes over me, you are the bright image that woos me to the land of dreams." But he was also continually frustrated by an inability to render his own romance as ably as his sentimental authors had rendered theirs. Partly, he contended, it was "the poverty of words" that made it impossible to capture his love in language. But partly, too, his affections had gotten beyond his simple ability to express them. "I feel at a loss how to write you," he wrote Elodie helplessly. "The rehearsal of my love must have become tiresome.... I wish I could write you in beautiful language how deeply you are loved and how much I feel your absence from me." Occasionally, Dawson relied on other authors for his prose, not cribbing so much as citing places where Elodie might do some supplemental reading. "I wish I could describe my love as eloquently as Bulwer has made Claude Menotte declare his for Pauline," he wrote her. "Get the play [Lady of Lyons] and read it, imagining yourself Pauline as addressed by me." But more often Dawson hoped his beloved would accept his imperfect rendering of devotion and forgive him the "unstudied language" of his heart. "I imagine no picture of the future that is not gilded by your presence," he told her plainly. "[I] think of no joy that is not doubled by having you to share it, and no privation that is not lessened because you will divide it with me." It was not an eloquent notion, he admitted, but it had the advantage of being "the plainer language of truth."[21]

Elodie was certainly flattered by the strength of Dawson's affection, but she was wary of it too. Though young, Elodie Todd was not without a certain savvy. She wondered that Dawson could know her at all from their short engagement and teased him that his love would prove a fading fancy. "It does well enough for you to *write about such things*," she told him, "but you must remember I have brothers-in-law and possess a wee portion of knowledge about gentlemen." Admitting she was a novice at love, she nevertheless made it clear that Dawson should not think her innocent in the ways of the world. Her love for him was not a little girl's reverie or the first blush of womanhood. When Dawson asked if she had "any fears about being deceived or not realizing all" her dreams for marriage, she answered, "not one." "Do you suppose I allowed myself to be drawn into an engagement," she asked, "without giving the subject serious reflection, such a serious and important step in life? I have seen and observed too much to be hasty about this matter." Indeed, Elodie had screened her suitors carefully. Her mother had begun to suppose she would never marry and claimed "if she were a suitor she would bring a clergyman with her when she asked the important question and have it over at once if the answer was favorable." Elodie, though, was confident and told her mother, "just wait until I see the right one."[22]

Elodie's initial impression of Dawson, however, was not favorable. "You must know," she told him, "that before our acquaintance began and I never saw you to know you until our meeting in Montgomery, I used to hear very much of you and fancied I knew you." Then she had thought him "so cold, not unfeeling, but reserved [and] unde-monstrative," a man who "did not care for friendship or love either." She had been surprised when Dawson began his suit—and more so by its warmth. Possessing a sturdy set of defense mechanisms herself, Elodie sympathized with Dawson's and forgave him his icy exterior. Her public presentation could be fairly prickly, too, and she tended to give her barbed wit a wide license. In her heart, though, she knew that "love is as essential to my life and happiness as the air I breathe." Dawson had passed a first muster, "writing so often" and generally "playing the *devoted*." It remained to be seen if it would last.[23]

So Elodie set about testing his sincerity. In veiled and playful ways, she reminded him that she was not an angel or a shrinking violet and delicately corrected the rosy excesses of his domestic reveries. Under Elodie's careful management, their letters became a kind of flirtatious negotiation, Dawson setting grand goals, Elodie reigning him in. When he called her beautiful, she called him a flatterer and insincere. When he called her gentle, she advised him that she had a temper of her own and not the amiability he "*lover-like*" attributed to her. Partly, of course, she was just being coy. A woman of irreverent wit, she could not resist poking occasional fun at Dawson's chronic ardor. A few days into his army service, Dawson managed to drop a trunk on his head—the gash required stitches and left a permanent scar. "I am sorry to hear that you are *battling* already," Elodie wrote sympathetically. "[I] would prefer your escaping as many scars as possible but do not think of returning home *without some* as you will never be accounted *brave and bold*. Kittie says she fears you will come home limping or without arms, Matt says without a head, so you can see what a subject of concern you are in the family." Even after Manassas, Elodie could be darkly comic about decapitation. "I would prize your war steed very much," she wrote him, "but to be a Hero you must have it killed under you in some way—have its head shot off, I think that would appear the funniest." Elodie's playfulness, however, could not mask her deeper concerns, partially for Dawson's physical well-being, partially for their relationship. Where Dawson indulged his anticipations, Elodie laid out the dangers of indulgence. "Do you not think," she asked him, "that we cause ourselves often unhappiness by allowing these bright and beautiful anticipations and imaginary pictures to take possession of us?" By giving thought to their hopes, they but strengthened the desire to have them realized until "almost unconsciously we build our air castles and it is not until they totter and fall that we realize they were but the baseless fabric of a vision." And this, of course, was Elodie's central fear—that Dawson was infatuated less with her than with his own love, that he would prove disappointed and intractable when their married life became routine.[24]

Dawson sensed this fear but pronounced it baseless. "You say we hardly know each other," he wrote Elodie, but "I think differently. I know you from your letters intimately." "Had I not been a volunteer," he noted, "I never would have known how rich were the imaginings of your mind and how pure and beautiful were the flowers that grow in the garden of your heart." With each exchange of letters, the couple revealed some new confession, admission, desire that brought them closer together. By the time "we are joined in the holy bonds of marriage," Dawson claimed, "we will have discovered in each other many latent qualities of head and heart that, otherwise, would have been known only after long years of association." Certainly the distance was a hardship; certainly nothing could compare to spending time together. But while most couples had a merely perfunctory and artificial courtship, Elodie and Nathaniel were enduring a trial by fire. "Do you not think," Dawson asked her, "that the circumstances which will prevent our marriage at any certain time will have a tendency to strengthen and increase our love for each other? When tried and made to pass thro' an ordeal we generally come out stronger and better." In Dawson's mind, then, distance did not so much compromise their love as help to constitute it. As the chasm that opened between them grew deeper, their longing grew deeper to fill it; the forced space tested and redoubled their devotion. Dawson had opened his very first letter to Elodie with this same sentiment: "We

are speeding on our way over the water and at each revolution of the
wheels the distance between us is lengthened but the ties which bind
us are only increased." Time, he believed, would bear him out.[25]

The problem, though, is that Dawson was speaking mostly for himself. "Circumstances have made me love you more than I dreamed
that I was capable of," he admitted to Elodie—but he never examined
the circumstances. At a thousand miles distant, surrounded by "comforts of home" that seemed in Dawson's dim recollection "perfectly
fabulous," Elodie inevitably became a glorified abstraction, an embodiment of all he would return to, a reason in the meantime to pull
on his boots and slog through the mud. Compared with this, what
had the Confederacy to offer: honor and duty and state's rights and
white home rule. Dawson certainly understood the language of these
notions, but he could not live them and feel them the way he could
Elodie. Dawson, after all, had spent most of his life in Selma proper,
partially abstracted from his own plantation. It had become in his
memory a sort of bucolic retreat, a vacation spot he always meant to
return to someday. "I am sometimes inclined to prefer a life upon
the plantation," he wrote Elodie, "where I could devote myself to you
and the pursuits of domestic life, which are not incompatible with
literature and books." These musings, however, were as close as he
had ever come to moving there, and he did not indulge them often.
He took up the subject of slavery even less frequently and never in
its connection to the war. Dawson was fighting, then, for the only
force in which he had a perfect faith—his own love of woman. Elodie
embodied that faith and became, symbolically and literally, all that
was worth living and dying for. Lying "in the rain, on the ground
. . . covered with one blanket," Dawson was "supported by the knowledge" that he did it all for her. "I . . . confess that I am calmed and
satisfied when I take this view of the war," he told Elodie, and "I
frequently think how just and right it is that I should be fighting for
you and my little girls, defending my country and vindicating *your
rights and liberties*." What exactly those rights and liberties might be,
Dawson did not say, likely did not know, but as long Elodie and his
country remained roughly synonymous in his mind, he was willing
to fight. Traveling to Evansport for supplies, he ran into Brigadier
Generals French, Wigfall, and Whiting and their large retinue of

aides on an inspection tour of the division. "It was a splendid cavalcade of gallant gentlemen," Dawson wrote home, "all in uniform and
mounted upon noble steeds. As the train rode, at a gallop, over hill
and dale, thro' the woods, beautiful in their autumnal robes of crimson, my mind reverted to the days of Ivanhoe, and I thought the
comparison would have been complete if my Elodie had been in the
lead, upon a black charger." For three months, this was Dawson's
view of the war—wet blankets and whist on the one hand, Ivanhoe
and Elodie on the other.[26]

On the morning of July 21, a Union column of ten thousand men
forded the sluggish stream of Bull Run and managed to surprise an
enemy that was expecting them. The Confederates gave ground
grudgingly but were rocked back on their heels. Dawson himself was
making good time in reverse when a cannonball struck a fence he
was negotiating and sent him flying ten feet to the ground. Now at
the rear of a retreating division, musket fire pouring down on him,
Dawson, along with the two colonels of the Fourth Alabama, Egbert
J. Jones and Evander M. Law, scrambled to catch up to their fleeing
infantrymen. Though the Confederates would eventually rally and
launch a devastating counterattack, the Fourth Alabama did not fully
regain its composure until the battle was over. Dawson himself
watched as Colonel Jones and then Major Charles Scott fell on his
left and right, and he spent the rest of the afternoon hobbling around
the rear of the battlefield, tending to the wounded and trying unsuc-
cessfully to locate his scattered men. Though the Fourth Alabama's
overall conduct was unimpeachable, 38 killed and 208 wounded out
of 750 engaged, rumors that Dawson had shamefully fled the field
quickly circulated in camp and around Selma. For a man of Dawson's
quiet dignity, the imputation of cowardice was almost too much to
bear. He made minute accounts of his conduct to anyone who would
listen, including the newspapers, and confessed to one of his friends
that it might be better if he never returned from the war. He fan-
tasized about throwing himself into the path of enemy gunfire and
promised to meet with pistols any man willing to repeat the charges
to his face. The rumors were, of course, baseless and were eventually
traced to a disgruntled Selmian who resented Dawson's social standing
and was himself infatuated with Elodie Todd; nevertheless, the ex-

perience soured Dawson on the military and convinced him that petty politicking would ruin the Confederacy. After Manassas, Dawson's mind never again "reverted to the days of Ivanhoe."[27]

Then, too, Dawson had begun to find the constraints of army life beset with almost unbearable indignities. For the company-grade officers, especially, army discipline marked the first time they were expected to do as they were told, not as their class prerogatives allowed. The most galling of these constraints from Dawson's perspective was the army's refusal to grant leaves of absence and its threat to force all volunteers to remain in service for the duration of the war. More than a breach of trust, these moves made it possible that Dawson would not be able to marry Elodie for a period of some years, a prospect he found offensive. "I am willing to lay down my life for you," he told Elodie, "but the idea that I am to do so without having been married to you is a harrowing one." Without the sanction of law and God, Dawson's relationship with Elodie, and through her his reason for fighting, was faced with illegitimacy. "I have never felt so anxious," he wrote, "upon any subject, as to close the term of my service in order that I might be with my loved Elodie. . . . I know that unless we are married this spring, I will become useless to the country." At the outset of the war, Dawson had determined to see the conflict as a defense of female integrity, as a vindication of Elodie's rights and liberties. Now the simple synonymity he had always assumed between his fiancée and his country was breaking down; the Confederacy was forcing him to choose between them, and he made the choice easily. "You tell me that you have made up your mind to be *secondary* to your country," Dawson wrote his beloved, but "*You are my country*, and can be *secondary* to nothing." His own life could be sacrificed, he agreed, and all that he had—except her. "I am not a Roman to give my wife for my country," he summed it up, because "without [you] I would have no country to live for and to die for."[28]

The fall and winter of 1861 brought more whist and more rain; Dawson began referring to his flooded tent as a boat, the flaps whipping "in the wind like sails," the whole structure threatening always to "capsize." These were the quietest months of the war—the North was suffering a crisis of confidence, lamenting Manassas and stewing in a "half-acknowledged martial inferiority" to the South. With little

going on, it seemed to Dawson that the army should let the twelve-
month men return home; they had done their duty and others stood
ready to take their place. Besides, he noted cynically, "our armies
have done little but throw up lines of fortification to be abandoned
when approached by the enemy. Our great men wrangle in Congress
over their pay" while the men in the field freeze. By late 1861 it was
not patriotism but duty to his men that secured Dawson's allegiance.
"When I reflect upon the condition of others so much more to be
pitied than mine," he noted, "I am warned that there is not in my
nature enough of gratitude." He did, after all, have a tent, a trunk,
a servant, an abundance of clothing—everything "absolutely necessary to contentment," while many of his men, "accustomed to the
same comforts," having "as warm firesides to welcome them back,"
were exposed to trials Dawson would never know. The point was
graphically illustrated by a young man who came to Dawson's tent
after returning from guard duty. He was "the only son of a widowed
mother" and was "shivering from cold and rain," but, taking a "vacant camp chair and sitting by the fire," he seemed "as happy as a
lord."[29]

We have already seen that women formed the foundation of Dawson's religion and his patriotism. He knew Elodie only through her
letters, yet she had somehow come to embody all that gave God and
country any meaning. It should not surprise us that when contemplating his men, Dawson grounded his egalitarian impulse in the
home; men were all equal before their hearths, all alike in their quest
for a good woman and a fire to keep her warm by. That manhood
should be grounded in womanhood, that the crush of early love should
deepen and color the affections of a man for his fellow man, for his
God and his country's cause, is not a revelation. But as Dawson himself dimly understood, this was not "the effusion of a mind diseased
with love." In a culture in which men surrender nothing easily to
each other, the natural appetite for submission to something larger
than the self can become unbearable. God was too distant, the Confederacy too vague; Dawson only felt comfortable granting his obei-
sance to a woman. "Yours will be a *reign of love*," he promised Elodie,
"I will always be inclined to be controlled by you." The statement,
of course, contains a paradox—if Dawson could incline to be con-

trolled, he could just as easily determine to be disinclined. And this, ultimately, was what God and country and women had in common, the thing that made them bleed so easily together—to them all Dawson could surrender his will with the perfect knowledge that he could always take it back. He did not comprehend this fully, of course; overawed by the strength of his own devotion, he was only partially able to understand its source within himself, only dimly able to see that he had fallen in love with negotiating the terms of his own surrender. But he knew enough to be confused, and with this problem, as with all others, he turned artlessly to Elodie for aid. "Is such love as I give worth anything?" he asked her, "Or is it simply the homage that man pays to your sex?" Elodie knew enough not to answer; she had after all "brothers in law [and a] wee portion of knowledge about gentlemen."[30]

Theodorick Montfort: Something to Love and Pett

On July 4, 1851, a train steamed across a new wooden trestle cresting the Flint River and pulled into Oglethorpe, Georgia, the new terminus of the Southwestern Railroad line. The meaning of the event was lost on none of the men and women who gathered to celebrate its arrival. Formerly a sleepy nowhere, Oglethorpe would now have its chance to become a bustling somewhere. Soon planters with their wagons full of cotton were trundling into town from the hinterlands, delighted to have a new means to market. Soon businesses were springing up to ensure that none of the wagons returned to the hinterlands empty. After loading their cotton onto the trains, the planters had money to spend, and surely they had earned a few whiskeys at Oliver's Hall. Surely their wives and daughters had earned the "Calicoes, Ginghams, and Muslins" to be found at J. Kaufman & Brothers or the "beautiful supply of Perfumery, Toilet Powders, and Paints" in the window of Fears Drug Store. At its apogee in 1855, Oglethorpe boasted eighty businesses, including ten cotton warehouses, eight livery stables, seven hotels, three groceries, two daguerreotypists, and a book store. An omnibus met every train, speculation in lots and land became a respectable profession, and the town's newspaper trumpeted all of the details to any who would listen. "It is a *great place*," gushed the editor, and destined to become the "greatest commercial city in the South."[31]

In 1857, a train steamed through Oglethorpe on its way to the railroad's new terminus at Albany. By 1858, the southbound trains didn't steam through Oglethorpe at all, preferring to take the spur at Smithville, north of town. In two years, Oglethorpe had become a nowhere again, its moment as a somewhere so brief it hadn't even been captured by the decennial census. In 1850, the town's white population was a scant 113. In 1860, it was a hardly more impressive 268. But between these dates, Oglethorpe, Georgia, had been the starry dream of thousands.[32]

One of those thousands was Theodorick Montfort. Born in 1823, Montfort married Maria Louisa Daniel in 1848 and settled with her and a few slaves on a small farm outside Oglethorpe. There he planted, practiced law, and raised a family until swept into the war as a lieutenant in the Twenty-Fifth Georgia Volunteer Infantry Regiment. From November 1861 until April 1862, Montfort and his men were part of the division defending Fort Pulaski from the besieging Yankees, an unenviable assignment as the Confederates were outgunned, undersupplied, and without prospects for reinforcements. A fort under siege is like a prison. Retreat is impossible; escape seems impossible. Time draws out, the walls close in, and the occupants can only wait, moving in ever tightening circles, cornered and claustrophobic. After two months, Pulaski began to run out of food. Montfort sent to his wife for his fishing pole and was quite successful catching dinner for his men. The practice also seems to have relaxed him, helping relieve the mental strain of the siege. "I feel much better this evening," he wrote his wife after an afternoon with the cane pole. "I wish it was possible for me to send you all some of the fish & oysters I have here. I shall catch thousands this Spring and summer if the Yankees will permit & they will have to be very watchful to keep me from fishing." Gradually though, Pulaski ran out of other supplies as well. "I am entirely out of liquor," Montfort wrote home, so "I have quit & do not now want it. I am reduced down to 1½ twist of tobacco. I have also concluded to quit that soon. My pants all have holes in them. Soon I shall quit wearing pants." Montfort wasn't entirely kidding about his impending pantlessness. "I don't know that we would suffer much by going naked," he wrote. "If our Company should be forced to it, we are going to make long shirts out of tents & wear them.... So soon as it becomes the fashion & style of Cockspur Island to wear long shirts only, it will look & answer well."[33]

Montfort knew clearly why he suffered such indignities. "I am discharging my duty to my ... family," he explained to his wife. "I am prepared to submit to any inconvenience, make any sacrifice, & face any danger that duty may require." Like many soldiers before and since, Montfort's war effort was primarily personal, familial. While he could not (or at least did not) articulate precisely the nature of the threat, he was convinced the Yankees threatened the South at its most vital and tender point—its women, children, and homes. "We are anxious for the hour to arrive when by the aid of a Just God ... [we will] avenge the damning insult & outrage that has been offered & promised ... our wives, daughters & sisters," he wrote Louisa. "[Only then can we] enjoy undisturbed from Yankee Invasion the happiness of home."[34]

Because Montfort's motivation to fight drew so deeply on his love of home, letters from his family became crucial to his continued willingness to endure deprivation and possible death. When he received a letter, he "cried & shouted like a child" and proclaimed himself "right side up & prepared for anything the Yankees may send." But when he did not he felt an "anxiety ... so great" it made him "sad & almost sick." Letters, in short, allowed Montfort to see himself as he was seen from home, as the tireless protector of a family, and so long as they arrived, he could bear all that was maddening and miserable about life under siege.[35]

In February 1862, the Union army completed its encirclement of Pulaski and severed the lines of communication with the fort. Unlike the disruption to the supply of food, liquor, or clothing, the cessation of the mails was not something Montfort could accept with stoicism or a sense of humor. "[I] cannot get content to be satisfied with not hearing from home," he admitted. Montfort's discontentment was not idle chatter. Together with several fellow officers, he commissioned a courier to sneak across enemy lines to attend to their personal correspondence. The mission, Montfort admitted, was a dangerous one. The man had to "select some dark night & walk ... five miles through a marsh from one to three feet deep in mud before [he would] pass the Yankees that are [patrolling] day & night." Three times the feat was attempted. Three times the couriers were captured, leaving Montfort with the certain knowledge that "the Yankees have had fine times reading our letters." Grudgingly, he admitted that "communication is now entirely & effectually cut off."[36]

Isolated within Pulaski, Theodorick Montfort lived a sort of double life. During the day he made preparations for war. "All is life, animation, & excitement," he wrote, "with the mere hope of a change & a fight. Such is the human heart. Men after being in camp a while become indifferent to danger & death. I begin to have that kind of feeling myself. A man looses his better feelings & becomes hardened & indifferent to evry thing." But during the evenings everything was not animation and excitement, hardness and indifference. "In the dead hour of night when all is silent," he noted, "when we feel alone in the presence & care of our Maker, then home with all its endearments come crowding upon our memory, then men who face & smile at danger, weep & pray for those dear ones at home." Such a double life was perfectly normal, of course; virtually every wartime soldier led it. Each day he screwed himself up to face death (or cause it); each night he unwound to embrace the life that remained to him. In Montfort's case, however, the tension of the siege coupled with the cessation of the mail seems to have disrupted this process. His home grew so far away his imagination could not find it. The war grew so close his mind could not purge it. Walled up in Pulaski, Montfort was himself besieged, imperiled not merely physically but psychologically.[37]

This psychological strain is most evident in Montfort's plaintive attempts to familiarize his surroundings. His special charge at Pulaski included three large casement guns, their carapaces, ammunition, and firing crews. To him fell not only the job of drilling the men who would fire the guns but the privilege of naming the guns themselves. "The 1st 64 pounder I have dubbed Addie Elizabeth after Ma," Montfort wrote home, "the 2nd 42 pounder Sarah, in honor of Mrs Hall, the 3d a 32 pounder Louisa after yourself. The names are hansomely written on each piece with white paint in large letters, they are known in Garrison as all the other guns are by their names." With the familiar names emblazoned on their barrels and his near constant contact with them, Montfort began, by his own admission, actually to fall in love with his guns, to create from them a sort of ersatz family to replace the real one receding from him:

> My guns feel to me as part of my family. You would be really amused to hear the endearing epithets & see the tender care & consideration that is paid to them. I love them on account of my frequent & almost hourly association with them; 2d I love them because they are willing & submissive instruments in my hands, to protect myself & my country; 3d I love them because it is human & natural to love & pett something (they are my Petts); 4th I love them because the names reminds me of home & my wife, my mother, my friends; & 5th I love them because the names act as an incentive to stimulate me to acts of bravery & to a faithful & unflinching discharge of my duty, in the protection of those dear ones at home—& when the hour of conflict comes (which I think will be soon) I hope & expect to be as faithful to my guns (or Petts) as I would to those whose names they represent—& if it should be my fate to fall it shall be in their midst. If I survive, neither my (Petts) nor those who in honor they are named shall feel ashamed or dishonored by me. So you see we find some thing to love & pett on this Island.

Desperate to domesticate his formidable surroundings, Montfort dressed his own instruments of death in the raiment of family life. Love, Protection, Faithfulness, Tenderness, Humanity, Endearment, Home, Wife, Mother, Friendship—all this hung in his casements, like wash drying on a line, obscuring in some small way the dread purpose of the machines.[38]

On March 31, with the Union army preparing its final assault on Pulaski, Montfort made a last inspection of his casements. They were, he said, as "neat & clean as my house," and for just a moment the determined defender lashed out. "We are nerved for the contest by the recollection of our homes, our families & our rights," he affirmed. "If the Fort is taken we want them to find nothing [but] ruin[ed] walls & mangled corpse[s]." Penning a last letter to be delivered in the event of his death, he remonstrated his wife to teach his children to "hate [Yankees] with that bitter hatred that will never permit them to meet under any circumstances without seeking to destroy each other. I know the breach is now wide & deep between us & the Yankees. Let it widen & deepen untill all Yankees or no Yankees are to live in the South." But Montfort was too decent a person to sustain such sentiments; his great wave of anger crested and broke on the shoals of his own goodness:

> Yet amidst all of our vindictive feelings & bitter hatred [of] our enemy there is something sad & melancholy in the preparation for Battle. To see so many healthy men prepareing for the worst by disposing of their property by Will, to see the surgeon sharping his instruments & whetting his saw to take [from] them those necessary member[s] of our body that God has given us for our indispensible use, to see men engaged in carding up & prepareing lint to stop the flow of human blood from cruel & inhuman wounds, is awful to contemplate. Yet there is still another preperation for battle still more sickening—The Casemates are cleared; nothing is allowed to remain that is combustible or would be in the way during an engagement ... the floor is covered around each gun with sand not for health or cleanliness but to drink up human blood as it flows from the veins & hearts of noble men, from the hearts of those that love & are beloved. This is necessary to prevent the floor from becoming slipery with blood so as to enable the men to stand & do their duty. These are some of the preperations for battle. How sad to contemplate, yet how awful must be the realization—What a calamity is war. When will men cease to fight, & love their neighbors as themselves? Not as long as the present generation lives I am certain.

The lawyers are drafting the wills. The sawbones are sharpening the instruments. The men are screwing themselves up to "stand & do their duty." But Montfort's mind is already flying ahead to the time when the men are dying, the saw is working, and the blood is pooling beneath his beloved "family." Montfort would not be able to domesticate these images. There was nothing here that he could "love and pett." The war with all its horrors had burst through his feeble defenses, and with nowhere else to turn, he had thrown himself on the

mercy of a cliché: "When will men cease to fight, & love their neighbors as themselves?" It is a sad and plaintive question, wretched with
impotence, the last gasp of a man who has come to understand that
in war there is neither mercy nor sense, just death.[39]

Conclusion

Unlike the other men paired in this study, Nathaniel Dawson and
Theodorick Montfort had similar temperaments. Each man drew his
energy from the inner rather than the outer world; each man possessed a tenderness of heart that ill-suited a soldier; each man looked
on his war service as a sacrifice for love. "*You are my country,*" Dawson had written to Elodie. "Without [you] I would have no country
to live for and to die for." Montfort felt exactly the same way: "I am
discharging my duty to my . . . family," he had explained to Louisa.
"I am prepared to . . . make any sacrifice . . . that duty may require."
The men diverged in the nature of their war experience, however.
Where Dawson's Elodie presented herself nightly in the face of the
moon, Montfort's Louisa seemed ever mantled in the darkness beyond
the fort walls. Ultimately, only one of these men could consistently
make the metaphysical journey home, and the consequences were
telling.

Writing home was a literal as well as a literary project. In concert
with wives and sweethearts, Confederate soldiers created ersatz domestic worlds integral to their continued participation in the world
of mud and marches. In war, as in the marketplace before the war,
men's individuality, which was their dignity, threatened always to
dissolve in the impersonal relations of figurative or literal battles. In
returning home, men became individuals again, heroes even, for their
labors on behalf of their households. During the Civil War, of course,
the journey home was a psychic rather than a physical one, but it
was no less important. Confederates were all the time writing, imagining, and dreaming home, not merely because they wanted to be
there but because they found there compensations for all the indignities they daily endured.

As the conflict dragged on, however, men found it increasingly difficult to find their way home; war began to dominate their inner understanding of themselves, and their houses and the families within them began to recede. Tally Simpson became so desperate to find a way home that he created a sponsor for his journey in a picture he cut from a magazine. Edwin Fay became so hardened that he could better imagine sleeping in his wife's flower yard than in her bed. Certainly there were some men, like Nathaniel Dawson, who flew home and back almost unimpeded. But there were an equal number like Theodorick Montfort who gradually lost their way, becoming estranged from former lives and former selves. For these men, home became a dwindling memory, an almost unwelcome revenant of a former age. Thomas Cobb is a fascinating example of this tendency. For the first year of the war, he spent his happiest hours in nocturnal revery. "[You] flit through my dreams ... like a smiling fairy," he told his wife, and when I wake I long only "to catch the broken thread and dream on." Like many soldiers, Cobb had placed his wife at the center of his war effort; he had only to close his eyes to conjure her image and remember the reasons for which he fought. A year later, however, Cobb took cold comfort in dreams. "I have dreamed so often," he admitted helplessly, "that ... I have a vague uneasy consciousness that it is *all* a dream." Cobb, like Montfort, had become a liminal man, occupying the otherworldly space between sleeping and waking, living and dying. Here dreams offered no respite; the war was always present, even when he closed his eyes. "I dreamed about you all last night," Cobb wrote his wife despondently. "You had married another man [and] I thought I saw little Sally standing *alone* just as I went into battle." Cobb's mind, like Montfort's, had raced far ahead to his inevitable death on the battlefield, when his daughter would whisper her ghostly good-byes and his wife would mourn him and move on.[40]

To his credit, Cobb determined that men had only themselves to blame for their predicament. "Each of us magnifies our own importance and supposes that without us the world would be nothing to a large circle," he admitted. Then "death comes and soon after oblivion. A ... widow here and there cherishes a husband's memory and weeps over his grave, but the tide sweeps over his resting place and [soon it] is as if he had never lived." The quest for immortality, as Cobb finally grasped, brought only early mortality and an empty life. "What folly it is to seek after fame," he admitted to his wife. "Oh for peace, darling, peace and Home and your embrace. Are these in store for me?" For a quarter million Confederates, Cobb included, the answer was no.[41]

EPILOGUE

But were that hope of pride and power
Now offered with the pain
Ev'n then I felt—that brightest hour
I would not live again.*

Laurence Massillon Keitt

Laurence Keitt eventually married Susan Sparks and whisked her away, as promised, to Europe. There they toured galleries and ruins and planned for Susan to continue her art instruction. As the disunion sentiment in the South reached fever pitch, however, Keitt found himself unable to stay away. He had worked for Southern independence his entire adult life, and as it became a possible, then a probable, and then an accomplished fact, Keitt was drawn irresistibly back into politics. Strangely, however, the former "Harry Hotspur of the South" did not enter into the fray with his characteristic zeal, and his friends remarked on it. Caught up and contented in his new role as husband and father, Keitt endured considerable teasing at the hands of former associates who taunted him for being a family man, henpecked and hassled by Sue. Even when he was a member of the Montgomery convention charged with setting up the Confederate

*Edgar Allan Poe, "The Happiest Day."

government, Keitt played a low-key role, only coming to life when his wife told him to go brush his hair.[1]

But really it was the Civil War that transformed Laurence Keitt. A colonel in the army, he spent considerable time away from his wife and daughters, and his letters reflect a man lonely and soulsick for home. Keitt's once florid writing style became spare and straightforward; his metaphors gave way to simplicity, his posturing to self-revelation. "I feel more keenly than ever my love for you," he told Sue from Sullivan's Island in 1862, "and how much you are bound up with my existence." "I don't think I fear death more than a gentleman ought," he wrote her. "I may say I know I don't—but I do hate to leave you." "I wish, Ma Belle Susie, you could see my heart; I think you would be satisfied both of the character, degree, and quality of the love it contains for you." Keitt said he would miss his daughters if he were killed, and it was "a sore and terrible anguish" to contemplate never seeing them again. But to part from his wife cracked "every chord of the spirit and soul." "You have grown a part of my higher and better nature," Keitt told her, "and have made me a good man. I almost fear that you are my religion."[2]

On February 1, 1864, the Confederate blockade runner *Presto* collided with a partially submerged wreck in Charleston Harbor. The captain of the boat had run off, and Keitt was in charge of recovering the ship's cargo. Federal troops had taken up positions around the inlet and hampered all attempts at salvaging the wreck. One shell passed within twenty feet of Keitt and would have killed him had it actually exploded. Over the next few days, Keitt and his company managed to recover the bulk of the shoes, blankets, flannels, pork, and beef the *Presto* had been carrying. His men were tired, hungry, cold, wet, ill shod, and ill clothed, and Keitt wanted to distribute the supplies to them, but he was forced to return it all to a central depot. The incident was the last straw in a war Keitt was beginning both to hate and to accept responsibility for. "I had as much to do probably as anyone else in bringing about this revolution," he noted, "and I must accept its consequences. I see thousands around me who knew nothing about it, who had but little at stake, and who hoped to gain but little. They were carried by us into the war and they are fighting it out. I can do no less."[3]

As a younger man, Keitt had dreamed of a titanic struggle in which the sons of the South rose up to erect the last, great glittering civilization of earth. But the Civil War was more butchery than chivalry; it was, he said, "hate without manliness; war without generosity; cruelty without courage; rapine without greatness." "Blood has been poured out like water," he told his wife, "undisciplined troops have taken blazing and guarded batteries, but their valor and blood have won" them nothing. The war, he said, had come to everybody—states, towns, villages, hamlets, and firesides—all felt it and all shared in it. And yet nowhere had anyone "risen up with a star on his forehead" to make the war worthy of the men who were dying. Keitt, of course, had always supposed that in a conflict between North and South he would emerge as just such a man to complete the singing of his epic poem. But instead Keitt's Promethean moment came in the salt and the sand of Charleston Harbor when he realized, finally, that his epic had astronomical costs for others. Looking into the faces of his men, tired and hungry, most of them, like himself, just wanting to go home, he understood, perhaps for the first time, that the nameless hosts and hordes of *Iliad* and *Odyssey* were composed of men who had lives of their own, poems of their own, shorter, smaller, humbler, but compelling in their very simplicity. Keitt had written Susan early in their courtship that as a boy groping his way through the Greek tragedies, he had been "enduringly impressed with a thought which grew out of the web of their fearful stories." No one who inflicted misery on others, however accidentally, was deemed wholly guiltless. Fate and the Furies hunted down even the unintentionally wicked until "after travail, laceration, and despair" the offender was brought quivering and bleeding to the very "storm throne of the gods." "Thus inflexibly and unsparingly," Keitt noted, "did Antique Fate pursue all who even unwittingly wronged others."[4]

Laurence Keitt was blown off of his horse on June 1, 1864, during some early skirmishing at Cold Harbor. The doctor had some difficulty convincing him that his wounds were mortal; to the end he believed his body would rise to this last, great challenge. His final words were "Oh, wife, wife."[5]

Nathaniel Dawson

Nathaniel Dawson survived the Civil War and adjusted easily to life in the New South. Never the fiercest of Confederates or the most vehement of slaveholders, Dawson took up his law practice and by dint of hard work recovered some of his prewar affluence. Besides, by May 1862 he had won most of what he had been fighting for in the first place, dignity enough to take Elodie as his wife. True to her savvy, Elodie Todd married a man whose love proved not a passing fancy but a steady regard. The Dawsons' marriage was, by all indications, a happy one. Both became Selma luminaries—Elodie with the Ladies Memorial Association and Nathaniel in various political capacities—and, as Nathaniel noted, they had the cries of their baby boys to drown out the troubles of the times.[6]

Dawson's affection for graveyards persisted well after his Confederate service. In the orderly plots and carefully etched stones, he continued to find the echo of his reserve and his civility; the notion that even death could be well-groomed appealed to him as much in old age as it had on the fields of Manassas. When Elodie died in 1877, Nathaniel began a cemetery project of staggering extravagance. Commissioning Italian sculptors to carve a life-sized marble model of Elodie, Dawson had it shipped in pieces to the United States and reassembled at Selma's Live Oak Cemetery. There it still stands, a monument to a man's enduring love for a woman he had called his country.[7]

Harry St. John Dixon

Harry Dixon eventually got his wish and left his Greenville home to join the Confederate army. A private in the Eleventh Mississippi Infantry Regiment, Dixon was fiercely devoted to the South and, taking his own temper as a guide, he correctly predicted that the war would be long and bloody. "Blind religious fanaticism on one side," he wrote home, "and outraged liberties on the other, will incite both parties to dire extremities." But just as he had on the plantation, Dixon chafed under the authority of his supposed superiors. "At home I was, at least, once a gentleman," he misremembered, "& I do not now altho'

The gravemarker of Elodie Todd Dawson. Nathaniel Dawson Papers, University of Alabama Library, Tuscaloosa.

a private choose to be made a dog of by any man or set of men. It is galling to a gentleman to be absolutely & entirely subject to the orders of men who in private life were so far his inferiors; who when they met him felt rather like taking off their hat to him than giving him law & gospel." Naturally, Harry compared his condition to a kind of slavery and panted for release from his "hellish thraldom." The surest release, of course, was death, and Harry came at this subject with his characteristic meticulousness. In November 1861 and in an emendation in June 1862, he drafted a careful will, disposing of his little property and giving explicit instructions for his burial and funeral service. His notebooks, entitled "Fragments," "References," and

"Quotations," were to be given to a cousin. Knowing his father's disinclination to poetry, Harry left his copy of Milton to his mother. To his father Harry bequeathed his copy of Macaulay's *British Essays*, believing it "would please and interest him, suiting his peculiar taste." Harry's beloved dog, Sam, was to remain with the family until death, when he was to be buried in a small coffin next to his fallen master.[8]

Harry devoted even more attention to his own funeral service. He was to be buried in a vault of specific thickness and dimensions, crowned with a square pillar broken raggedly across the top and inscribed with the words, "The paths of glory lead but to the grave." The vault was to be erected on the northwest corner of the family estate, under a "clump of box elder trees where I have spent so many days in quiet & pleasant study." His coffin was to be metallic, his sword and pistols were to be laid across its top, and it was to be arranged such that his head would always face south and his feet would always face north. Those who attended the funeral were to be solemn and well dressed and were to proceed to the graveside in meticulous male-female pairs.[9]

Such careful arrangements proved unnecessary. Harry Dixon survived the war and returned to Greenville. To escape the horrors of Reconstruction, his father, Richard, sent Harry and the rest of the family around the isthmus of Panama to a ranch in California he named Refuge. Richard himself preferred to set straight off across the plains. He was starting over again, just as he had when he came south on horseback with $75 and a loaf of gingerbread.[10]

In California, Harry Dixon took up the practice of law and in 1874 met and married Constance Maynard, herself descended from an aristocratic Virginia family. From their letters, it is obvious that Harry and Connie were very much in love. "I wonder if it can ever be less unspeakably sweet to me to think of you," wrote Connie to her husband, "[to] speak of you, write to you, as *'my husband,'* my very own, mine to love, to rejoice with in prosperity, to soothe in moments of anger, to sympathize with in sorrow & disappointment." Harry was similarly smitten: "Sweet little woman, you are as much as a sweet wife can be, as much as if we were yet in the romance of courtship! Please God it may always be so." Unfortunately it could not always be so. The venereal disease that Harry had contracted in his moment of "youthful indiscretion" was syphilis, and it ate steadily into his

Harry St. John Dixon in his Confederate uniform. Harry St. John Dixon
Papers, Southern Historical Collection, UNC.

mind and body. As his daughter remembered, Harry became by the
1880s subject to "terrible nervous tensions" and "uncontrollable irri-
tability, which he never turned upon his family but always upon some
wrong or injustice in the world at large." Ultimately, the disease
became so advanced that Harry could no longer stay at home. Two
brothers and a brother-in-law came to take him away: "There was no
hope," his daughter remembered, "and everybody knew it then."
Harry Dixon spent his last days in a hospital. His mind was still active
but his body ravaged, and he occupied his time in disassembling and
reassembling the watch his father had given him when he was seventeen, a token of his arrival at manhood.[11]

David Outlaw

David Outlaw did not remain in national politics long. He was too
moderate, too decent, and too awkward for Washington, and after his
defeat in 1852, he never went back. Picking up his Windsor law

practice again, however, he discovered that whatever his contempt for politics, he somehow couldn't live without it. "After a man has... gotten into public life," he once confessed, "it is not so easy to get out." Elected to the North Carolina General Assembly in 1854, 1856, and 1858, he was away from home when his wife Emily died suddenly in 1859. Grieved over her loss and preoccupied by his own declining health, he played little public role in the Civil War. He died in 1868, rheumatic, gouty, and nearly blind, but everyone who remembered him—and they were not many—unfailingly mentioned his unattractiveness on the one hand and his decency on the other.[12]

Theodorick Montfort

Theodorick Montfort was not killed during the Union bombardment and occupation of Fort Pulaski. For two days, the Yankees blasted away at the walls, finally exposing the northern magazine so completely that a single shot might have ignited the powder and demolished the fort entirely. Under the circumstances, the Confederates had no option but surrender. "This is the first work that has ever been exposed to the fire of the [new] rifled cannon," noted the Confederate commander, "and the result [has] proved that brick and mortar cannot stand before them." The Union's tactical victory had been so complete that the cost in human lives had been quite low, only one man dead and one wounded in more than a thousand engaged. Ironically, though, Montfort's vision of blood pooling beneath his forensic family proved accurate. While the Yankees were cleaning out one of the casemates, a man carrying a live shell accidentally tapped it against one of the supporting arches. Hearing the explosion, Union Sergeant Edwin Merriam

> went immediately on the parapet and saw the most horrid sight I ever saw, 5 men all mangled and blown to pieces. [One] was killed instantly and one died in five minutes. One poor fellow was so broken to pieces he could not be moved without falling to pieces and lived 5 hours, another died just as they got ready to take his legs off; the other has had his leg amputated and was alive this morning.

By the time the sawbones had seen to the pieces, however, Theodorick Montfort was on his way to a Union prison on Governor's

Montfort's casemate after the fall of Fort Pulaski. U.S. Army Military
History Institute, Carlisle, Pennsylvania.

Island, New York. There he was remembered by one of the guards
as an "ideal Georgia cracker in general appearance, thin almost to
emaciation, hollow in the temple, flat chested with sandy hair and
beard that were always dishevelled." "He did not make much of a
figure as a soldier," the guard admitted. "But his heart was true and

brave, his intellect keen and searching. Full of funny stories of past experiences [and] thoughtful reflection upon current events ... it was a pleasure to hear him hold forth on any subject." Despite this geniality of temper, Montfort sat sadly apart from the other inmates. The war had broken a small but essential part of him; his health was failing and with it his will to live. When the prisoners were taken out to bathe in the lake, Montfort attempted as he had at Pulaski to return to the remembered rhythms of an Oglethorpe summer when he would abandon his law office and try conclusions with the fishes. "No more humorous picture arises to my mind than his appearance on the days when the water gate was opened," remembered one Union guard. "While others bathed [Lieutenant Montfort] fished and his 'get up' on these occasions was unique. An old slouch hat on his head, a shirt and soldier's packet covering the upper part of the body, the slim legs bare and brogans on the feet.... On one arm he carried a basket of bait (worms dug up around the kitchens) and with the other he wielded [a] rod and line purchased from the sutler. No one ever heard of a fish being caught, but he repeated the performance each week with unflagging zeal and seeming enjoyment." In September 1862 Theodorick Montfort was paroled. The deprivations of prison life coupled with the exposures of the long journey to Georgia, however, proved more than his health could bear. He lived long enough to die in his own bed, three days after returning home.[13]

Henry Craft

Despite his presentiments of death—presentiments that amounted to wishes—Henry Craft survived to a ripe old age. He lived in Tennessee and worked as a lawyer until his death, becoming a respected, if not a very flashy, member of the Memphis bar. Before the war, he had looked with envy on the young men striding stiffly to their destinies. Henry was emotionally unequipped for such things, and he knew it. Let the others make their bids for greatness; Henry was content to sulk. "I am not a man," he confessed, "and have no business with a man's affairs or responsibilities." But sometime after the war, Henry Craft reconciled himself to himself, his feminine nature, and the quiet compensations of a life simply led. Greatness, he had come to believe, was a gewgaw, and the struggle to attain it left men foolish and failed, aloof and alone. Delivering a eulogy in 1880 for his friend Judge Trigg, Henry delivered what amounted to a eulogy for the entire male preoccupation with immortality: "To live worthily as a lawyer or a judge," he intoned, "and to be recognized by the fraternity as one who feels right, and does right, and, with conscience clear and garments unstained, to pass away, honored and regretted, is to live to very good purpose." "I do not claim," he continued,

> that [Judge Trigg] was a great man; nor, as his friend, do I regret to say so. I have always looked upon greatness as a sort of isolation inconsistent with happiness. The eagle, in his pride of place, is high and lifted up. The sweep of his imperial vision is very broad; but his look is ever downward—ever directed to what lies beneath. From his majestic flight he betakes himself to an eyrie among the crags, and dwells in an inaccessible solitude. His talons are strong, and his beak is fierce. He tears what he feeds upon, and stoops only to destroy. There may be grandeur in the stately poise, in an atmosphere so high, upon pinions so broad; and there may be complacency in the haughty sense of an outlook that takes cognizance only of what lies beneath, and even in the solitude that implies superiority; but, O, it seems cold and lonely and estranged—a sphere removed from genial sympathies, and from the joys and sorrows, and cares and companionship which span a lower life.

It was then to the joys and sorrows, cares and companionship of a lower life that men dedicated themselves in the postwar world. To be a great man involved too much hardship. It was better by far just to be a good one.[14]

NOTES

Introduction

1. Stanford E. Moses Papers, Southern Historical Collection, University of North Carolina at Chapel Hill (hereafter SHC).

2. Moses Papers, 9, 16, 47–48.

3. Moses Papers, 54, 55.

4. Moses Papers, 30, 32–33.

5. Moses Papers, 25, 70.

6. Judith Lee Hallock, ed., *The Civil War Letters of Joshua K. Callaway* (Athens: University of Georgia Press, 1997), 157, 85.

7. Hallock, *Civil War Letters*, 161–62.

8. Hallock, *Civil War Letters*, 44–45.

9. Mary Ann Cobb to Howell Cobb, December 9, 1860, quoted in William B. McCash, *Thomas R. R. Cobb: The Making of a Southern Nationalist* (Macon: Mercer University Press, 1983), 193.

10. Thomas Cobb to Mary Ann Cobb, February 11, 1861, Thomas R. R. Cobb Papers, Hargrett Library, University of Georgia (unless otherwise noted all references are to this collection); Thomas Cobb to Mary Ann Cobb, February 15, 1861; Tom Watson Brown, "The Military Career of Thomas R. R. Cobb," *Georgia Historical Quarterly*, 1961, 344–62.

11. Thomas Cobb to Mary Ann Cobb, March 19, 1862.

12. Because this book addresses in loose ways the question of "why they

fought," it is important to clearly define this question at the outset. "Why they fought" is in fact two questions, depending on who is meant by *they*. Where *they* are North and South, the separate political and cultural entities, the question can be equally rendered: What caused the war? Why did the two sides come to blows? The answer to this question is relatively straightforward. Disagreements over the right of slaveholding caused secession; disagreements over the right of secession caused the war. Thus slavery was, if not the direct cause of the war, the precipitating, the root, cause. Only since the war has there been any concerted attempt to deny this commonsense fact. What is less clear, however, is the answer to another version of "why they fought," where *they* refers to the millions of civilians in a democratic country who willingly endured hardship and death to become killers of their former countrymen. It is to this important question that this book is in part addressed. Readers interested in other perspectives should begin with James M. McPherson, *For Cause and Comrades: Why Men Fought in the Civil War* (New York: Oxford University Press, 1997).

13. Jacquelyn Dowd Hall and Anne Frior Scott, "Women in the South," in *Interpreting Southern History: Historiographical Essays in Honor of Sanford W. Higginbotham,* ed. John B. Boles and Evelyn Thomas Nolen (Baton Rouge: Louisiana State University Press, 1987), 454–509.

14. See especially Christopher J. Olsen, *Political Culture and Secession in Mississippi: Masculinity, Honor, and the Antiparty Tradition, 1830–1860* (New York: Oxford University Press, 2000).

15. While the literature on Southern masculinity is somewhat thin, much has been written on manhood in the Victorian period more generally. See, for instance, Leonard Ellis, "Men among Men: An Exploration of All-Male Relationships in Victorian America" (Ph.D. diss., Columbia University, 1982); Mark C. Carnes and Clyde Griffen, eds., *Meanings for Manhood: Constructions of Masculinity in Victorian America* (Chicago: University of Chicago Press, 1990); Nicole Etcheson, "Manliness and the Political Culture of the Old Northwest, 1790–1860," *Journal of the Early Republic,* 1995, 59–77; David G. Pugh, *Sons of Liberty: The Masculine Mind in Nineteenth-Century America* (Westport, Conn.: Greenwood, 1983); E. Anthony Rotundo, *American Manhood: Transformations in Masculinity From the Revolution to the Modern Era* (New York: Basic, 1993).

16. Henry Craft Diary, June 26, 1848, Craft, Fort, and Thorne Family Papers, SHC.

17. Here my perspective has been informed by emotional history (or emotions history as some prefer). So described, emotional history is in its infancy, though it clearly feeds on the more mature disciplines of psychohistory, intellectual and cultural history, conceptual history, gender and family history, and histories of mentalite. The first use of the term *emotional*

history that I have found is Burton Raffel, "Emotional History: An Exploratory Essay," *Biography*, 1984, 352–62; and Raffel, *American Victorians: Explorations in Emotional History* (Hamden: Archon, 1984). Though Raffel notes in his introduction to *American Victorians* that "emotional states progress, and change, with time," he does not go on to develop the idea. A professor of English, Raffel has been rightly criticized for inattention to the historical forces that shape the way emotions are felt and expressed. Carol Z. Stearns and Peter N. Stearns did not even feel it necessary to recognize Raffel's attempts in their "Introducing the History of Emotion," *Psychohistory Review*, 1990, 263–91. In the same volume, John E. Toews offers a criticism of the Stearns proposal, "Cultural History, the Construction of Subjectivity and Freudian Theory: A Critique of Carol and Peter Stearns' Proposal for a New History of the Emotions," *Psychohistory Review*, 1990, 303–18. Peter Stearns has gone on to refine his thinking in *American Cool: Constructing a Twentieth-Century Emotional Style* (New York: New York University Press, 1994) and *An Emotional History of the United States* (New York: New York University Press, 1998), edited with Jan Lewis. See also Joel Pfister and Nancy Schnog, *Inventing the Psychological: Toward a Cultural History of Emotional Life in America* (New Haven: Yale University Press, 1997).

18. Carol Bleser, ed., *Secret and Sacred: The Diaries of James Henry Hammond, a Southern Slaveholder* (New York: Oxford University Press, 1988), 150.

Chapter 1: All That Makes a Man

1. Anna to Lord, June 22, 1849, Thomas Butler King Papers, SHC. For a solid biography of Thomas Butler King, see Edward M. Steel Jr., *T. Butler King of Georgia* (Athens: University of Georgia Press, 1964). On the King family, see Steven M. Stowe, *Intimacy and Power in the Old South: Ritual in the Lives of the Planters* (Baltimore: Johns Hopkins University Press, 1987); Stephen W. Berry, "More Alluring at a Distance: Absentee Patriarchy and the Thomas Butler King Family," *Georgia Historical Quarterly*, Winter 1998, 863–96.

2. C. Vann Woodward, ed., *Mary Chesnut's Civil War* (New Haven: Yale University Press, 1981), 31.

3. Beverly Scafidel, "The Letters of William Elliott" (Ph.D. diss., University of South Carolina, 1978), 500–501.

4. James L. Petigru to Philip Porcher, June 16, 1851, in James Petigru Carson, ed., *Life, Letters, and Speeches of James Louis Petigru, The Union Man of South Carolina* (Washington: W. H. Lowdermilk, 1920), 289–90.

5. Steel, *T. Butler King of Georgia*.

6. Harvey Jackson, ed., *Letters from Alabama, Chiefly Relating to Natural History* (Tuscaloosa: University of Alabama Press, 1993), 156, 88; Faust, *James Henry Hammond and the Old South*, 131.

7. It has never been particularly clear what Aaron Burr was intending to do. Perhaps he wasn't himself sure. Interested readers should start with Thomas Perkins Abernethy, *The Burr Conspiracy* (New York: Oxford University Press, 1954). On John Murrell, see James Penick Jr., *The Great Western Land Pirate: John A. Murrell in Legend and History* (Columbia: University of Missouri Press, 1981). On the filibustering forays, see particularly Tom Chaffin, *Fatal Glory: Narciso Lopez and the First Clandestine U.S. War against Cuba* (Charlottesville: University Press of Virginia, 1996); Charles L. Dufour, *Gentle Tiger: The Gallant Life of Roberdeau Wheat* (Baton Rouge: Louisiana State University Press, 1999); and Charles Henry Brown, *Agents of Manifest Destiny: The Lives and Times of the Filibusters* (Chapel Hill: University of North Carolina Press, 1980).

8. "Manifest Destiny of the World: Its Republic and Its Empire," *Southern Literary Messenger*, September 1859, 207–9.

9. "Manifest Destiny of the World," 207; "A Few Thoughts on Southern Civilization," *Russell's Magazine*, December 1857, 218.

10. "Characteristics of Civilization," *Russell's Magazine*, November 1857, 97; "A Few Thoughts on Southern Civilization," 224; Edward Alfred Pollard, "Hints on Southern Civilization," *Southern Literary Messenger*, April 1861, 308–11.

11. The impact of classical education on Southern manhood has yet to be fully plumbed. Wayne K. Durrill makes a good start in "The Power of Ancient Words: Classical Teaching and Social Change at South Carolina College, 1804–1860," *Journal of Southern History*, 1999, 469–98. On classical education in the period more broadly, see Bruce A. Kimball, *Orators and Philosophers: A History of the Idea of Liberal Education* (New York: Teachers College Press, 1986). The study of Southern education more generally begins with Walter J. Fraser Jr., R. Frank Saunders Jr., and Jon Wakelyn, eds., *The Web of Southern Social Relations: Women, Family, and Education* (Athens: University of Georgia Press, 1985). For more on the South's sense of history, see James Britton, "The Decline and Fall of Nations in Antebellum Southern Thought: A Study of Southern Historical Consciousness, 1846–1861" (Ph.D. diss., University of North Carolina, 1988).

12. George R. Taylor, *The Transportation Revolution* (New York: Holt, Rinehart and Winston, 1951), 79; William C. Preston to Waddy Thompson, September 7, 1853, William C. Preston Papers, South Caroliniana Library, University of South Carolina. On the South's enthusiasm for and success in railroad building, see David L. Carlton, "The Revolution from Above: The National Market and the Beginnings of Industrialization in North Carolina,"

Journal of American History, 1990, 445–75; W. Kirk Wood, "U. B. Phillips and Antebellum Southern Rail Inferiority: The Origins of the Myth," *Journal of Southern History,* 1987, 173–87; Lacy K. Ford Jr., "Yeoman Farmers in the South Carolina Upcountry: Changing Production Patterns in the Late Antebellum Period," *Agricultural History,* 1986, 17–37. Particularly germane to the discussion is Ford's contention that the coming of the railroads in the 1850s marked a substantial change in the lives of Southern yeomen, who began to drift from a policy of agricultural self-sufficiency to raising cash crops for market. James Oakes catalogues other fundamental changes in the South in the late antebellum period in "From Republicanism to Liberalism: Ideological Change and the Crisis of the Old South," *American Quarterly,* 1985, 551–71.

13. James Everett Kibler Jr., ed., "The First Simms Letters: 'Letters from the West' (1826)," *Southern Literary Journal,* 1987, 81–91; Richard R. John, *Spreading the News: The American Postal System from Franklin to Morse* (Cambridge: Harvard University Press, 1995).

14. John Shofner to Michael Shofner, August 28, 1834, Michael Shofner Papers, SHC.

15. William Elliott to Ann Elliott, September 3, 1858, in Scafidel, "Letters of William Elliott," 914–15.

16. Robert Morrison to James Morrison, May 31, 1853, in Robert Hall Morrison Papers, SHC; "The Days We Live In," *Southern Literary Messenger,* December 1854, 758.

17. "The Mothers and Children of the Present Day," *Southern Literary Messenger,* May 1856.

18. James Henry Hammond to Harry Hammond, July 16, 1859, in Carol Bleser, ed., *The Hammonds of Redcliffe* (New York: Oxford University Press, 1981), 68; William Elliott to William Elliott Jr., June 19, 1849, Scafidel, "Letters of William Elliott," 579; William Elliott to Phoebe Elliott, April 26, 1854, Scafidel, "Letters of William Elliott," 765.

19. Sarah Woolfolk Wiggins, ed., *The Journals of Josiah Gorgas* (Tuscaloosa: University of Alabama Press, 1995), 17.

20. Joseph G. Baldwin, *The Flush Times of Alabama and Mississippi: A Series of Sketches* (New York: Appleton, 1853), 227; Woodward, *Mary Chesnut's Civil War,* xxxiv.

21. J.E.B. Stuart to his cousin Bettie Hairston, October 28, 1853, in Peter W. Hairston, ed., "J.E.B. Stuart's Letters to His Hairston Kin, 1850–1855," *North Carolina History Review,* 1974, 304.

22. "Leaves from a Dreamer's Diary," *Russell's Magazine,* October 1858, 30, 32.

23. John M. Lincoln to cousin Sue Heiskell, November 12, 1857, Edward Marvin Steel Papers, SHC.

24. April 18, 1849, entry in Everard Baker Diary, SHC.

25. Richard Smith Elliott, *Notes Taken in Sixty Years* (St. Louis: R. P. Studley, 1883), 3.

26. Anna King to Florence King, August 7, 1851, King-Wilder Papers, Georgia Historical Society, Savannah; William Gilmore Simms quoted in John McCardell, "Poetry and the Practical: William Gilmore Simms," in Michael O'Brien and David Moltke-Hansen, eds., *Intellectual Life in Antebellum Charleston* (Knoxville: University of Tennessee Press, 1986), 204.

27. Wallace Cumming to Harriet Alexander, August 6, 1852, Alexander-Hillhouse Papers, SHC; Scafidel, "Letters of William Elliott," 497–98.

28. Giles J. Patterson, *Journal of a Southern Student, 1846–48, with Letters of a Later Period* (Nashville: Vanderbilt University Press, 1944), 51.

29. "Modern Oratory," *Southern Literary Messenger*, June 1852, 370.

30. *Boston Daily Star*, November 25, 1845, 2. For newspaper editorials detailing Poe's Lyceum appearance, see Kent P. Ljungquist, "Poe's 'Al Aaraaf' and the Boston Lyceum: Contributions to Primary and Secondary Bibliography," *Victorian Periodicals Review*, 1995, 199–216. For more background on the incident, consult Katherine Hemple Prown, "The Cavalier and the Syren: Edgar Allan Poe, Cornelia Wells Walter, and the Boston Lyceum Incident," *New England Quarterly*, 1993, 110–23.

31. "Edgar A. Poe," *Southern Literary Messenger*, April 1854, 250, 252; Daniel Hoffman, *Poe Poe Poe Poe Poe Poe Poe* (Baton Rouge: Louisiana State University Press, 1998), 34. Poe was skeptical about progress, but he could never fully shake the grandiosity of ambition ushered in by the romantic movement. The result was a man tragically at war with himself, given over to vain imaginings that were at once splendid and fantastic, morbid and doomed. In this, of course, he was anticipated by Byron: "The way to riches, to Greatness, lies before me," the poet wrote to his mother at age fifteen. "I can, I will cut myself a path through the world or perish." Most helpful in my readings of Poe were David Leverenz, "Poe and Gentry Virginia: Provincial Gentleman, Textual Aristocrat, Man of the Crowd," in Ann Goodwyn Jones and Susan V. Donaldson, eds., *Haunted Bodies: Gender and Southern Texts* (Charlottesville: University Press of Virginia, 1997), 79–108; Scott Peeples, *Edgar Allan Poe Revisited* (New York: Twayne, 1998); Louis D. Rubin, *The Edge of the Swamp: A Study in the Literature and Society of the Old South* (Baton Rouge: Louisiana State University Press, 1989); Larzer Ziff, "The Self Divided by Democracy: Edgar Allan Poe and the Already-Answered Question," in Ziff, *Literary Democracy: The Declaration of Cultural Independence in America* (New York: Viking, 1981), 67–86; J. Gerald Kennedy, "The Violence of Melancholy: Poe against Himself," *American Literary History* 8, no. 3 (1996): 533–51; Lawrence Frank, " 'The Murders in the Rue Morgue': Edgar Allan Poe's Evolutionary Reverie," *Nineteenth-Century Literature* 50, no. 2 (1995): 168–88; Burton R. Pollin, "A

New Englander's Obituary Eulogy of Poe," *American Periodicals* 4 (1994): 1–11; Joan Dayan, "Amorous Bondage: Poe, Ladies, and Slaves," *American Literature* 66, no. 2 (1994): 239–73; James Livingston, "Subjectivity and Slavery in Poe's Autobiography of Ambitious Love," *Psychohistory Review* 21, no. 2 (1993): 175–96; "A Posthumous Assessment: The 1849–1850 Periodical Press Response to Edgar Allan Poe," *American Periodicals* 2 (1992): 6–50; John Cleman, "Irresistible Impulses: Edgar Allan Poe and the Insanity Defense," *American Literature* 63, no. 4 (1991): 623–40; Elizabeth Fox-Genovese, "The Fettered Mind: Time, Place, and the Literary Imagination of the Old South," *Georgia Historical Quarterly* 74, no. 4 (1990): 622–50; Shawn Rosenheim, "The King of 'Secret Readers': Edgar Poe, Cryptography, and the Origins of the Detective Story," *English Literary History* 56, no. 2 (1990): 375–400; Kenneth Alan Hovey, "Critical Provincialism: Poe's Poetic Principle in Antebellum Context," *American Quarterly* 39, no. 3 (1987): 341–54; Michael Lawrence Burduck, "Phobic Pressure Points in Poe: The Nineteenth-Century Reader and His Fears" (Ph.D. diss., University of Mississippi, 1984); Richard Godden, "Edgar Allan Poe and the Detection of Riot," *Literature and History* 8, no. 2 (1982): 206–31, 272; Barnaby Conrad, "Genius and Intemperance," *Horizon* 23, no. 12 (1980): 33–40; C. Hugh Holman, "Another Look at Nineteenth-Century Southern Fiction," *Southern Humanities Review* 14, no. 3 (1980): 235–45; Jack Kaufhold, "The Humor of Edgar Allan Poe," *Virginia Cavalcade* 29, no. 3 (1980): 136–43; J. Gerald Kennedy, "Poe and Magazine Writing on Premature Burial," *Studies in the American Renaissance*, 1977, 165–78; Stuart Levine, "Poe and American Society," *Canadian Review of American Studies* 9, no. 1 (1978): 16–33; Allan Smith, "The Psychological Context of Three Tales by Poe," *Journal of American Studies* 7, no. 3 (1973): 279–92; Charles L. Sanford, "Edgar Allan Poe: A Blight upon the Landscape," *American Quarterly* 20, no. 1 (1968): 54–66; Claude Richard, "Poe and the Yankee Hero: An Interpretation of Diddling Considered as One of the Exact Sciences," *Mississippi Quarterly* 21, no. 2 (1968): 93–109; Madeleine B. Sterne, "Poe: 'The Mental Temperament' for Phrenologists," *American Literature* 40, no. 2 (1968): 155–63; Miriam Weiss, "Poe's Catterina," *Mississippi Quarterly* 19, no. 1 (1966): 29–33; Joseph M. Garrison Jr., "The Function of Terror in the Work of Edgar Allan Poe," *American Quarterly* 18, no. 2 (1966): 136–50; Curtis Dahl, "The American School of Catastrophe," *American Quarterly* 11, no. 3 (1959): 380–90.

Long after his death, Poe was generating ambivalent column inches for the *Southern Literary Messenger* and other antebellum magazines. For contemporary reviews and opinions of Edgar Allan Poe, see especially John Moncure Daniel, "Edgar Allan Poe," *Southern Literary Messenger*, March 1850, 172–87 ("Among all his poems, there are only two or three which are not execrably bad. The majority of his prose writings are the children of want and dyspepsia, of printer's devils and of blue devils."); "Edgar A. Poe,"

Southern Literary Messenger, April 1854, 249–53 ("Surely none of the hybrids which geology has dug out of the graves of Chaos and exhibited to our shuddering view is half so strange a compound as was Edgar A. Poe."); "Edgar Allan Poe," *Ladies' Repository*, July 1859, 419–23 ("Edgar Allan Poe was incontestably one of the most worthless persons of whom we have any record in the world of letters."); P. Pendleton Cooke, "Edgar Allan Poe: His Literary Merits Considered," *Southern Literary Messenger*, January 1848, 34–38 ("That he [Poe] would be a greater favorite with the majority of readers if he brought his singular capacity for vivid and truthlike narrative to bear on subjects nearer ordinary life, and of a more cheerful and happy character, does not I think admit of a doubt."); John Reuben Thompson, "The Late Edgar A. Poe," *Southern Literary Messenger*, November 1849, 694–97 ("It is remarkable . . . that a mind so prone to unrestrained imaginings should be capable of analytic investigation or studious research. Yet few excelled Mr. Poe in power of analysis or patient application. Such are the contradictions of the human intellect. He was an impersonated antithesis."); "The Raven— By Edgar A. Poe," *Southern Literary Messenger*, November 1857, 331–35 (Poe's scribblings sound "like the utterances of a full heart poured out—not for the sake of telling its sad story to a sympathizing ear—but because he is mastered by his emotions and cannot help giving vent to them."); and W. W. Kinsley, "The Province of Gloom in Literature," *Ladies' Repository*, January 1862, 45–47 (Poe "lived a life whose wickedness was equaled only by its melancholy; he came upon the very confines of moral sentiment without having one ray of its celestial light warming his heart.").

32. Bleser, *Secret and Sacred*, 263.

Chapter Two: Two Separate Yet Most Intimate Things

1. Poe explored the reverie of doomed ambition in much of his work. See especially J. Gerald Kennedy, "The Violence of Melancholy: Poe against Himself," *American Literary History*, 1996, 533–51; and Joan Dayan, "Amorous Bondage: Poe, Ladies, and Slaves," *American Literature*, 1994, 239–73. Quotes here come from Poe's *Tamerlane*. Interestingly, there are some strikingly similar lines in *Tamerlane* and *Hamlet*. Guildenstern's comment, "Which dreams, indeed, are ambition; for the very substance of the ambitious is merely the shadow of a dream" (2.2) is echoed by Poe: "Yet *more* than worthy of the love / My spirit struggled with, and strove, / When, on the mountain peak, alone, / Ambition lent it a new tone— / . . . / That was new pleasure—the ideal, / Dim, vanities of dreams by night— / And dimmer nothings which were real— / (Shadows—and a more shadowy light!)."

2. Henry Hughes Diary, May 21, 1848, April 30, 1848, and March 4, 1849, Mississippi Department of Archives and History. Remarkably, Hughes even dreamed of a return to Tamerlane's mountain, to a time before the bugle had awakened him. "O Ambition," he lamented. "My hand clenches,

my brow knits, I groan in Spirit. The name of a great man, an allusion to glory, makes my heart sink and [my] blood flow back until I almost faint. Would I were a Shepherd boy, remote from the busy haunts of men. . . . Oh, Oh! Let me not be compelled to live forever. Let me forever sleep and dream not." Hughes Diary, February 25, 1849, and January 14, 1849.

3. Hughes Diary, January 9, 1853.

4. Allan Nevins, *The Emergence of Lincoln: Douglas, Buchanan and Party Chaos, 1857–1859* (New York: Scribner's, 1950), 287–88; Roy F. Nichols, *The Disruption of American Democracy* (New York: Macmillan, 1948), 164–65; John Holt Merchant Jr., "Laurence M. Keitt: South Carolina Fire-Eater" (Ph.D. diss., University of Virginia, 1976), 160–73; William Henry Trescott to William Porcher Miles, February 7, 1858, William Porcher Miles Papers, SHC. Although it is difficult to piece together the true facts of the altercation, it seems probable that Grow knocked the (already tipsy) Keitt to the floor. "No harm came of the quarrel & consequent *row* in the House," noted Josiah Gorgas in his diary. "Mr. K[eitt] made a full apology, but has no recollection of being knocked down by Grow as asserted by the letter writers. He is a good deal laughed at by the opposition press, because his friends assert that he stumbled & fell.' " Josiah Gorgas to wife, February 26, 1858, in Wiggins, *Journals of Josiah Gorgas,* 16. Keitt, of course, had earlier distinguished himself for his involvement in Preston Brooks's caning of Charles Sumner. When Brooks first hatched the idea, Keitt begged to be allowed to carry it out. Brooks of course refused, but Keitt was nearby when Brooks began his assault, and made sure the "licks were well laid on" by threatening any man who moved to interrupt the flogging. Keitt helped Brooks dress a wound above his eye inflicted by the recoil of the cane, and both congressmen resigned their seats in protest—only to be resoundingly reelected. For a sustained treatment of the caning, see Harlan Gradin, "Losing Control: The Caning of Charles Sumner and the Breakdown of Antebellum Political Culture" (Ph.D. diss., University of North Carolina, 1991). The only sustained treatment of Keitt that has been published is a prosopographical chapter on him and Louis Wigfall in Eric H. Walther, *The Fire-Eaters* (Baton Rouge: Louisiana State University Press, 1992), 160–94.

5. Merchant, "Laurence M. Keitt," 15.

6. Laurence Massillon Keitt to Susan Sparks, January 20, 1855, Special Collections Library, Duke University (hereafter, unless otherwise noted, all references are to this collection); Keitt to Sparks, March 16, 1855; Keitt to Sparks, February 14, 1855.

7. Keitt to Sparks, February 14, 1855; Keitt to Sparks, January 20, 1855.

8. Merchant, "Laurence M. Keitt," 206–7; *Harper's Weekly*, December 22, 1860, 802.

9. Merchant, "Laurence M. Keitt," 14–16; Keitt to Sparks, January 20, 1855.

10. Keitt to Sparks, September 19, 1855; Merchant, "Laurence M. Keitt."

11. James Everett Kibler Jr., *Poetry and the Practical* (Fayetteville: University of Arkansas Press, 1992), 6–7, 15, 17, 88–94. Scholars interested in Simms should begin with Drew Gilpin Faust, *A Sacred Circle: The Dilemma of the Intellectual in the Old South, 1840–1860* (Baltimore: Johns Hopkins University Press, 1977); John McCardell, "Poetry and the Practical: William Gilmore Simms," in O'Brien and Moltke-Hansen, *Intellectual Life in Antebellum Charleston*, 186–210; John Caldwell Guilds, ed., *"Long Years of Neglect:" The Work and Reputation of William Gilmore Simms* (Fayetteville: University of Arkansas Press, 1988); John Caldwell Guilds, *Simms: A Literary Life* (Fayetteville: University of Arkansas Press, 1992); and John Caldwell Guilds and Caroline Collins, eds., *William Gilmore Simms and the American Frontier* (Athens: University of Georgia Press, 1997). Simms was often little more than a forge, churning out a regional literature that is marred equally by his hurry, his petulance, his grinding discipline, and his inability to forget himself when he wrote of others. (Simms himself seemed to understand this. His self-composed epitaph reads: "Here lies one who after a reasonably long life, distinguished chiefly by unceasing labors, left all his better works undone.") In fairness, it should be noted that Simms had moments, rare but delightful, when he wrote with verve and lilt and brooded with deep passion on the problems that beset his region and his country. Never did he do so better than in *Poetry and the Practical*.

The poetic proclivity of antebellum Southerners has yet to be fully explored. In the pages of the South's literary magazines, a battle was being waged between romantics and classicists, and the poetics of Simms and Keitt needs to be understood in this context. Both Simms and Keitt fell somewhere in the middle, exploring classical themes with a romantic flourish. Scholars wishing for a start on this subject might begin with Elizabeth Fox-Genovese, "The Fettered Mind: Time, Place, and the Literary Imagination of the Old South," *Georgia Historical Quarterly*, 1990, 622–50; Edd Parks, *Henry Timrod* (New York: Twayne, 1964); Edd Winfield Parks, *The Essays of Henry Timrod* (Athens: University of Georgia Press, 1942); Richard J. Calhoun, ed., *Witness to Sorrow: The Antebellum Autobiography of William J. Grayson* (Columbia: University of South Carolina Press, 1990).

12. Keitt to Sparks, September 19, 1855. While it is difficult to prove that Keitt read these lectures, there is some circumstantial evidence to support the theory. On October 22, 1855, Keitt wrote to Sue: "I do not know when Simms will be at Darlington C[ourt]. H[ouse]. Sometime in the winter. He came to see me in Charleston, but I was ill from exposure, as I had gone down in the night train from Barnwell. The talk between us was general. He has just written me a letter, but all he says is that he will be over here in a few weeks. Pray go to hear him, for his lectures are admirable."

13. Kibler, *Poetry and the Practical*, 88; Keitt to Sparks, October 13, 1855; Keitt to Sparks, April 30, 1856; Keitt to Sparks, June 19, 1856.

14. Keitt to Sparks, April 30, 1855; Keitt to Sparks, undated June 1855. Again, when laid side by side, Keitt's extended romantic diatribe against stagnation (as revealed in his letters to Susan Sparks) and Simms's *Poetry and the Practical* yield many points of agreement. Keitt's sense of politics as epic poem, for instance, almost certainly drew on Simms's work: "The soul of art is Imagination! That high reaching genius which perpetually craves to soar—to spread abroad the wing of conquest—to cast over all things the eye of discovery—to penetrate the depths of matter,—to explore the mysteries of space; and by lifting the soul of man in search, urge upon him the sleepless necessity which makes him rejoice forever in the development of his own wondrous powers! What you have done—what you are—is due wholly to this own faculty. It is the soul of all the rest. The race is simply brutal, until spiritualized by this crowning gift, and the radical differences existing between men and races, are due to the unequal distribution of it in their allotment! This faculty has been your pioneer, has hewn out your way through rock and forest, has taken for you the seals from off the mysterious portals of the deep. It has informed your courage, your enterprise—lighted up your whole career, so that, though you may not have written, you have lived a glorious epic poem!" Here poetry has burst its confines as we understand them. Simms is calling for a poetry of practice, wherein men live out their imaginations, build their dreams, and found, thereby, a Civilization. Keitt was seduced by just such a romantic project, and we must therefore take seriously his claim to be living an epic poem.

15. Keitt to Sparks, June 6, 1855; Keitt to Sparks, July 11, 1855; Keitt to Sparks, undated June 1855.

16. Keitt to Sparks, July 29, 1855; Keitt to Sparks, July 11, 1855; Keitt to Sparks, January 20, 1855; Keitt to Sparks, June 6, 1855; Keitt to Sparks, undated June 1855; Keitt to Sparks, July 29, 1855. Keitt's discussion here suggests that we should study the impact of Europe's 1848 revolutions on the American psyche, with particular attention to how American disintegration, in the form of sectionalism, was folded into a growing sense that the entire Atlantic world was poised on the brink of revolutionary consolidation.

17. Keitt to Sparks, September 11, 1855; Keitt to Sparks, May 29, 1856. As might be expected, Keitt saw the Sumner caning not merely as a blow for proslavery forces but as further fuel for his coming apocalypse: "Brooks that day flogged Sumner of Massachusetts, and he did it well and soundly. He combined in happy proportions freedom of speech and freedom of the cudgel. Sumner had slandered Judge Butler in his absence. The feeling is pretty much sectional. If the northern men had stood up, the city would now float with blood. The fact is the feeling is wild and fierce. The Kansas fight has just occurred and the times are stirring. Everybody here feels as if we are upon a volcano. I am glad of it, for I am tired of stagnation" (Keitt to Sparks, May 29, 1856).

18. Keitt to Sparks, undated February 1855; Keitt to Sparks, May 3, 1855; Keitt to Sparks, March 9, 1855.

19. Keitt to Sparks, undated February 1855.

20. Keitt to Sparks, undated February 1855; Keitt to Sparks, February 14, 1855; Keitt to Sparks, March 16, 1855; Keitt to Sparks, May 3, 1855.

21. Keitt to Sparks, May 9, 1855.

22. Keitt to Sparks, April 13, 1856; Keitt to Sparks, June 19, 1856; Keitt to Sparks, May 9, 1856; Keitt to Sparks, May 30, 1856; Keitt to Sparks, undated June 1855; Keitt to Sparks, May 30, 1855; Keitt to Sparks, May 9, 1855.

23. Keitt to Sparks, September 26, 1855; Keitt to Sparks, February 2, 1856.

24. Keitt to Sparks, undated June 1855; Keitt to Sparks, November 8, 1855.

25. Keitt to Sparks, February 17, 1856.

26. Keitt to Sparks, July 7, 1856.

27. Hubert H. McAlexander, "Flush Times in Holly Springs," *Journal of Mississippi History*, 1986, 1–13; Henry Craft Diary, July 30, 1848, Craft, Fort, and Thorne Family Papers, SHC (hereafter, unless otherwise noted, all references are to this collection). Also on the history of Holly Springs, see William Baskerville Hamilton, *Holly Springs, Mississippi, to the year 1878* (Holly Springs: Marshall County Historical Society, 1984). For other contemporary perspectives on Mississippi's startling transformation from frontier to cotton kingdom, see J.F.H. Claiborne, *Mississippi, as a Province, Territory, and State: With Biographical Notices of Eminent Citizens* (Jackson: Power & Barksdale, 1880); and Percy L. Rainwater, ed., *Random Recollections of Early Days in Mississippi, by H. S. Fulkerson* (Baton Rouge: Otto Claitor, 1937). For secondary sources, consult John Hebron Moore, *The Emergence of the Cotton Kingdom in the Old Southwest: Mississippi, 1770–1860* (Baton Rouge: Louisiana State University Press, 1988); and Bradley G. Bond, *Political Culture in the Nineteenth-Century South: Mississippi, 1830–1900* (Baton Rouge: Louisiana State University Press, 1995). On the effect of these changes on the aboriginal population, see Daniel H. Usner Jr., "American Indians on the Cotton Frontier: Changing Economic Relations with Citizens and Slaves in the Mississippi Territory," *Journal of American History*, 1985, 297–317.

28. Henry Craft Diary, April 8, 1848; Henry Craft Diary, April 11, 1849.

29. Henry Craft Diary, April 28, 1848; Henry Craft Diary, April 30, 1848.

30. Henry Craft Diary, April 30, 1848.

31. Henry Craft Diary, May 4, 1848.

32. Henry Craft Diary, July 12, 1848.

33. Henry Craft Diary, July 30, 1848.

34. Henry Craft Diary, October 29, 1848.

35. Henry Craft Diary, April 8, 1848.

36. Henry Craft Diary, April 8, 1848; Henry Craft Diary, May 9, 1848; Henry Craft Diary, April 28, 1848.

37. Henry Craft Diary, April 30, 1848.

38. Henry Craft Diary, June 25, 1848; Henry Craft Diary, June 26, 1848. On the fondness of romantics for overindulging in the mourning of a beautiful woman, see much of Poe and Michael O'Brien, "Politics, Romanticism, and Hugh Legare: 'The Fondness of Disappointed Love,' " in his *Rethinking the South: Essays in Intellectual History* (Baltimore: Johns Hopkins University Press, 1988), 57–83.

39. Henry Craft Diary, April 30, 1848; Henry Craft Diary, June 26, 1848. Clearly, Henry Craft suffered from some form of depression or melancholia that went well beyond his mourning for Lucy. Today such problems can be treated, but in the nineteenth century feelings of self-loathing and unworthiness became self-perpetuating as depressed men and women blamed themselves for being abnormal. For a longer view on the history of depression, see Stanley W. Jackson, *Melancholia and Depression: From Hippocratic Times to the Modern Times* (New Haven: Yale University Press, 1986); and Aaron T. Beck, John Paul Brady, and Jacques M. Quen, *The History of Depression* (New York: Psychiatric Annals, 1977).

40. Henry Craft Diary, June 25, 1848; Henry Craft Diary, July 2, 1848.

41. Henry Craft Diary, July 2, 1848; Henry Craft Diary, June 26, 1848; Henry Craft Diary, July 12, 1848.

42. Henry Craft Diary, June 25, 1848; Henry Craft to Matt, February 3, 1848; Henry Craft Diary, October 8, 1848.

43. Henry Craft Diary, October 29, 1848; Henry Craft Diary, November 3, 1848.

44. Henry Craft Diary, June 26, 1848; Henry Craft Diary, October 8, 1848.

45. Henry Craft Diary, August 28, 1859.

46. Henry Craft Diary, October 25, 1860; Henry Craft Diary, May 20, 1860.

47. Henry Craft Diary, August 12, 1860.

48. Henry Craft Diary, December 30, 1860; Henry Craft Diary, August 19, 1860.

49. Henry Craft Diary, December 2, 1860.

50. Henry Craft Diary, August 12, 1860.

51. Henry Craft Diary, August 19, 1860; Henry Craft Diary, May 2, 1859; Henry Craft to sister, February 3, 1848; Henry Craft Diary, August 12, 1860.

52. Henry Craft Diary, December 30, 1860; Henry Craft Diary, December 31, 1860.

Chapter 3: Across a Great Divide

1. Childs, *Rice Planter and Sportsman*, 71–72; Charles L. Dufour, *Gentle Tiger: The Gallant Life of Roberdeau Wheat* (Baton Rouge: Louisiana State

University Press, 1957), 75; "Courtship Made Easy," *Southern Literary Messenger*, July 1857, 14.

2. Carson, *Life, Letters, and Speeches of James Louis Petigru*, 246.

3. Lord King to brother Thomas Butler King Jr., January 31, 1858, Thomas Butler King Papers; "Courtship Made Easy," 18; the man is identified only as "Alexander," in "Courtship Made Easy," 13–14.

4. F. W. Shelton, "On Old Bachelors," *Southern Literary Messenger*, April 1853, 223–28; "Courtship Made Easy," 15.

5. Harriet Alexander to William Cumming, August 4, 1852, Alexander and Hillhouse Family Papers, SHC; Toosie (last name unknown) to Lordy King, Thomas Butler King Papers. On letter writing as genre, see Lenore Hoffman and Margo Culley, eds., *Women's Personal Narratives: Essays in Criticism and Pedagogy* (New York: Modern Language Association, 1985); Steven M. Stowe, "The Rhetoric of Authority: The Making of Social Values in Planter Family Correspondence," *Journal of American History*, 1987, 916–33, and "Singleton's Tooth: Thoughts on the Form and Meaning of Antebellum Southern Family Correspondence," *Southern Review*, 1989, 323–33. On letter writing and courtship, see Stowe, *Intimacy and Power*; and Dykstra, *Searching the Heart*.

6. Wes Halliburton to Juliet Halliburton, April 17, 1861, John Wesley Halliburton Papers, SHC.

7. Harry St. John Dixon Diary, June 6, 1861, SHC; Wes Halliburton to Juliet Halliburton, April 30, 1861.

8. Wes Halliburton to Juliet Halliburton, April 3, 1861, April 14, 1861.

9. George Peddy Cuttino, ed., *Saddle Bag and Spinning Wheel, Being the Civil War letters of George W. Peddy, M.D., Surgeon, 56th Georgia Volunteer Regiment, C.S.A., and his wife Kate Featherston Peddy* (Macon: Mercer University Press, 1981), 175; William M. Cash and Lucy Somerville Howorth, eds., *My Dear Nellie: The Civil War Letters of William L. Nugent to Eleanor Smith Nugent* (Jackson: University Press of Mississippi, 1977), 100.

10. William W. Hassler, ed., *The General to His Lady: The Civil War Letters of William Dorsey Pender to Fanny Pender* (Chapel Hill: University of North Carolina Press, 1962), 185–86, 122.

11. Cash and Howorth, *My Dear Nellie*, 25–26; Cuttino, *Saddle Bag and Spinning Wheel*, 25–26; Hassler, *General to His Lady*, 57–58, 43–44, 45–46. William Nugent's sense that his wife could be an iconoclast to the religion he made of her is echoed by Laurence Keitt: "I go soon away, and to a tempest-swept arena where the fierce storm spirit will be unchained, and where I shall meet the conflict now with a steadier eye and a stronger arm, and will clutch the laurel of victory with a readier grasp because of you. My triumphs now—if any such I win—will be for you and mainly because of you. Then, dear Sue, be not an iconoclast to my heart and trouble not and deface not its best image" (Keitt to Sparks, November 8, 1855, Laurence Keitt Papers).

12. Rev. R. Q. Mallard to Mary Sharpe Jones, November 3, 1856, in Robert Manson Myers, ed., *The Children of Pride: A True Story of Georgia and the Civil War* (New Haven: Yale University Press, 1972), 2590; George Fitzhugh, "The Women of the South," *DeBow's Review*, August 1861, 148, 152. Scholars interested in the life of antebellum Southern women should begin with Elizabeth Fox-Genovese's *Within the Plantation Household* (Chapel Hill: University of North Carolina Press, 1988). Slavery and rural isolation, Fox-Genovese believes, defined Southern women's experience in ways significantly different from that of their Northern counterparts. While granting the major thrust of recent historiography—that Southern women's involvement in politics, reform, education, and unruliness needs to be taken seriously—this book places the stress where Fox-Genovese placed it—on the harrowing confinement of the planter woman's sphere, a confinement that could be compensated for, but never fully assuaged, by associational involvement and a few trips to town. (For a very thoughtful review of Fox-Genovese's book, see Suzanne Lebsock, "Complicity and Contention: Women in the Plantation South," *Georgia Historical Quarterly*, 1990, 59–83).

13. Laura Cole to her cousin, Cecelia, undated, Brumby and Smith Family Papers, SHC, 59.

14. Cash and Howorth, *My Dear Nellie*, 58; Cuttino, *Saddle Bag and Spinning Wheel*, 184, 133; Harriet Alexander to William Cumming, October 12, 1852, Alexander and Hillhouse Family Papers.

15. Anna Page to Hannah Page, March 1, 1823, Thomas Butler King Papers; Anna King to Thomas King, June 9, 1842, Thomas Butler King Papers.

16. Anna King to Thomas King, April 11, 1850, Thomas Butler King Papers; Anna King to Lord King, July 11, 1849, Thomas Butler King Papers; Anna King to Lord King, September 24, 1848, Thomas Butler King Papers; Anna King to Florence King, January 14, 1852, King-Wilder Papers, Georgia Historical Society–Savannah; Anna King to Florence King, December 14, 1851, King-Wilder Papers; Anna King to Florence King, February 29, 1852, King-Wilder Papers; Anna King to Hannah Couper, October 5, 1852, William Audley Couper Papers, SHC.

17. Anna King to Florence King, undated 1851 or 1852, King-Wilder Papers; Anna King to Lord King, May 15, 1849, Thomas Butler King Papers; Anna King to Lord King, June 12, 1849, Thomas Butler King Papers; Anna King to Hannah Couper, June 15, 1852, William Audley Couper Papers; Anna King to Hannah Couper, June 19, 1852, William Audley Couper Papers; Anna King to Hannah Couper, June 26, 1852, William Audley Couper Papers; Anna King to Florence King, October 14, 1851, King-Wilder Papers; Anna King to Florence King, November 13, 1851, King-Wilder Papers; Anna King to Hannah Couper, September 22, 1852, William Audley Couper Papers; Anna to Florence, undated 1851 or 1852, King-Wilder Papers.

18. Anna King to Hannah Couper, July 10, 1852, William Audley Couper

Papers; Anna King to Thomas King, June 25, 1848, Thomas Butler King Papers.

19. Anna King to Florence King, September 22, 1851, King-Wilder Papers; Anna King to Hannah Couper, December 21, 1856, William Audley Couper Papers.

20. Anna King to Thomas King, April 7, 1848, Thomas Butler King Papers; Anna King to Thomas King, June 9, 1842, Thomas Butler King Papers; Anna King to Florence King, August 21, 1851, Thomas Butler King Papers; Anna King to Hannah Couper, July 3, 1852, William Audley Couper Papers; Anna King to Hannah Couper, September 25, 1852, William Audley Couper Papers.

21. Anna to Floyd and Tip, January 21, 1859, King-Wilder Papers; Anna King to Georgia King, July 8, 1859, King-Wilder Papers; Anna King to Thomas King, April 2, 1859, Thomas Butler King Papers.

22. Anna King to Thomas King, April 2, 1859, Thomas Butler King Papers; Anna King to Georgia King, June 25, 1859, King-Wilder Papers; Anna King to Georgia King, July 19, 1859, King-Wilder Papers; Anna King to Georgia King, July 30, 1859, King-Wilder Papers; Anna King to Georgia King, August 10, 1859, King-Wilder Papers; Anna King to Florence King, December 14, 1851, King-Wilder Papers; Florence King to Floyd King, May 25, 1860, Thomas Butler King Papers.

23. On Sarah Ann Haynsworth Gayle, see Fox-Genovese, *Within the Plantation Household*, 1–35; Mary Chesnut, *A Diary from Dixie* (New York: D. Appleton, 1905), 124; Caroline Gilman, *Recollections of a Southern Matron*, 160. On the marriage of Benjamin and Elizabeth Perry, see Carol K. Bleser, "The Perrys of Greenville: A Nineteenth-Century Marriage," in Walter Fraser, ed., *The Web of Southern Social Relations*, 72–89. On the gendered experience of time, see Steven M. Stowe, "City, Country, and the Feminine Voice," in O'Brien and Moltke-Hansen, *Intellectual Life in Antebellum Charleston*, 295–324.

24. Susan Cornwall Diary, March 18, 1857, SHC; Cornelia Spencer Diary, undated July 1865, SHC; Sarah Morgan Diary, May 23, 1862, in Charles East, ed., *The Civil War Diary of Sarah Morgan* (Athens: University of Georgia Press, 1991), 83; Laura Cole to her cousin, Cecilia, undated, Brumby and Smith Family Papers, SHC, 58. Ms. Cole's disgust with the crimson velvet riding dress is echoed by an unidentified Selma diarist in Michael O'Brien's *An Evening When Alone*: "This afternoon has been greatly enlivened by the visit of a dutch pedlar! with silks and satins for sale, I was called upon for my opinion, I thought they were all hideous but did not say so before the soi-distant Polonois—and duly assisted Mary in choosing a small shawl[. T]his is quite an event, and will be very useful in furnishing us with a subject for conversation for one week at least—we are in the habit here of making the most of these matters" (paperback edition), 131. My

point, again, is not remotely to suggest that all women were unhappy. Rather, female unhappiness was a kind of emotional style that all women recognized as a grim potential. Elodie Todd, for instance, did not like to cry because she thought it might be habit-forming and take her down the very female road of indulgent loneliness and helpless fretting. "I regard my grief as too sacred to be seen by every eye," she noted, "and am selfish enough to *enjoy it entirely alone* when I have the inclination to indulge [in tears] which I very seldom do as I think matters will not be improved, and I have a great dread of an unhappy person who is a tax on any one, and you know the habit might increase. I am afraid of being like Mrs. Hardie, not only miserable myself but causing those around me to be so too" (Elodie Todd to Nathaniel Dawson, May 27, 1861, Nathaniel Henry Rhodes Dawson Papers, SHC).

25. Georgia King to Richard Cuyler King, May 14, 1860, Thomas Butler King Papers; East, *Civil War Diary of Sarah Morgan*, 352–53.

26. O'Brien, *An Evening When Alone*, 135; Scafidel, "Letters of William Elliott," 792; Tristram Skinner to Eliza Harwood, May 10, 1841, Skinner Family Papers; O'Brien, *An Evening When Alone*, 138.

27. O'Brien, ed., *An Evening When Alone*, 78; Elliott Ashkenazi, ed., *The Civil War Diary of Clara Solomon: Growing up in New Orleans, 1861–1962* (Baton Rouge: Louisiana State University Press, 1995); Virginia Ingraham Burr, *The Secret Eye: The Journal of Ella Gertrude Clanton Thomas, 1848–1889* (Chapel Hill: University of North Carolina Press, 1990).

28. East, *Civil War Diary of Sarah Morgan*, 248–49, 155–56.

29. O'Brien, ed., *An Evening When Alone*, 137, 135.

30. Woodward, ed., *Mary Chesnut's Civil War*, 25; East, *Civil War Diary of Sarah Morgan*, 155; Sarah Wadley Diary (typescript), SHC, 119–20.

31. Margaret Ann (Meta) (Morris) Grimball Diary, March 15, 1861 and March 20, 1861, SHC; Elizabeth Clitherall Diary, November 20, 1860, SHC.

Chapter 4: Purity and Desire

1. William Elliott, *Carolina Sports by Land and Water: including incidents of devil-fishing, wild-cat, deer and bear hunting, etc.* (New York: Derby & Jackson, 1859); William Elliott to Ann Elliott, August 27, 1855, Scafidel, "Letters of William Elliott," 820–21.

2. On Southerners as Victorians, see Carol Bleser, ed., *In Joy and in Sorrow: Women, Family, and Marriage in the Victorian South, 1830–1900* (New York: Oxford University Press, 1991). In the introduction, C. Vann Woodward notes, "The term 'Victorian' in the general title is to be understood as more than a chronological designation, or one taken to suggest conventional notions of propriety, authority, and prim conduct. 'Victorian' South differed

from Victorian England and Victorian New England." (xxi). See also "Rediscovering the Victorians," *Wilson Quarterly*, Spring 1997, 15–55.

3. R.F.W. Allston to Ben Allston, February 25, 1852, Allston Papers, South Carolina Historical Society.

4. Ibid.

5. Ibid.

6. David Outlaw to Emily Outlaw, January 29, 1849, David Outlaw Papers, SHC (hereafter, unless otherwise noted, all references are to this collection); David Outlaw to Emily Outlaw, July 28, 1848. On the general tenor of the House during the debates that would culminate in the Compromise of 1850, see Holman Hamilton, *Prologue to Conflict: The Crisis and Compromise of 1850* (Lexington: University of Kentucky Press, 1964); Michael F. Holt, *The Political Crisis of the 1850s* (New York: Wiley, 1978); Edwin Charles Rozwenc, *The Compromise of 1850* (Boston: D. C. Heath, 1957); and Merrill D. Peterson, *The Great Triumvirate: Webster, Clay, and Calhoun* (New York: Oxford University Press, 1987). Outlaw's assessment that "negroes" constituted the "everlasting topic" of debate before the assembly echoes that of Thomas Hart Benton, senator from Missouri, who likened the omnipresence of the slavery issue in 1848 to a biblical plague: "You could not look upon the table but there were frogs. You could not sit down at the banquet table but there were frogs. You could not go to the bridal couch and lift the sheets but there were frogs. We can see nothing, touch nothing, have no measures proposed, without having this pestilence thrust before us."

7. David Outlaw to Emily Outlaw, February 3, 1848; David Outlaw to Emily Outlaw, August 5, 1848; David Outlaw to Emily Outlaw, February 20, 1848; Emily Outlaw to David Outlaw, January, 19, 1850. Outlaw's particularities on the subject of vanity and pride put one in mind of Jane Austen's musings on the same: "Vanity and pride are different things, though the words are often used synonimously. A person may be proud without being vain. Pride relates more to our opinions of ourselves, vanity to what we would have others think of us" (*Pride and Prejudice*, Penguin Classics, 20). If Outlaw read Austen, he does not mention it.

8. David Outlaw to Emily Outlaw, June 6, 1850; Emily Outlaw to David Outlaw, May 28, 1852; Emily Outlaw to David Outlaw, January 29, 1850.

9. David Outlaw to Emily Outlaw, February 4, 1848; David Outlaw to Emily Outlaw, July 24, 1850.

10. David Outlaw to Emily Outlaw, December 16, 1847; David Outlaw to Emily Outlaw, February 12, 1848; David Outlaw to Emily Outlaw, July 27, 1848; David Outlaw to Emily Outlaw, March 12, 1848.

11. David Outlaw to Emily Outlaw, December 8, 1850; David Outlaw to Emily Outlaw, May 23, 1850.

12. David Outlaw to Emily Outlaw, December 7, 1847; David Outlaw to Emily Outlaw, August 10, 1848; David Outlaw to Emily Outlaw, undated

January 1848; David Outlaw to Emily Outlaw, February 7, 1848; David Outlaw to Emily Outlaw, December 14, 1847; David Outlaw to Emily Outlaw, January 16, 1848; David Outlaw to Emily Outlaw, December 14, 1847.

13. David Outlaw to Emily Outlaw, March 13, 1848; David Outlaw to Emily Outlaw, August 1, 1848; David Outlaw to Emily Outlaw, February 15, 1848; David Outlaw to Emily Outlaw, December 4, 1849; David Outlaw to Emily Outlaw, May 5, 1850; David Outlaw to Emily Outlaw, undated January 1848.

14. A delightful study of crusty (small-r) republicanism is Harry L. Watson, "Squire Oldway and His Friends: Opposition to Internal Improvements in Antebellum North Carolina," *North Carolina Historical Review*, 1977, 105–19.

15. Mrs. Clay's famous study of Washington in the period, it should be remembered, was written after the fact, with that peculiar romantic hindsight Southerners brought to the examination of all things antedating the Unpleasantness. In her memory, at least, Washington was a resplendent court at "the very apex of its social glory." Fewer states meant fewer representatives, making society "correspondingly select." Moreover, she noted, "many distinguished men . . . retained their positions in the political foreground for . . . many years," and when they finally died or retired their sons often succeeded them, "inheriting, in some degree, their ancestors friends" and creating "a social security" that lent "charm and prestige to the fashionable coteries of the Federal centre." Troubled by the irksome instabilities of the democratic process, Mrs. Clay chose in retrospect to emphasize the degree to which the political cream rose to the top and stayed there. True courtiers, after all, cannot be swanking about the backcountry prostrating themselves for votes when they need to be composing bad poetry for the court belles. Virginia Tunstall Clay, *A Belle of the Fifties; Memoirs of Mrs. Clay, of Alabama, Covering Social and Political Life in Washington and the South, 1853–66* (New York: Doubleday, 1905), 28, 29, 86, 87. For other contemporary perspectives on Washington society, see T. C. DeLeon, *Four Years in Rebel Capitals: An Inside View of Life in the Southern Confederacy, from Birth to Death; From Original Notes, Collated in the Years 1861 to 1865* (Mobile: Gossip Printing Company, 1892); Francis J. Grund, ed., *Aristocracy in America. From the Sketchbook of a German Nobleman* (London: R. Bentley, 1839); John von Sonntag de Havilland, *A Metrical Description of a Fancy Ball Given at Washington, 9th April, 1858* (Washington: F. Philip, 1858); Elizabeth Keckley, *Behind the scenes, or, Thirty Years a Slave and Four Years in the White House*, with an introduction by James Olney (New York: Oxford University Press, 1988); Elizabeth Lomax, *Leaves from an Old Washington Diary, 1854–1863* (Mount Vernon: Golden Eagle, 1941); Benjamin Perley Poore, *Perley's Reminiscences of Sixty Years in the National Metropolis* (New York: W. A.

Houghton, 1886); Margaret Bayard Smith, *The First Forty Years of Washington Society, Portrayed by the Family Letters of Mrs. Samuel Harrison Smith* (New York: Scribner, 1906); and Anne Hollingsworth Wharton, *Social Life in the Early Republic* (Williamstown: Corner House, 1970).

16. David Outlaw to Emily Outlaw, December 21, 1847; David Outlaw to Emily Outlaw, July 3, 1850; David Outlaw to Emily Outlaw, December 12, 1848; David Outlaw to Emily Outlaw, January 7, 1848; David Outlaw to Emily Outlaw, December 6, 1847; David Outlaw to Emily Outlaw, January 27, 1850; David Outlaw to Emily Outlaw, December 14, 1850.

17. David Outlaw to Emily Outlaw, February 21, 1848; David Outlaw to Emily Outlaw, January 7, 1848; David Outlaw to Emily Outlaw, February 7, 1849; Virginia Tunstall Clay, *A Belle of the Fifties*, 37; David Outlaw to Emily Outlaw, March 26, 1848.

18. David Outlaw to Emily Outlaw, March 12, 1848; David Outlaw to Emily Outlaw, February 5, 1848; David Outlaw to Emily Outlaw, January 27, 1849; David Outlaw to Emily Outlaw, February 15, 1848; David Outlaw to Emily Outlaw, January 27, 1849.

19. David Outlaw to Emily Outlaw, August 7, 1850; David Outlaw to Emily Outlaw, January 16, 1848; David Outlaw to Emily Outlaw, February 18, 1848; David Outlaw to Emily Outlaw, December 18, 1850; David Outlaw to Emily Outlaw, January 16, 1850; David Outlaw to Emily Outlaw, January 10, 1850; David Outlaw to Emily Outlaw, January 18, 1851; David Outlaw to Emily Outlaw, February 11, 1850; David Outlaw to Emily Outlaw, February 11, 1851; David Outlaw to Emily Outlaw, December 16, 1847; David Outlaw to Emily Outlaw, February 25, 1850.

20. David Outlaw to Emily Outlaw, February 6, 1850; David Outlaw to Emily Outlaw, February 11, 1850; David Outlaw to Emily Outlaw, February 3, 1849; David Outlaw to Emily Outlaw, February 11, 1848; David Outlaw to Emily Outlaw, March 12, 1848; David Outlaw to Emily Outlaw, January 30, 1849; David Outlaw to Emily Outlaw, August 7, 1850.

21. David Outlaw to Emily Outlaw, January 18, 1851; David Outlaw to Emily Outlaw, August 10, 1848; David Outlaw to Emily Outlaw, March 26, 1848.

22. David Outlaw to Emily Outlaw, June 16, 1850; David Outlaw to Emily Outlaw, June 26, 1850; David Outlaw to Emily Outlaw, June 16, 1850; David Outlaw to Emily Outlaw, July 27, 1850; David Outlaw to Emily Outlaw, December 4, 1849.

23. David Outlaw to Emily Outlaw, June 16, 1850; David Outlaw to Emily Outlaw, December 8, 1850; David Outlaw to Emily Outlaw, June 16, 1850; David Outlaw to Emily Outlaw, March 17, 1848; David Outlaw to Emily Outlaw, June 25, 1850. Given Outlaw's sense that he was himself defiled by his association with Washington, much might be made of the fact that he appears to have been a chronic bather. Even in the dead of winter

he tended to bathe in cold water and in the summers he took a "shower bath every morning" and washed himself "from head to foot with cold water" every afternoon. I have resisted interpreting these habits for want of evidence but merely mention Outlaw's belief that "it is a real luxury to feel that you are clean." Certainly Outlaw was not the only one to feel the stink of the city upon him. As a friend wrote William Porcher Miles in 1858, "Don't let Washington spoil you. I am afraid that continual intercourse with those abolitionists will hurt any decent man and that the Halls of congress are like a *dirty privy*, a man will carry off some of the stink even in his clothes" (Benjamin Evans to William Porcher Miles, March 4, 1858, William Porcher Miles Papers, SHC).

24. Harry St. John Dixon Diary, June 29, 1860, Harry St. John Dixon Papers, SHC (hereafter, unless otherwise noted, all references are to this collection); Richard Dixon to Harry Dixon, November 4, 1860; Dixon Diary, August 29, 1860; April 12, 1860. Harry tells the story of his father's childhood in a long diary entry. The entry is not dated but runs from page 66 through page 71 of the second volume of the diary.

25. Dixon Diary, August 30, 1860; Dixon Diary, June 9, 1860.

As the watch chain vignette suggests, even the greatest macrohistorical events (like John Brown's raid) are experienced in deeply personal, highly individualized ways by those who live through them. This is not at all to suggest that generalizations cannot be drawn about how a society reacts as a whole. In the case of John Brown's raid this has been done quite effectively in Steve Channing, *Crisis of Fear: Secession in South Carolina* (New York: Norton, 1970). Rather, it is to note that it is important to be ever mindful that a collection of individual responses always comprises the larger one.

The Dixon diaries resonate with the stories of gamboling boyhood written by Mark Twain and with Katherine Du Pre Lumpkin's study of the psyche of young masters. Scholars interested in this subject should consult: Katharine Du Pre Lumpkin, *The Making of a Southerner* (Athens: University of Georgia Press, 1991) and Chris Mayfield, ed., *Growing Up Southern: Southern Exposure Looks at Childhood, Then and Now* (New York: Pantheon, 1981). On the history of childhood more generally in the period, see Joseph F. Kett, *Rites of Passage: Adolescence in America 1790 to the Present* (New York: Basic, 1977) and Robert Hamlett Bremner, *Children and Youth in America: A Documentary History*, vol. 1, *1600–1865* (Cambridge: Harvard University Press, 1970).

26. Dixon Diary, March 27, 1860; April 12, 1860.

27. Harry Dixon to Richard Dixon, March 3, 1860; Dixon Diary, July 27, 1860; July 29, 1860; April 24, 1860.

28. Dixon Diary, April 1, 1860.

29. Dixon Diary, April 12, 1859; April 13, 1859; April 3, 1860; March 18, 1860.

30. Dixon Diary, May 25, 1859; July 24, 1860; November 26, 1859.

31. Dixon Diary, August 20, 1860; June 8, 1859; September 7, 1860; April 27, 1860; October 24, 1859; June 25, 1859.

32. Dixon Diary, July 10, 1859; September 16, 1860; June 27, 1860; March 22, 1860; August 14, 1860.

33. Dixon Diary, March 3, 1860.

34. Dixon Diary, April 8, 1860; May 31, 1860.

35. Dixon Diary, May 21, 1859; April 15, 1859; April 24, 1859; May 7, 1859; May 11, 1859; May 3, 1859; May 16, 1859.

36. Dixon Diary, October 24, 1859; October 27, 1859; November 18, 1859.

37. Dixon Diary, March 9, 1860.

38. Dixon Diary, April 19, 1860; April 20, 1860; May 9, 1860; August 5, 1860.

39. Dixon Diary, June 19, 1860; June 20, 1860; April 7, 1860; May 5, 1860.

40. Dixon Diary, September 15, 1860; September 17, 1860.

41. Dixon Diary, September 18, 1860; September 21, 1860.

42. Dixon Diary, September 26, 1860; September 27, 1860.

43. Dixon Diary, October 23, 1860; December 22, 1860; June 19, 1861.

44. Dixon Diary, October 21, 1860; Harry Dixon to Richard Dixon, February 10, 1861; Julia Dixon to Harry Dixon, March 20, 1861; Dixon Diary, January 24, 1861. On how sons at college related to their fathers in the South, see Jon L. Wakelyn, "Antebellum College Life and the Relations between Fathers and Sons," in Walter J. Fraser Jr., R. Frank Saunders Jr., and Jon Wakelyn, eds., *The Web of Southern Social Relations*. On Charlottesville in the period, see Virginius Dabney, *Mr. Jefferson's University: A History* (Charlottesville: University Press of Virginia, 1981).

45. Harry Dixon to Richard Dixon, April 28, 1861; Dixon Diary, November 24, 1861; December 23, 1860; November 15, 1860.

46. Harry Dixon to Richard Dixon, December 16, 1860; Harry Dixon to Richard Dixon, May 5, 1861; Richard Dixon to Harry Dixon, April 27, 1861; Dixon Diary, June 19, 1861; Harry Dixon to Richard Dixon, March 22, 1861; Harry Dixon to Richard Dixon, May 5, 1861; Harry Dixon to Richard Dixon, April 17, 1861.

47. Dixon Diary, April 27, 1861; October 27, 1860; December 24, 1860.

48. Dixon Diary, April 27, 1861; May 13, 1861; April 26, 1861.

Chapter 5: A Fountain of Waters

1. The literature on secession is almost as vast as the literature on the war itself and cannot be surveyed here. Scholars interested in gendered reads of secession should begin with Christopher J. Olsen, *Political Culture and*

Secession in Mississippi: Masculinity, Honor, and the Antiparty Tradition, 1830–1860 (New York: Oxford University Press, 2000).

2. Meta Grimball Diary, January 30, 1861; Margaret Ann (Meta) Morris Grimball Diary; William Bingham to his cousin, Mag, December 22, 1860, Lenoir Family Papers, SHC; Joan Cashin, *Our Common Affairs*, 281; Martin Crawford, ed., *William Howard Russell's Civil War: Private Diary and Letters, 1861–1862* (Athens: University of Georgia Press, 1992), 23.

3. Richard B. Harwell, ed., "Louisiana Burge: The Diary of a Confederate College Girl," *Georgia Historical Quarterly*, 1952, 144–49.

4. Mark Twain, "Private History of a Campaign That Failed," 866; Eggleston, *A Rebel's Recollections*, 21; C. O. Bailey to Charley, February 24, 1861, James B. Bailey Papers, SHC; John Henderson to Archibald Henderson, January 13, 1861, John Steele Henderson Papers, SHC; Cashin, *Our Common Affairs*, 286; J. G. deRoulhac Hamilton, ed., *The Papers of Randolph Abbott Shotwell* (Raleigh: North Carolina Historical Commission, 1929), 40.

5. Vignette of Keitt's receiving secession news appears in *Reminiscences of Peace and War* by Mrs. Roger A. Pryor (New York, 1905), quoted in Philip Van Doren Stern, ed., *Prologue to Sumter: The Beginnings of the Civil War from the John Brown Raid to the Surrender of Fort Sumter, Woven into a Continuous Narrative by Philip Van Doren Stern* (Bloomington: Indiana University Press, 1961), 180; Lord King to Thomas Butler King, April 7, 1848, Thomas Butler King Papers; Henry Lord Page King Diary, April 25, 1860, Thomas Butler King Papers; Edward G. Butler to Mary Susan Ker, January 2, 1861, Mary Susan Ker Papers, SHC; Daniel Hamilton to son, November 10, 1860, Ruffin, Roulhac, and Hamilton Family Papers, SHC.

6. William Thomson Sr. to William Thomson Jr., November 23, 1860, William Sydnor Thomson Papers, Emory University (all further notes will refer to this collection); Thomson Jr. to Thomson Sr., November 29, 1860; Thomson Sr. to Thomson Jr., December 3, 1860; Thomson Jr. to Thomson Sr., December 22, 1860; Thomson Sr. to Thomson Jr., December 27, 1860.

7. Thomson Jr. to Thomson Sr., February 2, 1861; Thomson Jr. to "my dear Kind friend," February 1, 1861; Thomson Sr. to Thomson Jr., December 27, 1860; Thomson Sr. to Thomson Jr., January 9, 1861; Thomson Jr. to Thomson Sr., March 24, 1861; Thomson Sr. to Thomson Jr., March 15, 1861; Thomson Sr. to Thomson Jr., March 10, 1861.

8. Meta Grimball Diary, December 29, 1860; James Petigru Carson, ed., *Life, Letters, and Speeches of James Louis Petigru*, 370–71.

9. William to Fanny Pender, May 18, 1861, in Hassler, *The General to His Lady*, 23; Quoted in introduction to *"Dear Mother: Don't grieve about me. If I get killed, I'll only be dead": Letters from Georgia Soldiers in the Civil War* (Savannah: Beehive, 1977), x.

10. Eggleston, *Rebel's Recollections*, 21, 33; John Kent Folmar, ed., *From That Terrible Field: Civil War Letters of James M. Williams, Twenty-First Alabama Infantry Volunteers* (University: University of Alabama Press, 1981), 1; Hassler, *General to His Lady*, 12; John Rozier, ed., *The Granite Farm Letters: The Civil War Correspondence of Edgeworth and Sallie Bird* (Athens: University of Georgia Press, 1988), 30. Little can be conclusively proven about an increase in the number of men who availed themselves of prostitutes in the heady atmosphere of the early war. Though official records were kept on incidents of venereal disease, they are spotty, particularly for the Confederacy. Victorian propriety and obvious issues of shame ensure that most references to the subject are veiled at best. Still, one notes in women's correspondence, particularly, oblique references to the excesses of camp life. "Sad hearts are many about here," noted a member of the Lenoir family, even "if they should escape being killed, I fear most of our young men will be ruined. Camp life is not at all conducive to religion or morality" ("R.N. Tellinghart" to cousin "Aunt Sade," April 12, 1861, Lenoir Family Papers, SHC. Names are in quotes because it is suspected that they are nicknames of Lenoir family members). "I shall be thankful for this excitement & camp life to cease," noted Georgia King, "thank God! since Mally [her brother] is more happy he does not seem to care to go to the camp now. At one time I felt like cursing the camp from my own heart" (Georgia King to Lord King, March 16, 1861, Thomas Butler King Family Papers, SHC). Still more evidence can be found in the correspondence of men who, while assuring their wives of their own moral probity, did not shrink from charging their fellows with loose living: "If every one loved home and their family as I do," wrote Winston Stephens to his beloved, "there would not be so much room for complaint among the sex you belong to, but some are destitute of all honor to their Wives, or love of home as I have evidence of here in many cases. Men come here and forget the embraces of their dear Wives and throw themselves away upon the common *strumpet*, but My Dear 'though I say it that should not say' you may trust your old man as God knows my marriage vow has been kept and I have never felt the least inclination to break it so help me God." Quote from Arch Frederic Blakey, Ann Smith Lainhart, and Winston Bryant Stephens Jr., eds., *Rose Cottage Chronicles: Civil War Letters of the Bryant-Stephens Families of North Florida* (Gainesville: University Press of Florida, 1998), 92–93.

11. Charles W. Turner, ed., *My Dear Emma: War Letters of Col. James K. Edmondson, 1861–1865* (Verona: McClure, 1978), 99; Judith Lee Hallock, ed., *The Civil War Letters of Joshua K. Callaway* (Athens: University of Georgia Press, 1997), 24.

12. Cash and Howorth, *My Dear Nellie*, 182–83; Bell Irvin Wiley, ed., *"This Infernal War": The Confederate Letters of Sgt. Edwin H. Fay* (Austin: University of Texas Press, 1958), 209.

13. Hallock, *Civil War Letters of Joshua K. Callaway*, 30; *"Dear Mother: Don't grieve about me. If I get killed, I'll only be dead,"* 257; Wiley, *"This Infernal War,"* 118–19; Folmar, *From That Terrible Field*, 26.

14. For a sound discussion of Confederate tactics and strategy, see Gabor S. Boritt, ed., *Why the Confederacy Lost* (New York: Oxford University Press, 1992).

15. Hallock, *Civil War Letters of Joshua K. Callaway*, 16, 35; Cash and Howorth, *My Dear Nellie*, 97.

16. *"Dear Mother: Don't grieve about me. If I get killed, I'll only be dead,"* 21; Folmar, *From That Terrible Field*, 91; Hallock, *Civil War Letters of Joshua K. Callaway*, 131; Wiley, *"This Infernal War,"* 127–32, 300–302, 51.

17. Cash and Howorth, *My Dear Nellie*, 132; Hallock, *Civil War Letters of Joshua K. Callaway*, 44–45.

18. Wiley, *"This Infernal War,"* 203; Guy R. Everson and Edward H. Simpson Jr., eds., *"Far, Far from Home": The Wartime Letters of Dick and Tally Simpson Third South Carolina Volunteers* (New York: Oxford University Press, 1994), 214; Blakey et al., *Rose Cottage Chronicles*, 229.

19. Cash and Howorth, *My Dear Nellie*, 156; Alto Loftin Jackson, ed., *So Mourns the Dove: Letters of a Confederate Infantryman and His Family* (New York: Exposition, 1965), 30.

20. *"Dear Mother: Don't grieve about me. If I get killed, I'll only be dead,"* 30; Wiley, *"This Infernal War,"* 61; Cash and Howorth, *My Dear Nellie*, 204; *"Dear Mother: Don't grieve about me. If I get killed, I'll only be dead,"* 314.

21. Wiley, *"This Infernal War,"* 338–39; Cash and Howorth, *My Dear Nellie*, 128–29; R. Lockwood Tower, ed., *Lee's Adjutant: the Wartime Letters of Colonel Walter Herron Taylor, 1862–1865* (Columbia: University of South Carolina Press, 1995), 71. On the process by which men anchored their patriotism in romantic love, see Stephen W. Berry, "When Mail Was Armor: Envelopes of the Great Rebellion, 1861–1865," *Southern Cultures*, Fall 1998, 69–71.

22. Wiley, *"This Infernal War,"* 211; Folmar, *From That Terrible Field*, 118.

23. Hallock, *Civil War Letters of Joshua K. Callaway*, 144; Cuttino, *Saddle Bag and Spinning Wheel*, 54; Wiley, *"This Infernal War,"* 68, 121.

24. Everson and Simpson, *"Far, Far from Home,"* 215; Blakey et al., *Rose Cottage Chronicles*, 252–53; Rozier, ed., *The Granite Farm Letters*, 191; Folmar, *From That Terrible Field*, 70.

25. It is not exactly clear how the Capertons and Kings were acquainted, but the families were often in each other's company throughout the 1850s.

26. John Floyd King to Lin Caperton, August 4, 1861, Thomas Butler King Papers (all further citations refer to this collection); Floyd to Lin, November 28, 1861; Lin to Floyd, September 15, 1861.

27. Floyd to Lin, February 14, 1860; Floyd to Lin, November 27, 1861; Floyd to Lin, January 9, 1862; Floyd to Lin, December 3, 1861.

28. Floyd to Lin, January 5, 1862; Floyd to Lin, November 27, 1861; Floyd to Lin, December 3, 1861.

29. Everson and Simpson, *"Far, Far from Home,"* 14–15, 141.

30. Everson and Simpson, *"Far, Far from Home,"* 199, 259, 241.

Chapter 6: Looking Homeward

1. Wiley, *"This Infernal War,"* 292.

2. Cash and Howorth, *My Dear Nellie,* 164–65; Blakey et al., *Rose Cottage Chronicles,* 310. Winston Stephens was killed on March 1, 1864, during some skirmishing near Tallahassee. A few days later Tivie bore his only child, a boy.

3. William C. Davis, *A Government of Our Own: The Making of the Confederacy* (New York: Free Press, 1994); Virginia K. Jones, ed., "A Contemporary Account of the Inauguration of Jefferson Davis," *Alabama Historical Quarterly* 23 (1961): 273–77.

4. Nathaniel Dawson to Elodie Todd, October 22, 1861, Nathaniel Henry Rhodes Dawson Papers, SHC (hereafter, unless otherwise noted, all references are to this collection).

5. Nathaniel Dawson to Elodie Todd, December 8, 1861.

6. Nathaniel Dawson to Joel Matthews, April 11, April 26, May 30, and November 10, 1861, all in N.H.R. Dawson Papers, Special Collections Library, Duke University.

7. Nathaniel Dawson to Elodie Todd, June 26, 1861; Elodie Todd to Nathaniel Dawson, May 9, 1861.

8. Elodie Todd to Nathaniel Dawson, April 1, 1862; Elodie Todd to Nathaniel Dawson, October 13, 1861; Elodie Todd to Nathaniel Dawson, July 23, 1861; Elodie Todd to Nathaniel, May 9, 1861; Elodie Todd to Nathaniel Dawson, June 12, 1861.

9. Elodie Todd to Nathaniel Dawson, September 1, 1861. See also Norman F. Boas, "Unpublished Manuscripts: Recollections of Mary Todd Lincoln by Her Sister Emilie Todd Helm; An Invitation to a Lincoln Party," *Manuscripts* 43, no. 1 (1991): 23–34. For more on the Mary Todd Lincoln and her Confederate relations, see Justin G. Turner, *Mary Todd Lincoln: Her Life and Letters* (New York: Knopf, 1972); and Jean H. Baker, *Mary Todd Lincoln: A Biography* (New York: Norton, 1987).

10. Baker, *Mary Todd Lincoln.*

11. Elodie Todd to Nathaniel Dawson, November 9, 1861; Elodie Todd to Nathaniel Dawson, July 23, 1861; Elodie Todd to Nathaniel Dawson, August 4, 1861.

12. Elodie Todd to Nathaniel Dawson, September 29, 1861; Elodie Todd

to Nathaniel Dawson, December 22, 1861; Elodie Todd to Nathaniel Dawson, January 5, 1862. On Selma during the period, see Claude C. Grayson, *Yesterday and Today; Memories of Selma and Its People* (New Orleans: Pelican, 1948); John Hardy, *Selma: Her Institutions and Her Men* (Selma: Bert Neville and Clarence DeBray, 1957); Walter Mahan Jackson, *The Story of Selma* (Birmingham, 1954); and *Selma and Dallas County: 150 years* (Selma: Selma and Dallas County Chamber of Commerce, 1969). On the Confederate home front in Alabama generally, see William Warren Rogers Jr., *Confederate Home Front: Montgomery during the Civil War* (Tuscaloosa: University of Alabama Press, 1999).

13. Nathaniel Dawson to Elodie Todd, September 13, 1861; Nathaniel Dawson to Elodie Todd, May 18, 1861.

14. Nathaniel Dawson to Elodie Todd, October 7, 1861.

15. Nathaniel Dawson to Elodie Todd, October 16, 1861; Elodie Todd to Nathaniel Dawson, July 14, 1861; Nathaniel Dawson to Elodie Todd, June 23, 1861; Nathaniel Dawson to Elodie Todd, May 24, 1861; Nathaniel Dawson to Elodie Todd, November 7, 1861; Nathaniel Dawson to Elodie Todd, September 16, 1861. I want to restate that I am not remotely suggesting that Dawson had any, even latent, homosexual tendencies. Rather, it is my intention to suggest that, given their touchiness, men's relationships with one another were often cramped and awkward. Historians researching the history of homosexuality are often apt to force it into places it doesn't belong, and I don't wish to be counted in their number. In *About Time: Exploring the Gay Past* (New York: Meridian, 1991), Martin Duberman recounts the story of James Henry Hammond and Thomas Wither's playful exploration of each other's erections, suggesting that this should be regarded as a homosexual encounter. Rather, I think the vignette suggests so raucous a sense of heterosexuality that it burst over and through "normal" confines without so much as a hiccup (Martin Duberman, " 'Writhing Bedfellows' in Antebellum South Carolina: Historical Interpretation and the Politics of Evidence," in *About Time*, 3–23).

16. Nathaniel Dawson to Elodie Todd, November 25, 1861; Nathaniel Dawson to Elodie Todd, May 30, 1861.

17. Nathaniel Dawson to Elodie Todd, November 2, 1861; Nathaniel Dawson to Elodie Todd, May 20, 1861; Nathaniel Dawson to Elodie Todd, October 22, 1861.

18. Nathaniel Dawson to Elodie Todd, August 18, 1861; Nathaniel Dawson to Elodie Todd, October 22, 1861; Nathaniel Dawson to Elodie Todd, June 30, 1861; Nathaniel Dawson to Elodie Todd, May 30, 1861; Elodie Todd to Nathaniel Dawson, August 4, 1861; Nathaniel Dawson to Elodie Todd, May 28, 1861.

19. Nathaniel Dawson to Elodie Todd, June 17, 1861; Nathaniel Dawson to Elodie Todd, May 18, 1861.

20. Nathaniel Dawson to Elodie Todd, December 11, 1861; Nathaniel Dawson to Elodie Todd, January 24, 1862.

21. Nathaniel Dawson to Elodie Todd, December 8, 1861; Nathaniel Dawson to Elodie Todd, March 15, 1862; Nathaniel Dawson to Elodie Todd, July 14, 1861; Nathaniel Dawson to Elodie Todd, June 2, 1861; Nathaniel Dawson to Elodie Todd, May 14, 1861; Nathaniel Dawson to Elodie Todd, May 19, 1861.

22. Elodie Todd to Nathaniel Dawson, May 19, 1861; Elodie Todd to Nathaniel Dawson, December 15, 1861; Elodie Todd to Nathaniel Dawson, November 2, 1861.

23. Elodie Todd to Nathaniel Dawson, August 4, 1861; Elodie Todd to Nathaniel Dawson, July 7, 1861.

24. Elodie Todd to Nathaniel Dawson, December 15, 1861; Elodie Todd to Nathaniel Dawson, May 15, 1861; Elodie Todd to Nathaniel Dawson, November 9, 1861; Elodie Todd to Nathaniel Dawson, October 20, 1861.

25. Nathaniel Dawson to Elodie Todd, August 21, 1861; Nathaniel Dawson to Elodie Todd, May 17, 1861; Nathaniel Dawson to Elodie Todd, May 20, 1861; Nathaniel Dawson to Elodie Todd, April 26, 1861.

26. Nathaniel Dawson to Elodie Todd, June 19, 1861; Nathaniel Dawson to Elodie Todd, May 15, 1861; Nathaniel Dawson to Elodie Todd, June 6, 1861; Nathaniel Dawson to Elodie Todd, April 10, 1862; Nathaniel Dawson to Elodie Todd, July 2, 1861; Nathaniel Dawson to Elodie Todd, November 21, 1861.

27. Nathaniel Dawson to Elodie Todd, July 21, 1861; Nathaniel Dawson to Elodie Todd, August 29, 1861.

28. Nathaniel Dawson to Elodie Todd, July 2, 1861; Nathaniel Dawson to Elodie Todd, December 18, 1861; Nathaniel Dawson to Elodie Todd, January 8, 1862; Nathaniel Dawson to Elodie Todd, August 21, 1861.

29. Nathaniel Dawson to Elodie Todd, November 2, 1861; Nathaniel Dawson to Elodie Todd, April 2, 1862; Nathaniel Dawson to Elodie Todd, November 27, 1861.

30. Nathaniel Dawson to Elodie Todd, May 30, 1861; Nathaniel Dawson to Elodie Todd, May 29, 1861; Nathaniel Dawson to Elodie Todd, June 26, 1861.

31. Details of Oglethorpe's rise and fall are drawn from the introduction of Spencer B. King, Jr., ed., *Rebel Lawyer: Letters of Theodorick W. Montfort, 1861–1862* (Athens: University of Georgia Press, 1965), 1–18.

32. King, *Rebel Lawyer*, 9 n. 29. For a detailed account of the Union army's successful campaign against Pulaski, see Herbert M. Schiller, *"Sumter Is Avenged": The Siege and Reduction of Fort Pulaski* (Shippensburg: White Mane, 1995).

33. King, *Rebel Lawyer*, 53, 59, 61.

34. King, *Rebel Lawyer*, 49.

35. King, *Rebel Lawyer*, 66–68.

36. King, *Rebel Lawyer*, 52, 55, 57–58, 61, 75.

37. King, *Rebel Lawyer*, 55.

38. King, *Rebel Lawyer*, 56.

39. King, *Rebel Lawyer*, 65, 71–72.

40. Thomas Cobb to Mary Ann Cobb, February 21, 1861, June 23, 1862, March 12, 1862, Thomas R. R. Cobb Papers.

41. Thomas Cobb to Mary Ann Cobb, March 16, 1862, Thomas R. R. Cobb Papers.

Epilogue

1. Merchant, "Laurence M. Keitt," 351.

2. Laurence Keitt to Susan Keitt, May 1, 1862, Laurence Massillon Keitt Papers.

3. Laurence Keitt to Susan Keitt, January 24, 1864.

4. Laurence Keitt to Susan Keitt, February 11, 1864; Laurence Keitt to Susan Sparks, May 9, 1855.

5. Dr. Theodoric Pryor to Susan Keitt, June 17, 1864.

6. Kit C. Carter and Jerry C. Oldshue, "N.H.R. Dawson: Soldier, Statesman, and U.S. Commissioner of Education," *Alabama Review*, 1981, 202–13.

7. Ibid. For a sketch of Elodie Dawson's grave marker, see Obituaries: Mrs. Dawson's Folder, N.H.R. Dawson Papers, University of Alabama Library, Tuscaloosa.

8. Harry Dixon to Richard Dixon, March 24, 1861, Harry St. John Dixon Papers; Will of Harry St. John Dixon, as composed in a letter to his parents, November 1862, Harry St. John Dixon Papers.

9. Will of Harry St. John Dixon, Harry St. John Dixon Papers; Dixon's inscription is of course borrowed from Thomas Gray, "Elegy Written in a Country Church-Yard": "The boast of heraldry, the pomp of power / And all that beauty, all that wealth e'er gave / Awaits, alike, th' inevitable hour: / The paths of glory lead but to the grave."

10. Rebecca Dixon Chambers letter, 1958, Harry St. John Dixon Papers.

11. Rebecca Dixon Chambers letter, 1958; Connie Dixon to Harry Dixon, September 16, 1874; Harry Dixon to Connie Dixon, July 12, 1874; Rebecca Dixon Chambers letter, 1958, all in Harry St. John Dixon Papers.

12. David to Emily Outlaw, May 23, 1850. Pulaski Cowper, "Colonel David Outlaw," *Wake Forest Student*, 1896, 287–95; "Sketches of Members of the Convention of 1835, by a Member of That Body," *Economist*, Elizabeth City, North Carolina, April 22, 1872.

13. Herbert M. Schiller, *"Sumter Is Avenged,"* 135–36; King, *Rebel Lawyer*, 11–12.

14. Henry Craft, "Memorial to the Honorable Connally F. Trigg," 1880, Craft, Fort, and Thorne Family Papers.

BIBLIOGRAPHY

Manuscript Sources

SOUTHERN HISTORICAL COLLECTION, UNIVERSITY OF NORTH CAROLINA
AT CHAPEL HILL

James W. Albright Books
Alexander and Hillhouse Family Papers
Augustus Octavius Bacon Papers
James B. Bailey Papers
Everard Green Baker Diaries
Daniel Hoard Baldwin Letters
Lucy Plummer Battle Papers
Battle Family Papers
William Beavans Books
Berry Benson Papers
Robert Bingham Papers
Macon Bonner Papers
John Bratton Papers
R. H. Browne Papers
Brumby and Smith Family Papers
George W. Bryan Papers
Lucy Wood Butler
Caroline Eliza Clitherall Diaries

Laura Beecher Comer Papers
James Conner Letters
Dabney Cosby Papers
William Audley Couper Papers
Craft, Fort, and Thorne Family Papers
Nathaniel Henry Rhodes Dawson Papers
Harry St. John Dixon Papers
Samuel W. Eaton Papers
Elliott and Gonzales Family Papers
Chesley D. Evans Letters
Julia Johnson Fisher Diary
George Loyall Gordon Papers
David Gavin Diary
Josiah Gorgas Papers
Margaret Ann (Meta) Morris Grimball Diary
Grimball Family Papers
Bryan Grimes Papers
James Gwynn Papers
George Hairston Diary
Joseph B. Harrell Diary
John Steele Henderson Papers
Mary Ferrand Henderson Papers
William Thomas Humphrey Papers
Eugene Janin Papers
J. A. Johnson Letters
Benjamin B. Kendrick Papers
Mary Susan Ker Papers
Ker Family Papers
Thomas Butler King Papers
Alexander Robert Lawton Papers
Emma Leconte Diary
Lenoir Family Papers
William Gaston Lewis Papers
Henry Armand London Papers
Samuel Catawba Lowry Recollections and Diary
Albert Moses Luria Diary
Bartlett Yancey Malone Diary
Manigault, Morris, and Grimball Family Papers
Andrew McCollam Papers
Neill McLeod Civil War Letters Manuscript
J. R. (James Robert) McMichael Diary
Paul Agalus McMichael Papers

Mercer Family Papers
George Anderson Mercer Diary
George Knox Miller Papers
Theodore Davidson Morrison Papers
Stanford E. Moses Papers
William Porcher Miles Papers
William Page Papers
Peek Family Papers
James Louis Petigru Papers
William Beverley Pettit Papers
Pettigrew Family Papers
Phifer Family Papers
Proffit Family Letters
Quitman Family Papers
James Ryder Randall Papers
W. R. Redding Papers
William McKendree Robbins Papers
Ruffin, Roulhac, and Hamilton Family Papers
Thomas Ruffin Papers
Ruffin and Meade Family Papers
Scott Family Papers
Michael Shofner Papers
Jane Sivley Letters
Skinner Family Papers
Hartwell Percy Spain Diary
Cornelia Phillips Spencer Papers
James H. Stanley Papers
Theodore Osborn Stark Papers
John Kennedy Street Papers
Charles W. Sydnor Letters
Elizabeth Webb Strudwick Papers
John Dudley Tatum Letters
Paul Turner Vaughan Papers
James T. Wallace Diary
Joseph Walters Letters
Thomas Ware Diary
Lewis Henry Webb Papers
Benjamin F. White Diary
Williamson Whitehead Papers
Edmund Jones Williams Letters
Mary Ann Covington Wilson Papers
John Q. Winfield Letters

Anita Dwyer Withers Diary
Wright and Herring Family Papers
Asa John Wyatt Diary

SPECIAL COLLECTIONS, DUKE UNIVERSITY

Nathaniel Henry Rhodes Dawson Papers
Lawrence Massillon Keitt Papers

SPECIAL COLLECTIONS, EMORY UNIVERSITY

William Sydnor Thomson Papers

GEORGIA HISTORICAL SOCIETY, SAVANNAH

Thomas Butler King Papers
King-Wilder Papers

SOUTH CAROLINA HISTORICAL SOCIETY

Allston Papers

UNIVERSITY OF GEORGIA

Thomas Reade Rootes Cobb Papers

Published Primary Sources

Anderson, John Q., ed. *Brokenburn: The Journal of Kate Stone, 1861–1868.*
Baton Rouge: Louisiana State University Press, 1995.
Baer, Elizabeth R., ed. *Shadows on My Heart: The Civil War Diary of Lucy
Rebecca Buck of Virginia.* Athens: University of Georgia Press, 1997.
Baldwin, Joseph G. *The Flush Times of Alabama and Mississippi: A Series
of Sketches.* New York: Appleton, 1853.
Beatty, Richmond Groom, ed. *Journal of a Southern Student, 1846–1848, with
Letters of a Later Period.* Nashville: Vanderbilt University Press, 1944.
Blakey, Arch Frederic, Ann Smith Lainhart, and Winston Bryant Stephens
Jr., eds. *Rose Cottage Chronicles: Civil War Letters of the Bryant-Stephens
Families of North Florida.* Gainesville: University Press of Florida, 1998.
Bleser, Carol, ed. *The Hammonds of Redcliffe.* New York: Oxford University
Press, 1981.
———. *Secret and Sacred: The Diaries of James Henry Hammond, a South-
ern Slaveholder.* New York: Oxford University Press, 1988.
———. *Tokens of Affection: The Letters of a Planter's Daughter in the Old
South.* Athens: University of Georgia Press, 1996.
Brady, Patricia, ed. *George Washington's Beautiful Nelly: The Letters of
Eleanor Parke Custis Lewis to Elizabeth Bordley Gibson, 1794–1851.* Co-
lumbia: University of South Carolina Press, 1991.
Burr, Virginia Ingram, ed. *The Secret Eye: The Journal of Ella Gertrude*

Clanton Thomas, 1848–1889. Chapel Hill: University of North Carolina, 1990.

Calhoun, Richard James, ed. *Witness to Sorrow: The Antebellum Autobiography of William J. Grayson*. Columbia: University of South Carolina Press, 1990.

Carson, James Petigru, ed. *Life, Letters, and Speeches of James Louis Petigru, The Union Man of South Carolina*. Washington: W. H. Lowdermilk, 1920.

Cash, William M., and Lucy Somerville Howorth, eds. *My Dear Nellie: The Civil War Letters of William L. Nugent to Eleanor Smith Nugent*. Jackson: University Press of Mississippi, 1977.

Cashin, Joan, ed. *Our Common Affairs: Texts from Women in the Old South*. Baltimore: Johns Hopkins University Press, 1996.

Crabtree, Beth G., and James W. Patton, eds. *Journal of a Secesh Lady: The Diary of Catherine Ann Devereux Edmondston, 1860–1866*. Raleigh, NC: Division of Archives and History, 1979.

Crist, Lynda Lasswell, and Mary Seaton Dix, eds. *The Papers of Jefferson Davis*. Baton Rouge: Louisiana State University Press, 1971–.

Cuttino, George Peddy, ed. *Saddle Bag and Spinning Wheel, Being the Civil War Letters of George W. Peddy, M.D., Surgeon, 56th Georgia Volunteer Regiment, C.S.A., and His Wife Kate Featherston Peddy*. Macon: Mercer University Press, 1981.

DeButts, Mary, ed. *Growing Up in the 1850s: The Journal of Agnes Lee*. Chapel Hill: University of North Carolina, 1984.

DeLeon, T. C. *Four Years in Rebel Capitals: An Inside View of Life in the Southern Confederacy, from Birth to Death; From Original Notes, Collated in the Years 1861 to 1865*. Mobile: Gossip Printing Company, 1892.

Dimond, E. Grey, ed. *Letters from Forest Place: A Plantation Family's Correspondence, 1846–1861*. Jackson: University Press of Mississippi, 1993.

East, Charles, ed. *The Civil War Diary of Sarah Morgan*. Athens: University of Georgia Press, 1991.

Eggleston, George Cary. *A Rebel's Recollections*. New York: Hurd & Houghton, 1875.

Everson, Guy R., and Edward H. Simpson Jr., eds. *"Far, Far from Home": The Wartime Letters of Dick and Tally Simpson Third South Carolina Volunteers*. New York: Oxford University Press, 1994.

Folmar, John Kent, ed. *From That Terrible Field: Civil War Letters of James M. Williams, Twenty-First Alabama Infantry Volunteers*. University: University of Alabama Press, 1981.

Freehling, William W., and Craig M. Simpson, eds. *Secession Debated: Georgia's Showdown in 1860*. New York: Oxford University Press, 1992.

Fulkerson, H. S. *Random Recollections of Early Days in Mississippi*. Vicksburg: Vicksburg Printing & Publishing, 1885.

Hallock, Judith Lee, ed. *The Civil War Letters of Joshua K. Callaway*. Athens: University of Georgia Press, 1997.

Hamilton, J. G. deRoulhac, ed. *The Papers of Randolph Abbott Shotwell*. Raleigh: North Carolina Historical Commission, 1929.

Hassler, William W., ed. *The General to His Lady: The Civil War Letters of William Dorsey Pender to Fanny Pender*. Chapel Hill: University of North Carolina Press, 1962.

Inscoe, John C., ed. "Fatherly Advice on Secession: Edward Jones Erwin to His Son at Davidson College, 1860–1861." *American Presbyterians*, 1991, 97–109.

Jackson, Alto Loftin, ed. *So Mourns the Dove: Letters of a Confederate Infantryman and His Family*. New York: Exposition, 1965.

Jackson, Harvey H., ed. *Letters from Alabama, Chiefly Relating to Natural History*. Tuscaloosa: University of Alabama Press, 1993.

King, Spencer B., ed. *Rebel Lawyer: Letters of Theodorick W. Montfort, 1861–1862*. Athens: University of Georgia Press, 1965.

Lane, Mills, ed. *"Dear Mother: Don't grieve about me. If I get killed, I'll only be dead": Letters from Georgia Soldiers in the Civil War*. Savannah: Beehive, 1977.

Lomax, Elizabeth Lindsay. *Leaves from an Old Washington Diary, 1854–1863*. Mount Vernon: Golden Eagle, 1941.

Masur, Louis P., ed. *The Real War Will Never Get in the Books: Selections from Writers during the Civil War*. New York: Oxford University Press, 1993.

Moore, John Hammond, ed. *A Plantation Mistress on the Eve of the Civil War: The Diary of Keziah Goodwyn Hopkins Brevard, 1860–1861*. Columbia: University of South Carolina Press, 1993.

Myers, Robert Manson, ed. *The Children of Pride: A True Story of Georgia and the Civil War*. New Haven: Yale University Press, 1972.

Nelson, Dana D., ed. *Principles and Privilege: Two Women's Lives on a Georgia Plantation*. Ann Arbor: University of Michigan Press, 1995.

O'Brien, Michael, ed. *An Evening When Alone: Four Journals of Single Women in the South, 1827–1867*. Charlottesville: University Press of Virginia, 1993.

Oliphant, Mary C. Simms, Alfred Taylor Odell, and T. C. Duncan Eaves, eds. *The Letters of William Gilmore Simms*. Columbia: University of South Carolina Press, 1952–.

Parks, Edd Winfield, ed. *The Essays of Henry Timrod*. Athens: University of Georgia Press, 1942.

Rosengarten, Theodore, ed. *Tombee: Portrait of a Cotton Planter with the Journal of Thomas B. Chaplin (1822–1890)*. New York: William Morrow, 1986.

Rozier, John, ed. *The Granite Farm Letters: The Civil War Correspondence of Edgeworth and Sallie Bird.* Athens: University of Georgia Press, 1988.

Turner, Charles W., ed. *My Dear Emma: War Letters of Col. James K. Edmondson, 1861–1865.* Verona, Va.: McClure, 1978.

Wakelyn, Jon L., ed. *Southern Pamphlets on Secession, November 1860–April 1861.* Chapel Hill: University of North Carolina Press, 1996.

Wiggins, Sarah Woolfolk, ed. *The Journals of Josiah Gorgas.* Tuscaloosa: University of Alabama Press, 1995.

Wiley, Bell Irvin, ed. *"This Infernal War": The Confederate Letters of Sgt. Edwin H. Fay.* Austin: University of Texas Press, 1958.

Wilson, Clyde, ed. *Selections from the Letters and Speeches of the Hon. James H. Hammond of South Carolina.* Spartanburg: Reprint Company, 1978.

Woodward, C. Vann, ed. *Mary Chesnut's Civil War.* New Haven: Yale University Press, 1981.

Selected Secondary Sources

Allmendinger, David F. *Ruffin: Family and Reform in the Old South.* New York: Oxford University Press, 1990.

Auer, J. Jeffrey, ed. *Antislavery and Disunion, 1858–1861: Studies in the Rhetoric of Compromise and Conflict.* New York: Harper & Row, 1963.

Ayers, Edward L. *Vengeance and Justice: Crime and Punishment in the Nineteenth-Century American South.* New York: Oxford University Press, 1984.

Barney, William L. "Patterns of Crisis: Alabama White Families and Social Change, 1850–1870." *Sociology and Social Research*, 1979, 524–43.

———. "Resisting the Republicans: Georgia's Secession Debate." *Georgia Historical Quarterly*, 1993, 71–85.

———. *The Road to Secession: A New Perspective on the Old South.* New York: Praeger, 1972.

———. *The Secessionist Impulse: Alabama and Mississippi in 1860.* Princeton: Princeton University Press, 1974.

———. "An Undiagnosed Fever: Political Radicalism in South Carolina." *Reviews in American History*, 1983, 214–18.

Barton, Michael. *Goodmen: The Character of Civil War Soldiers.* University Park: Pennsylvania State University Press, 1981.

Bell, Malcolm, Jr. *Major Butler's Legacy: Five Generations of a Slaveholding Family.* Athens: University of Georgia Press, 1987.

Beringer, Richard E. "Jefferson Davis's Pursuit of Ambition: The Attractive Features of Alternative Decisions." *Civil War History*, 1992, 5–39.

———. *Why the South Lost the Civil War.* Athens: University of Georgia Press, 1986.

Blake, Russel L. "Ties of Intimacy: Social Values and Personal Relationships of Ante-Bellum Slaveholders." Ph.D. diss., University of Michigan, 1978.

Bleser, Carol, ed. *In Joy and in Sorrow: Women, Family, and Marriage in the Victorian South, 1830–1900.* New York: Oxford University Press, 1992.

Bode, Frederick A. "A Common Sphere: White Evangelicals and Gender in Antebellum Georgia." *Georgia Historical Quarterly*, 1995, 775–809.

Borrit, Gabor S., ed. *Why the Confederacy Lost.* New York: Oxford University Press, 1992.

Breen, T. H. "Horses and Gentlemen: The Cultural Significance of Gambling among the Gentry of Virginia." *William and Mary Quarterly*, 1977, 239–57.

Britton, James Clinton, III. "The Decline and Fall of Nations in Antebellum Southern Thought: A Study of Southern Historical Consciousness, 1846–1861." Ph.D. diss., University of North Carolina, 1988.

Bruce, Dickson D., Jr. "The Conservative Use of History in Early National Virginia." *Southern Studies*, 1980, 128–46.

————. "Hunting: Dimensions of Antebellum Southern Culture." *Mississippi Quarterly*, 1977, 259–81.

————. *Violence and Culture in the Antebellum South.* Austin: University of Texas Press, 1979.

Burton, Orville Vernon. *In My Father's House Are Many Mansions: Family and Community in Edgefield, South Carolina.* Chapel Hill: University of North Carolina Press, 1985.

Burton, Orville Vernon, and Robert C. McMath Jr., eds. *Class, Conflict, and Consensus: Antebellum Community Studies.* Westport, Conn.: Greenwood, 1982.

Bynum, Victoria E. *Unruly Women: The Politics of Social and Sexual Control in the Old South.* Chapel Hill: University of North Carolina Press, 1992.

Campbell, Randolph B. *An Empire for Slavery: The Peculiar Institution in Texas, 1821–1865.* Baton Rouge: Louisiana State University Press, 1989.

Carnes, Mark C., and Clyde Griffen, eds. *Meanings for Manhood: Constructions of Masculinity in Victorian America.* Chicago: University of Chicago Press, 1990.

Cashin, Joan E. " 'Decidedly Opposed to the Union': Women's Culture, Marriage, and Politics in Antebellum South Carolina." *Georgia Historical Quarterly*, 1994, 735–59.

————. *A Family Venture: Men and Women on the Southern Frontier.* New York: Oxford University Press, 1991.

————. "The Structure of Antebellum Planter Families: 'The Ties That Bound Us Was Strong.' " *Journal of Southern History*, 1990, 55–70.

————. "Women at War." *Reviews in American History*, 1990, 343–48.

Censer, Jane Turner. *North Carolina Planters and Their Children, 1800–1860.* Baton Rouge: Louisiana State University Press, 1984.

———. " 'Smiling through Her Tears': Antebellum Southern Women and Divorce." *American Journal of Legal History*, 1981, 24–47.

———. "Southwestern Migration among North Carolina Planter Families: The Disposition to Emigrate." *Journal of Southern History*, 1991, 407–26.

Channing, Steven A. *Crisis of Fear: Secession in South Carolina*. New York: Norton, 1970.

Clinton, Catherine. "Equally Their Due: The Education of the Planter Daughter in the Early Republic." *Journal of the Early Republic*, 1982, 39–60.

Clinton, Catherine, and Nina Silber, ed. *Divided Houses: Gender and the Civil War*. New York: Oxford University Press, 1992.

Cott, Nancy F. "Notes toward an Interpretation of Antebellum Childrearing." *Psychohistory Review*, 1978, 4–20.

Coulter, E. Merton. "The Great Georgia Railway Disaster Hoax on the London Times." *Georgia Historical Quarterly*, 1972, 25–50.

Crofts, Daniel W. *Reluctant Confederates: Upper South Unionists and the Secession Crisis*. Chapel Hill: University of North Carolina Press, 1989.

Crowther, Edward R. "Holy Honor: Sacred and Secular in the Old South." *Journal of Southern History*, 1992, 619–36.

Davis, David Brion. *The Slave Power Conspiracy and the Paranoid Style*. Baton Rouge: Louisiana State University Press, 1969.

Davis, Michael. *The Image of Lincoln in the South*. Knoxville: University of Tennessee Press, 1971.

Davis, William C. *A Government of Our Own: The Making of the Confederacy*. New York: Free Press, 1994.

Dean, Eric. "We Will All Be Lost and Destroyed: Posttraumatic Stress Disorder and the Civil War." *Civil War History*, 1991, 138–53.

DeBats, Donald A. "An Uncertain Arena: The Georgia House of Representatives, 1808–1861." *Journal of Southern History*, 1990, 423–56.

Degler, Carl N. "Thesis, Antithesis, Synthesis: The South, the North, and the Nation." *Journal of Southern History*, 1987, 3–18.

Ellis, Leonard. "Men among Men: An Exploration of All-Male Relationships in Victorian America." Ph.D. diss., Columbia University, 1982.

Etcheson, Nicole. "Manliness and the Political Culture of the Old Northwest, 1790–1860." *Journal of the Early Republic*, 1995, 59–77.

Faust, Drew Gilpin. *The Creation of Confederate Nationalism: Ideology and Identity in the Civil War South*. Baton Rouge: Louisiana State University Press, 1988.

———. *James Henry Hammond and the Old South: A Design for Mastery*. Baton Rouge: Louisiana State University Press, 1982.

———. *Mothers of Invention: Women of the Slaveholding South in the American Civil War*. Chapel Hill: University of North Carolina Press, 1996.

―――. *Southern Stories: Slaveholders in Peace and War.* Columbia: University of Missouri Press, 1992.

Forgie, George B. *Patricide in the House Divided: A Psychological Interpretation of Lincoln and His Age.* New York: Norton, 1979.

Foster, Gaines M. *Ghosts of the Confederacy: Defeat, the Lost Cause, and the Emergence of the New South, 1865–1913.* New York: Oxford University Press, 1987.

―――. "Guilt over Slavery: A Historiographical Analysis." *Journal of Southern History,* 1990, 665–94.

Fox-Genovese, Elizabeth. "The Fettered Mind: Time, Place, and the Literary Imagination of the Old South." *Georgia Historical Quarterly,* 1990, 622–50.

―――. *Within the Plantation Household: Black and White Women of the Old South.* Chapel Hill: University of North Carolina Press, 1988.

Gorn, Elliott J. " 'Gouge and Bite, Pull Hair and Scratch': The Social Significance of Fighting in the Southern Backcountry." *American Historical Review,* 1985, 18–43.

Gradin, Harlan Joel. "Losing Control: The Caning of Charles Sumner and the Breakdown of Antebellum Political Culture." Ph.D. diss., University of North Carolina, 1991.

Greenberg, Kenneth S. *Honor and Slavery: Lies, Duels, Noses, Masks, Dressing as a Woman, Gifts, Strangers, Humanitarianism, Death, Slave Rebellions, the Proslavery Argument, Baseball, Hunting, and Gambling in the Old South.* Princeton: Princeton University Press, 1996.

―――. *Masters and Statesmen: The Political Culture of American Slavery.* Baltimore: Johns Hopkins University Press, 1985.

Heidler, David Stephen. "Fire Eaters: The Radical Secessionists in Antebellum Politics." Ph.D. diss., Auburn University, 1985.

Higginbotham, R. Don. "The Martial Spirit in the Antebellum South: Some Further Speculations in a National Context." *Journal of Southern History,* 1991, 3–26.

Inscoe, John C. "Mountain Masters: Slaveholding in Western North Carolina." *North Carolina Historical Review,* 1984, 143–73.

Jimerson, Randall C. *The Private Civil War: Popular Thought During the Sectional Conflict.* Baton Rouge: Louisiana State University Press, 1988.

Johnson, Michael P. "Planters and Patriarchy: Charleston, 1800–1860." *Journal of Southern History,* 1980, 45–72.

―――. *Toward a Patriarchal Republic: The Secession of Georgia.* Baton Rouge: Louisiana State University Press, 1977.

Jones, Ann Goodwyn, and Susan V. Donaldson, eds. *Haunted Bodies: Gender and Southern Texts.* Charlottesville: University Press of Virginia, 1997.

Kimmel, Michael. *Manhood in America: A Cultural History.* New York: Free Press, 1996.

Klement, Frank L. *Dark Lanterns: Secret Political Societies, Conspiracies, and Treason Trials in the Civil War.* Baton Rouge: Louisiana State University Press, 1984.

Lebsock, Suzanne. "Complicity and Contention: Women in the Plantation South." *Georgia Historical Quarterly*, 1990, 59–83.

Lewis, Jan. *The Pursuit of Happiness: Family and Values in Jefferson's Virginia.* Cambridge: Cambridge University Press, 1983.

Linderman, Gerald F. *Embattled Courage: The Experience of Combat in the American Civil War.* New York: Free Press, 1987.

Lystra, Karen. *Searching the Heart: Women, Men, and Romantic Love in Nineteenth-Century America.* New York: Oxford University Press, 1989.

Marks, Stuart A. *Southern Hunting in Black and White: Nature, History, and Ritual in a Carolina Community.* Princeton: Princeton University Press, 1991.

May, Robert E. *John A. Quitman: Old South Crusader.* Baton Rouge and London: Louisiana State University Press, 1985.

———. "Psychobiography and Secession: The Southern Radical as Maladjusted Outsider." *Civil War History*, 1988, 46–69.

———. "Southern Elite Women, Sectional Extremism, and the Male Political Sphere: The Case of John A. Quitman's Wife and Female Descendants, 1847–1931." *Journal of Mississippi History*, 1988, 251–85.

Mayfield, John. " 'The Soul of a Man': William Gilmore Simms and Myths of Southern Manhood." *Journal of the Early Republic*, 1995, 477–500.

———. "The Theatre of Public Esteem: Ethics and Values in Longstreet's *Georgia Scenes*." *Georgia Historical Quarterly*, 1991, 566–86.

McCurry, Stephanie. *Masters of Small Worlds: Yeoman Households, Gender Relations, and the Political Culture of the Antebellum South Carolina Low Country.* New York: Oxford University Press, 1995.

———. "The Two Faces of Republicanism: Gender and Proslavery Politics in Antebellum South Carolina." *Journal of American History*, 1992, 1245–64.

McMillen, Sally G. *Motherhood in the Old South: Pregnancy, Childbirth, and Infant Rearing.* Baton Rouge: Louisiana State University Press, 1990.

McPherson, James M. "Antebellum Southern Exceptionalism: A New Look at an Old Question." *Civil War History*, 1983, 230–44.

———. *Battle Cry of Freedom: The Civil War Era.* New York: Oxford University Press, 1988.

———. *For Cause and Comrades: Why Men Fought in the Civil War.* New York: Oxford University Press, 1997.

McPherson, James M., and William J. Cooper Jr., eds. *Writing the Civil War: The Quest to Understand.* Columbia: University of South Carolina Press, 1998.

Mitchell, Reid. *Civil War Soldiers.* New York: Viking, 1988.

————. *The Vacant Chair: The Northern Soldier Leaves Home.* New York: Oxford University Press, 1993.

Moore, John Hebron. *The Emergence of the Cotton Kingdom in the Old Southwest: Mississippi, 1770–1860.* Baton Rouge: Louisiana State University Press, 1988.

Neely, Mark E. "Was the Civil War a Total War?" *Civil War History,* 1991, 5–28.

Nichols, Roy Franklin. *The Disruption of American Democracy.* New York: Collier, 1962.

O'Brien, Michael. *Rethinking the South: Essays in Intellectual History.* Baltimore: Johns Hopkins University Press, 1988.

O'Brien, Michael, and David Moltke-Hansen. *Intellectual Life in Antebellum Charleston.* Knoxville: University of Tennessee Press, 1986.

Oakes, James. *Slavery and Freedom: An Interpretation of the Old South.* New York: Random House, 1990.

Olsen, Christopher J. *Political Culture and Secession in Mississippi: Masculinity, Honor, and the Antiparty Tradition, 1830–1860.* New York: Oxford University Press, 2000.

Osterweis, Rollin G. *Romanticism and Nationalism in the Old South.* New Haven: Yale University Press, 1949.

Pugh, David G. *Sons of Liberty: The Masculine Mind in Nineteenth-Century America.* Westport, Conn.: Greenwood, 1983.

Rable, George C. *Civil Wars: Women and the Crisis of Southern Nationalism.* Urbana: University of Illinois Press, 1989.

————. *The Confederate Republic: A Revolution against Politics.* Chapel Hill: University of North Carolina Press, 1994.

Rose, Alan Henry. *Demonic Vision: Racial Fantasy and Southern Fiction.* Hamden: Archon, 1976.

Rose, Anne C. *Victorian America and the Civil War.* Cambridge: Cambridge University Press, 1992.

Rotundo, E. Anthony. *American Manhood: Transformations in Masculinity From the Revolution to the Modern Era.* New York: Basic, 1993.

Rubin, Louis D. *The Edge of the Swamp: A Study in the Literature and Society of the Old South.* Baton Rouge: Louisiana State University Press, 1989.

Scafidel, Beverly. "The Letters of William Elliott." Ph.D. diss., University of South Carolina, 1978.

Steel, Edward M., Jr. *T. Butler King of Georgia.* Athens: University of Georgia Press, 1964.

Stowe, Steven M. *Intimacy and Power in the Old South: Ritual in the Lives of the Planters.* Baltimore: Johns Hopkins University Press, 1987.

————. "Intimacy in the Planter Class Culture." *Psychohistory Review,* 1982, 141–64.

————. "Private Emotions and a Public Man in Early Nineteenth Century Virginia." *History of Education Quarterly*, 1987, 75–81.

————. "The Rhetoric of Authority: The Making of Social Values in Planter Family Correspondence." *Journal of American History*, 1987, 916–33.

————. "Singleton's Tooth: Thoughts on the Form and Meaning of Antebellum Southern Family Correspondence." *Southern Review*, 1989, 323–33.

————. " 'The Thing, Not Its Vision': A Woman's Courtship and Her Sphere in the Southern Planter Class." *Feminist Studies*, 1983, 113–30.

————. "The 'Touchiness' of the Gentlemen Planter: The Sense of Esteem and Continuity in the Ante-Bellum South." *Psychohistory Review*, 1979, 6–15.

Taylor, William R. *Cavalier and Yankee: The Old South and the American National Character*. Cambridge: Harvard University Press, 1957.

Walther, Eric H. *The Fire-Eaters*. Baton Rouge: Louisiana State University Press, 1992.

Watson, Ritchie Devon, Jr. *Yeoman versus Cavalier: The Old Southwest's Fictional Road to Rebellion*. Baton Rouge: Louisiana State University Press, 1993.

Wayne, Michael. "An Old South Morality Play: Reconsidering the Social Underpinnings of the Proslavery Ideology." *Journal of American History*, 1990, 838–63.

Whites, LeeAnn. *The Civil War as a Crisis in Gender: Augusta, Georgia, 1860–1890*. Athens: University of Georgia Press, 1995.

Wiggins, Sarah Woolfolk. "Josiah Gorgas, A Victorian Father." *Civil War History*, 1986, 229–46.

Woods, James M. "The Enigma of Secession: Recent Historiography on Southern Disunion." *Journal of Confederate History*, 1990, 111–23.

————. *Rebellion and Realignment: Arkansas's Road to Secession*. Fayetteville: University of Arkansas Press, 1987.

Wyatt-Brown, Bertram. *Southern Honor: Ethics and Behavior in the Old South*. New York: Oxford University Press, 1982.

————. *Yankee Saints and Southern Sinners*. Baton Rouge: Louisiana State University Press, 1985.

INDEX

African Americans. See Race; Slavery

Alexander, Harriet, 89–90, 96–97, 106

Allston, Benjamin, 115–17

Alston, J. Mote, 86

Ambition, 12, 18; and Civil War 7, 171–72; and deflation of, 9, 37–38, 40–44, 193–96, 216, 236–37; and conflation with love, 45–47, 80, 85–86, 171–72, 182–83

Averitt, James, 205–6

Bailey, C.O., 167

Baker, Everard, 37–38

Baldwin, Joseph, 35

Barksdale, William, 48

Benjamin, Judah, 8

Bingham, William, 164, 165

Bird, Edgeworth, 173, 186

Brown, John, 137–38

Bryant, Willie, 181

Burge, Louisiana, 166

Burr, Aaron, 22–23

Butler, Edward, 168

Callaway, Joshua, 6–7, 9, 174, 175, 176–77, 178, 179, 184

Caperton, Lin, 186–89

Chesnut, Mary, 19, 104, 109

Civil War: men's motivations in, 10, 166–69, 171–73, 182–84, 191–92, 193–96; men's experiences of, 173–82; 185–87

Civilization building, as male impulse and pursuit, 21, 26–27, 34, 43, 112–13

Clay, Henry, 132

Clay, Virginia Tunstall, 127, 257

Clemens, Samuel, 166

Clitherall, Eliza, 111–12

Cobb, Howell, 8

Cobb, Thomas Reade Rootes, 7–9, 225–26

Cole, Laura, 95–96, 105

Cole, Thomas, 27

Corbin, Richard, 171

Cornwall, Susan, 104

Correspondence: as incubator of courtship, 89–90; during Civil War, 184–86

Courtship, 86–94

Craft, Henry: and boyhood, 64–65; and courtship of Lucy Hull, 65–68; at

283

Craft, Henry (*Continued*)
  Princeton, 68–70; and grieving, 68–73;
  and journalizing, 74, 76; and marriage
  to Ella, 74–77; and affection for son, 77–
  78; and post-war career, 236–37; and
  attitude toward greatness, 236–37
Cumming, Wallace, 39, 89

Dancing, 93, 132–33
Davis, Jefferson, 8, 156, 196
Dawson, Nathaniel Henry Rhodes:
  boyhood of, 197; early career of, 197–
  98; and courtship of Elodie, 199, 207–8,
  210–11, 213–15; and domestic
  imagination, 204–5, 207; and relations
  with other men, 205–7; and romantic
  reading, 207, 210–11; and death, 209–
  10; and Confederate cause, 214–15, 216–
  17; and Manassas, 215–16; and Elodie's
  death, 250
DeBow's Review, 95
Demographics, maturation of the South
  and, 28–29
Depression, 42–44, 46
Diarists: men as, 74; women as, 107–9
Dickey, William, 182
Dixon, Harry St. John: and relationship
  with father, 136; racial attitudes of, 137–
  38, 155–56; attitudes toward slavery,
  137–38, 155; and boyhood, 140–41; and
  attitudes toward women, 141–48; and
  sex, 142–46; and coming-of-age, 148–
  51; at UVA, 152–58; and secession, 155–
  57; and venereal disease, 158, 232–33;
  during Civil War, 180, 230–31; will of,
  231–32; marriage of, 232; death of, 232–
  33
Dixon, Julia, 137, 138
Dixon, Richard, 136, 137, 138–39
Domestic imagination, 204–5, 222
Douglass, Ella, 74–77

Economic development, in South, 28–30
Edmonston, James, 174
Education, men's collegiate, 36–37
Eggleston, George, 167, 172

Elliott, Richard, 38
Elliott, William, 30, 32–33, 39–40, 106,
  114–15
Emotions, men and, 11–12
Expansionism, 23–26

Family, 111–12
Fashion, 83–84
Father-son relations, 32–34, 71, 154
Fay, Edwin, 175, 176, 178–79, 181, 182,
  183, 193
Fighting, in Congress, 47–49, 125–26
Fitzhugh, George, 95
Fort, John, 182
Fort Pulaski, 219–24, 234
Founding Fathers, attitudes toward
  expansion of, 29
Franklin, Benjamin, 34–35
Friendship, men and, 39–40; 205–7

Gayle, Sarah, 103
God, men's attitudes toward, 43–44, 70,
  91–94, 208
Gorgas, Josiah, 34–35
Gosse, Philip Henry, 22
Grieving, men and, 68–73, 198
Grimball, Meta, 110, 164, 165, 171
Grow, Galusha, 47–48

Halliburton, Wes, 90, 91
Hamilton, Daniel, 168–69
Hamilton, James, 23
Hammond, James Henry, 12–13, 22, 32–
  34, 43–44, 117
Henderson, John, 167
Honor, 20–21
Horses, 105–6
Hughes, Henry, 46–47
Hull, Lucy, 65–68

Jackson, Benjamin, 181
Jones, Egbert J., 215

Keitt, Laurence: and altercation with
  Galusha Grow, 47–49, 247; others'
  opinions of, 48–49, 55; boyhood of, 49–

50; as fire-eater, 51; and Sumner
caning, 59, 249; and courtship of
Susanna Sparks, 59–64; and reaction to
news of secession, 168; and Civil War,
227–29; death of, 229
King, Anna, 38, 97–103
King, Georgia, 105–6
King, John Floyd, 186–89
King, Henry Lord Page, 87, 90, 168
King, Mallery, 105–6
King, Thomas Butler, 17–18, 21
King, Thomas Butler Jr., 102–3

Land piracy, 23
Law, Evander M., 215
Lee, Robert E., 8
Lieber, Francis, 52
Lincoln, Abraham, 203–4
Lincoln, John, 37
Lincoln, Mary Todd, 201–2
Love: men and, 12–13. See also Sexuality;
Courtship
Lunt, Dolly, 166
Luria, Albert, 3–6, 9
The Lustful Turk, 142

Manhood: Civil War as test of, 9–10, 171–
73; historiography on, 10–13; pressures
of, 77–78
Marriage, 172–73, 207
Masturbation, 115–17
McDowell, Amanda, 167
McGuire, Judith, 165
McLaws, Lafayette, 178
Men: motivations of, 12–13; and coming-
of-age in 1850s, 31–32, 35–36; and
college, 36–37; friendships among, 39–
40, 153; and self-loathing, 42–44, 46,
70–71; and courtship, 86–94; and
grieving, 68–73, 198; and desire, 141–
46; and secession, 166–72; as soldiers,
173–92; in defeat, 193–96
Miles, William Porcher, 48
Montfort, Theodorick: and siege of Fort
Pulaski, 219–24; and fishing, 219, 236;
motivations of, 220; and

correspondence, 220–21; and
psychological strain of siege, 221–22;
capture of, 234–35; death of, 236
Morgan, Sarah, 106, 107–8, 109
Morrison, Robert, 31
Moses, Eliza, 3–6
Mother-son relations, 154
Murrell, John, 23
Music, 106–7

Napoleon, 38
North-South comparisons, 33, 34
North-South tensions, 133–34
Nugent, William, 93, 96, 174–75, 177,
179, 181, 182, 183, 194

Oglethorpe, Georgia, 218–19
Oratory, men's affection for, 40–41
Outlaw, David: as congressman,118, 124,
133–34; and love for Emily, 119–23; as
correspondent, 121–22; attitudes toward
Washington, D.C., of, 124–34; sexual
mores of, 129–34; post-congressional
career of, 233–34; death of, 234

Paternalism, 20
Patterson, Giles, 40–41
Peddy, George, 93, 96, 184–85
Peddy, Kate, 96
Pender, William, 92–94, 171, 172
Petigru, James, 20–21, 86–87, 171
Poe, Edgar Allan, 39, 42–43, 45–46, 244–
46
Poetry, 40–41, 54–56
Poetry and the Practical, 54–56, 248
Preston, William C., 28
Princeton University, 68–70
Professions: men's struggles to choose, 36,
72
Prostitution, 157–58, 262

Quitman, John, 47

Race, Southern attitudes toward, 137–38
Railroads, expansion in South, 28
Religion, 91–94

Retreat Plantation, St. Simons Island,
    Georgia, 97–103, 105–6
Ruffin, Elizabeth, 107
Russell's Magazine, 25, 36
Russell, William, 165

Scott, Charles, 215
Secession, 7–8, 155–57, 163–73, 196–97
Selma, Alabama, 203–4
Sex: nineteenth-century attitudes toward,
    115–17, 129–34
Shofner, John, 29–30
Simms, William Gilmore, 39; and *Poetry
    and the Practical*, 54–56, 248
Simpson, Tally, 185, 189–91
Slavery, 21–22, 24–26, 118–19, 137–38,
    155
Soldiers: motivations of, 4, 182–84, 191–
    92, 216, 222–23; and coping with
    death, 7, 173–74; indignities of, 174–75;
    attitudes toward army, 175–76; and
    discipline, 176–77; and loss of self, 177–
    79; and letters home, 184–85
Soloman, Clara, 107
Southern Literary Messenger, 23–24, 31,
    32, 41, 42, 86, 87–89
South Carolina College, 40, 52
Sparks, Susanna, 59–64
Spencer, Cornelia, 104
Stephens, Alexander, 8, 47
Stephens, Winston, 185–86, 193–94, 195
Stuart, J.E.B., 26
Sumner, Charles, caning of, 59, 249

Tamerlane, 45–46
Taylor, Walter, 183

Thomas, Ella, 107
Thomson, William, 169–71
Thomson, William Jr., 169–70
Todd, Elodie: and opinion of herself, 199–
    200; and relations with sister Mary,
    201–2; and feelings toward divided
    family, 202–3; and social divisions in
    Selma, 203–4; and romantic
    negotiations with Nathaniel, 211–13;
    death of, 230
Todd family, 200–2
Toombs, Robert, 8
Trescott, William, 48–49

Venereal disease, 157–58
Victoria, Queen, 114–15
Victorianism, 114–15
Virginia Military Institute, 53

Walker, William, 23
Washburn, Cadwallader, 48
Washington, D.C., 50–51, 122–23, 124–34
Wet dreams, 144–46
Wheat, Roberdeau, 86
Williams, James, 172, 176, 178, 186
Women: and hope, 38; and dress, 84–85;
    and courtship, 89–90; and size, 96; and
    dealing with men, 95–97; and crushing
    confinement, 97–111; and horses, 105–6;
    as makers of music, 106–7; and
    journalizing, 107–9; and marriage, 108–
    9; mortality of, 110–11; as
    embodiments of Civilization, 112–13;
    and sexual double-standards, 117

Yancey, William, 198